whoever dies first wins

KAREN JOYCE BONOFIGLIO

whoever dies first wins

SURVIVING DEVASTATING TRAUMA AND CHOOSING TO LIVE AGAIN

Copyright ©2024 Karen Joyce Bonofiglio
All rights reserved.

No part of this publication may be reproduced or transmitted in any form or by any means, electronic or mechanical, including photography, recording, or any information storage and retrieval system, without permission in writing from the author. Requests for permission to make copies of any part of the work should be emailed to the following address: docbono@comcast.net.

Neither the publisher nor the author shall be liable for any loss of profit or any other commercial damages, including but not limited to special, incidental, consequential, personal, or other damages.

Published and distributed by Merack Publishing
San Diego, USA
www.merackpublishing.com

Library of Congress Control Number: 2024912107
Bonofiglio, Karen
Whoever Dies First… Wins: Surviving Devastating Trauma and Choosing to Live Again

ISBN
Paperback 978-1-949635-58-4
Hardcover 978-1-949635-40-9
eBook 978-1-949635-70-6

For Bono
My Love
My Life
My Everything

You were here, and then you were gone. I lost my breath, my spark, my essence. Yet, you gave it all back to me again from behind the Veil.

> As far as I can see, grief will never truly end. It may become softer over time, more gentle, and some days will feel sharp. But grief will last as long as love does—forever.
>
> —Lexi Behrndt, Scribbles & Crumbs

CONTENTS

Foreword	1
INTRODUCTION "If I Could Turn Back Time"	5
EXPECT THE UNEXPECTED: Essential Guideposts for Navigating my Grief Journey	7
SECTION I · BONO'S PASSING	**13**
CHAPTER 1 "LAST KISS"	15
CHAPTER 2 JOURNEY TO HELL	29
CHAPTER 3 "ALL MY LOVING"	37
CHAPTER 4 SPARKS FLEW	57
CHAPTER 5 "HOLD ME NOW"	77
CHAPTER 6 "MOURNING GIRL"	87
CHAPTER 7 "BABY ELEPHANT WALK"	99
CHAPTER 8 "DOWNTOWN"	109

CHAPTER 9
"FEELIN' ALRIGHT" — 121

SECTION II · FOR YOUR GROWTH — 127

CHAPTER 10
"FOR YOUR GROWTH" — 129

CHAPTER 11
"SUNSHINE" AND SPIRITUAL AWAKENINGS — 135

SECTION III · TACKLING GRIEF — 145

CHAPTER 12
HONORING GRIEF EACH DAY — 147

CHAPTER 13
"TIPTOEING THROUGH THE TULIPS" — 163

CHAPTER 14
"FREE YOUR MIND" — 173

CHAPTER 15
IT TAKES A BREAKDOWN TO HAVE A BREAKTHROUGH — 181

CHAPTER 16
"UNCHAINED MELODY" — 189

CHAPTER 17
"PRESERVE YOUR MEMORIES" — 221

CHAPTER 18
"DRAG"GED DOWN BY FAMILIAL "NET" LOSS — 235

CHAPTER 19
"HELP!" — 259

CHAPTER 20
"I NEED YOU" — 275

SECTION IV · "ELEVATION"   283

CHAPTER 21
MY EPIPHANIES   285

CHAPTER 22
"ALL YOU NEED IS LOVE"   293

CHAPTER 23
"A CELEBRATION" TIME?   301

CHAPTER 24
"YOU ARE SO BEAUTIFUL"   317

CHAPTER 25
GRIEF IS THE PRICE OF LOVE   333

SECTION V · "SHADOWS OF THE NIGHT"   347

APPENDIX I
"Oogum Boogum":   351

APPENDIX II:
"Silly Love Songs": Bono's Playlist   365

APPENDIX III:
"Sunshine of Your Love":Some More Loving Encounters from Beyond the Veil   367

APPENDIX IV:
List of Recommended Readings   379

Bibliography   381

Acknowledgments   387

About the Author   391

FOREWORD

Listen to your heart instead of your mind while reading this book—it has more wisdom.

—KAREN BONOFIGLIO

It is a privilege to be a hospice nurse. We're allowed (rarely enthusiastically and mostly reluctantly) into one of the most intimate, stressful, heartbreaking, joyous (I'm not kidding), and meaningful times of people's lives. We meet as strangers, and—if we're very lucky—emerge at the other end as dear friends. Such is how I met Karen.

I had the true joy of caring for Karen's parents during the final stages of their lives. First, I looked after her ornery dad (who couldn't stand me initially because I was "too bossy"; as his dementia progressed, he forgot he didn't like me, and I became one of his favorites.). Afterward, I cared for her beautiful mom, from whom I received my very favorite honorific, Nursey Beth.

Through that two-year end-of-life journey, Karen and I worked closely together to maximize her parents' comfort and quality of life. It's normal and expected for the hospice nurse to have to earn the trust of patients and family members, but Karen was an especially hard nut to crack. Initially, Karen was seriously not buying what I was selling.

Our philosophies toward medicine were—and are—very different, so we talked A LOT and learned from each other what mattered and what each of us was comfortable with. And trust grew. This collaboration resulted in beautiful, peaceful deaths for Ted and Ruth Joy, and in a lifelong friendship for Karen and me.

My name is Beth Gafur, RN, ADN, CHPN—also known as Nursey Beth. Karen asked me to write a little about my perspective on capital "G" Grief: on what I've learned, seen, and experienced throughout my career. Given all of the loss Karen has survived, she should be writing this part, but here goes…

In her book *On Death and Dying,* Elizabeth Kubler-Ross (1969) introduced us to her "Five Stages of Grief": Denial, Anger, Bargaining, Depression, and Acceptance—in that order.

But as anyone who's experienced it can attest, Grief isn't lived on a continuum, moving cleanly from one stage to the next. Plus, those five descriptors hardly cover it. Grief is squishy and messy. It's like a rollercoaster or sneaker wave, coming out of the blue to knock you sideways when you least expect it. It's gut-wrenching, all-encompassing, infuriating, a motherfucker, exhausting, guilt-inducing and crazy-making. It makes you think and act in ways you never thought possible. It's seemingly endless. It's the expression of the end of life as we've known it.

And it is. Grief is all of that. But it can also be surprising, beautiful, growth-inducing, expansive, creative, and opportunistic (in a good way). Just look at how Karen has channeled her loss and grief: from surviving on chocolate, tequila, and coffee, to writing a book that will help many others. I've been asked by families if the pain will ever go away, or if it will always hurt this much. The answer is no and no. The pain of loss never goes away, but our perception of it changes over time and through effort. What we do with our pain, and how we allow our lives to grow around and accommodate that loss, is what determines what our lives with Grief look like.

I've witnessed Grief experienced and expressed differently, and on different timelines, by members of the same family. While this is normal, it can be—and often is—a source of unwelcome stress and conflict. We "expect" others "should" feel, think, and act as we do; this is clearly unfair and untrue, but grief and clear thinking are largely incompatible. Some people become overwhelmed and incapacitated, while others feel nothing or have very complicated, mixed feelings. Estrangements and unresolved conflicts, whether they're between surviving family members or with the deceased person, add a whole different level of Grief to resolve.

It's hard to be gracious or think of others' feelings when we're sucked so far down the Grief hole, but we'd all do well to throw out all thoughts of "Expectation" and "Should," and just give each other grace. We're all entitled to our feelings. We all mess up. We all deserve grace.

So, how do we in the cheap seats demonstrate our support for those living the Grief? Be available, send cards, drop off appropriate dietary meals, pick up the phone when they call, clean their bathrooms, make grocery runs, text or call often and leave a message (they'll answer if they're up to it), invite them to events, and keep on inviting them—even when they've already said no to the previous twenty events. Listen to what they say, and support feelings expressed without judgment, comment, or—for the love of all things holy—making it about yourself. Be the cane that helps them walk again. And when you have no idea what to do or say, just sit with them in silence and hold space. THAT is sacred time.

I wish you the best possible on your own Grief journey.

Sincerely,
Nurse Beth Gafur RN, ADN, CHPN

Introduction
"IF I COULD TURN BACK TIME"

I thought I was going to die. On November 8, 2020, I ceased to be the person I knew all my life. I became non-existent, and I was thrown into the abyss of my own fiery inferno.

Me. Karen Bonofiglio. Just an average person with an average life. How wrong I was. My entire life had prepped me for what was to come, but I wouldn't realize it until years after I entered my own personal Hell. My life was changed forever in fundamental ways. I had no idea how I would survive—if I would survive. The pain was unimaginable and insurmountable.

Death. Grief. Trauma. Depression. Numbness. Loneliness. Anger. Thoughts of suicide. Can you relate to these words? If you've experienced a significant loss before, I believe you can.

I endured all these emotions and more and survived the tragic loss of three of my closest family members within a year. My father—a man who was so much a part of me—was dead and gone. My mother—instrumental in shaping my life from childhood onward—left to join him in Heaven a year later. My husband—three weeks after Mom—also died unexpectedly. In a span of thirteen months, I lost my three most prominent and cherished loved ones: those who'd lent me support, guided me, and accepted me with a special love and bond that never wavered.

I wanted to die. I wanted to join them. The pain was too great. I didn't care if I lived or died. God take me. But I didn't die. I learned to live again, and I used my nightmarish life experiences as a catalyst to help others who would also suffer from horrific losses of loved ones.

My story is of survival. My book takes you into the world of death and grief: a deep darkness most of us will experience. Yet, it can be used as a beacon of hope, and provides practical advice on how to survive the death of a loved one and once again thrive as a person.

Come with me on my journey. I survived. You can too.

Expect the Unexpected: ESSENTIAL GUIDEPOSTS FOR NAVIGATING MY GRIEF JOURNEY

My life as a schoolteacher was one of teaching, experiencing, and creativity. These themes are very prevalent in my book. You will discover alternate ways of looking at ideas, as they will be presented to you—the reader—in a variety of ways. This brief guide outlines these methods.

- Facebook Posts About Grief: These will be sprinkled throughout the book, mainly at the end of chapters. Each post is labeled with the date it was originally created, and this subsection of the book serves as a great example of the grieving process and all of its ups and downs in real time. Sharing my story and my experiences was a way for me to release my emotions and everything I was experiencing with my tragic losses. I continue to share my journey on Facebook with my friends, and we all love and support each other. I invite them to observe or become a part of my journey of grief and trauma during this tumultuous time. Many knew my husband and me as a couple. I'd always been a private person, but the pain was so searing that it was cathartic for me. I found, in return, I gained an even larger tribe of friends who helped and encouraged me.

- Music and Song: Music was an integral part of my and my husband's lives together, as he was a talented musician. After he passed, he sent me a myriad of songs for comfort. Some of the titles of these songs and of other thematically relevant ones have been incorporated into the chapter and heading titles of this book. It is a wonderful play on words and represents what you may experience when reading. I hope you listen to the songs before reading, or whenever it suits you. A playlist of songs my husband sent me can be found in Appendix II. While listening, you may shed some tears. You may laugh. Some you may not recognize, but they may touch you if you are grieving, nonetheless.

- Spiritual Messages from Behind the Veil: These will be presented through a section at the end of each chapter called "Forever in Touch: Unbroken Connection and Loving Encounters with Bono." My husband, parents, and others have not left my side, and they come to visit me and send me messages through the mysterious existence of life after death. It is quite comforting knowing they are just a thought away. Some more of such encounters can be found in Appendix III. They have sustained me through my grief.

- Definition Doggy Boxes (DDBs): My deceased puppies—Roosevelt, Vinni, and Isabel—have visited me from behind the Veil. Their personalities were uniquely different, and they will give you an unbiased flavor of the book with their explanations. Much of the language—particularly the spiritual vocabulary—I use throughout the book may be foreign to you: something you have not yet experienced. These boxes provide a breakdown of some of this content into easier terms for understanding.

- Spirit(ual) Boxes (SBs): These boxes will give you a glimpse into the spiritual world of my deceased loved ones. They allow the Spiritual forms of my husband, parents, and doggies to provide their own views on the events of my past, their deaths, and my journey through grief; these beloved family members tell stories of our lives together from their own points of view, while also clarifying certain information in the text. They offer a (spiritually) higher and different perspective from my own writing. The DDBs above are a specialized version of these boxes that define difficult concepts.

Clearly, I have written these boxes as well (they were not written by Spirit), so they are fictional in some sense; however, they are heavily based on conversations with these loved ones in life, the contents of spiritual encounters with them after death, and the personalities of these cherished family members. Therefore, they are heavily based in fact and experience—a form of historical fiction if you will. They also allow me to be more objective about my subjective experiences so as to offer readers (and myself) a well-rounded explanation of my journey through grief. Most importantly, these boxes are really fun. They offer some levity when things get dark. Here, I present you with your first Spirit Box, courtesy of my amazing husband, Dr. Carl Bonofiglio.

SPIRIT BOX #1: BONOFIED

"Carl Bonofiglio here. The bona fide article. Also known as: 'Carl,' 'Bono,' 'the husband,' 'Honey,' 'Baby,' 'Doc,' 'My Fireman'…and 'Mr. Perfect.' You know—all the usual.

"It looks like my wife's written a book about her folks and me departing for Heaven and leaving her behind. Poor Karen. I didn't realize how hard this would be on her when we left. She'll certainly give me a piece of her mind when she joins me. Maybe she'll be so happy to be together again, that being mad at me will be a faint memory.

"Peeking over her shoulder, it looks like Karen's separated her book into five sections. They appear to talk about: our lives and deaths with her and their effects on her; my big moment from beyond where I help her examine what's next for her; tackling grief and ways to cope; growing through grief; and more communications and encounters with us across the Veil, as well as some resources on grief and on spirituality. Sounds like a great book—but I'm biased.

"My wife's very spiritually inclined, but not everyone's on the same wavelength. She wants to help people through their grief in any way she can. We Spiritual forms have, in turn, decided to band together to help her out with this project. Here's how things will play out. You will find a symphony of 'Spirit(ual form) Boxes' interspersed throughout the book from loved ones who've left and moved behind the Veil. These tell stories from our lives together with Karen and give clarification and tips about the grieving process as well as spirituality. Read 'em or don't, but I definitely recommend it. Don't worry—I star in a lot of them.

"Buckle up. You're in for a ride."

SECTION I

BONO'S PASSING

"A SONG FOR YOU, MY LOVE"

chapter 1
"LAST KISS"

Grief is like the ocean; it comes on waves ebbing and flowing. Sometimes the water is calm, and sometimes it is overwhelming. All we can do is learn to swim.

VICKI HARRISON

THAT FATEFUL NIGHT

"No! No! NNNNNNNNNNNNNooooooooooooooo! Wake up! Wake up honey! Don't leave me! People come back into their bodies all the time—you can too!"

But my husband doesn't stir and lies lifeless on the floor. While I wait for my family to arrive, I lie next to him. I begin stroking his hair and telling him how much I love him—over and over.

THE PREVIOUS DAY: CELEBRATE THE GOOD TIMES

I felt so damn good. The kids were coming over to celebrate our daughter Victoria's birthday. Covid was rampant, and Bono—my husband—and

I didn't see the kids that much anymore due to everyone being in isolation. Victoria had chosen Indian food for our delicious dinner, and we feasted on takeout at home. The house was decorated, the perfect gift wrapped, and we waited with anticipation for everyone to arrive.

Oh, the fun we had. Just like old times before Covid. The kids, Nick and Victoria, picked on me. I am fair game, and it bonds them together. Lots of love, laughter, and good food was present at our gathering. It felt good to banter at the table, to honor our daughter, to have our voices chime in while singing the "Happy Birthday" song, and to enjoy each other as a family.

Indian food is a very heavy fare. It sits awkwardly in the gut, and that can be quite uncomfortable if one overeats. My husband LOVED most types of food, but Indian was his favorite. He ate with gusto, polished off a mini-Bundt cake, and then remarked that he wasn't feeling well. No wonder—he'd stuffed himself. I suggested that he go lie down and that I'd take care of the cleanup. Whenever we gathered for festivities, he'd relish every bite on his plate.

My husband's name was Carl: I started calling him Bono early on (his last name was Bonofiglio, and he was a musician), but he wouldn't allow anyone else to address him in this way. They could call him "Carl" or "Doc" (he was a well-loved chiropractor). Bono was a big man—in both stature and character—towering over everyone at 6'2". I am a mere 5'2", and I looked tiny next to him. The prominence of his height gave me comfort and protection. I loved it when he pulled me into his chest and held me close—to be enveloped in his arms was heavenly. This act made me feel safe. Feel protected. Feel loved, cherished, and cared for.

The love Bono and I shared was palpable, and our friends have constantly commented about it. They've said most marriages are not like this, and we were so lucky to have each other. Carl and I gave of ourselves completely to each other. I'd been married twice previously, and I'd allowed myself to lose my voice and be minimized in those marriages. He was the first husband who accepted me for who I was (a flawed human being) and who never tried to stifle my voice. He taught me to surrender and love completely, and we shared an incredible partnership. Other than the love from my father, I've never experienced such adoration from a man in my life.

Later that evening, I joined Bono upstairs, where he'd gone to rest. My place to relax was in bed, watching TV, while he preferred his big red fluffy chair downstairs. I noticed right away that he was lying on the bed in his jeans—he hadn't changed into more comfy attire. I looked at him quizzically and inquired about how he felt. Bono jumped up and declared that he was just fine.

My husband had always taken care of me and never wanted me to worry. For the last eight years, I'd taken care of my parents until they let go and took God's hand. My mom had died just three weeks earlier, and Bono knew that my heart was heavy and that I was suffering. Once again, he declared "he was fine" so as not to worry me or cause any alarm. When I look back now, him lying on the bed in his jeans was a sign that something was amiss. He would always change into his comfy clothes once he went upstairs. Bono had tried to shield me from pain. Taking care of my parents until the end of their days had taken a toll on my well-being, and my stress levels were always high. Losing Mom a few weeks earlier had been very rough for me.

A few hours later, I joined my husband downstairs and he enthusiastically remarked,

"Honey, I'm feeling better. I drank some apple cider vinegar!"

Looking at him, he appeared perfectly fine. His eyes were clear and happy, and a grin was on his face—my husband had simply overeaten. Life went back to normal as I took in his dancing eyes and smiling face. I returned his smile, and all was well in our world.

We had a nighttime ritual. I would sit on the couch between our two doggies and stroke them while Bono and I chatted. We would discuss our day, our upcoming day, and anything else on our minds. Nothing was off limits when we talked—our minds and hearts were open. I didn't know how special our routine was and how much I would cherish it until after he was gone.

I would arise, go over to him, and lean over and kiss him, my eyes looking into his. We both always said, "I love you." I am so grateful for our ritual. I am so grateful that my last words to him expressed the love I held in my heart for this phenomenal man. My everything. My rock. My fireman who would rescue me. My man who was always by my side creating the cohesion and security in our family. For twenty-six years, we had both taken care of each other through all the ups and downs of life—through the deaths of our parents. We were powerful together.

...THE NIGHT MY LIFE ENDED

It certainly gets tedious having to wake up each night to use the bathroom—a curse of getting older. I usually wake up at around 3 a.m., but tonight I woke up at 1:45 a.m. and noticed my husband was not in bed—I figured he was probably using the bathroom off our bedroom, so I went down the hall to the other bathroom.

Upon returning to bed, I called my husband as he was still not in bed, but he didn't answer—nothing unusual here. I'd gone to the bathroom on other nights, and my husband would be in there—at which time I would hear a booming voice say:

"What are you gonna do to me, woman? Sit on me?"

His voice usually startled me, but then it would bring laughter; however, on this night, there was no voice.

Tonight, I found my husband on the floor—partway in the bathroom and the other half in the bedroom. I could tell immediately that he was dead, as I'd already dealt with my parents' deaths months prior. Although my husband was dead, he looked so peaceful, but he was cold to the touch and his body was a different shade of color. Red. His body was red. Why would it be red? When Mom and Dad died, they didn't look red, but I did not find my husband immediately as was the case with my parents when they left.

I know about near-death experiences, so I tried to shake him to bring him back into his body. While the tears streamed from my face, my voice became hysterical, but he still wouldn't wake up, and he wouldn't come back. I lay next to him and stroked his hair, not knowing what to say. I covered him with my pink robe because he was cold, and I stayed by his side talking to him. I couldn't think. I couldn't reason. I couldn't believe he was lying on the floor with no breath.

WHERE DID IT ALL GO WRONG? WAITING FOR EVERYTHING TO MAKE SENSE

Somehow, following this unspeakable discovery, I made three phone calls:

- 911: "I just woke up, and my husband is dead. No, he isn't breathing. Tell the officers I have dogs; they'll bark but are friendly. Please don't shoot my dogs."
- My daughter (Victoria, nicknamed "Binks"): She didn't answer her phone.
- My son (Nick): I cried into the phone, "Bono is dead. No, I can't reach Binks."

Two policemen arrived first. When I reflect, my doggies had disappeared into the background and never barked at these officers. Nor did they come to greet my children when they arrived. My dogs are barkers, yet they knew their daddy was dead and they lay on their beds not moving while everything unfolded. They were observing it all, and not following me if I moved as per usual—just noticing how everything was playing out with huge, terrified eyes.

I walked with one officer upstairs to where my husband lay dead; unbeknownst to me, he was taking in the room and checking for foul play. We found my husband peacefully lying on the floor, and I explained that I'd covered up his body with my pink robe. I don't know why I did this. Was it because his body was cold? Due to him being naked? I felt he was vulnerable. I can't explain why. I noticed my other two robes were on the bed, and I asked the officer why they were there. He had no clue and said my husband must've put them there. What had happened to my husband prior to his passing? Had his brain been misfiring? What had he experienced? I'll never know, and I wish now that I would've been awake to help him. I wish I could've held him and called an ambulance—although he would've argued that we should wait until morning.

The officer didn't need to survey our room for signs of foul play. I loved and adored this man with every part of my being. He didn't know how deeply our love ran, how we cherished and worshipped each other, or that we'd each give our own life so that the other could live. Our bond was incredible: unbreakable. Yet, he was just doing his job and exploring every possibility.

I am sure my husband died shortly after he came to bed. I'd retired at 9:30 p.m., and felt him come to bed at 10:30 p.m. How I wish I would've rolled over and held him instead of going back to sleep. Would this have changed the circumstances of his death? Would I have been able to help him? I will never know, and those ideas continuously percolate in my mind.

FINAL FAMILY TIME TOGETHER

My son and his partner, Leah, arrived first and found me with a police officer at the table. My dogs didn't stir—they did not joyfully go to greet my son. There was no barking. Nick and Leah walked in and circled us, taking it all in. They both hung back and circled to me. I felt I was prey—like I was being circled by vultures. I felt so isolated, although my family had started to arrive. I answered my son's questions, sobbed in disbelief, and crumpled onto his chest. Tears were streaming down my face. Nick left to go upstairs and see Carl; Leah stayed behind.

Soon afterward, Victoria and Mitch repeated the same process, only Mitch came in first and Victoria was crying in the background. They, too, approached us the same way, and again I felt like I was being circled and would be offered up for sacrifice. Nick is a therapist, and he patiently listened to the officer while Mitch went up to see Carl. Victoria didn't go upstairs to see her dad as it was too much, and I'm grateful that she doesn't hold that memory. We were all in shock and disbelief. A few short hours ago, we were all enjoying a celebration and having a grand time. And now my husband lay dead upstairs.

We waited for the medical examiner to arrive, but—due to Covid and the officer not suspecting foul play—they never came. I don't know who called the funeral home, but they arrived shortly after that conversation. I'd gone back upstairs to be with my husband. I stroked his hair and sobbed over his body. I kept repeating over and over:

"I love you. I love you so much."

It was a mantra in my ears. I can't believe he is gone. Dead. Finito. He was going to live until he was ninety. He still had dreams and huge aspirations that he wanted to accomplish. This man was always learning, growing, and trying new things. He had a zest for life and embraced it fully. No one disturbed me during this time. I was able to repeat to Bono how much I loved him. I'd given up on trying to wake him. His body was quite cold and red at that point. He looked so peaceful—like he just knelt and fell asleep with his hands underneath him.

SPIRIT BOX #2: HERE TODAY, GONE TO PEE

"Wait. What happened? I feel so light and free. I feel encompassed in love. I'm not in my body, but feel so much alive…how can that be? Wasn't I just going to use the toilet?

"My wife is sleeping soundly, yet I put out robes for her on the bed. Was I expecting a fashion show later? I feel myself being pulled away, drawn apart from my beloved wife. I can't leave her. I'm not ready to leave yet. She and the kids need me. But somehow it feels necessary.

"I lean over her to give her my 'Last Kiss' before I'm taken from this earthly life. But don't worry too much, something tells me I'll be back to visit."

Nurse Beth (my parents' hospice care nurse and my good friend) and the police officer gave me some insight into the position of his body.

Nurse Beth asked me, "Karen, what do you do if you fall down?"

I didn't know how to respond.

"You put out your hands to break your fall. He didn't. His hands were under him."

She stated that he'd probably knelt down and was dead before he'd hit the floor. The officer also observed that he'd seen many bodies, and none had looked as peaceful as my husband's. I took solace in the fact that he did not suffer or feel great pain. In the back of my mind, I wished that he hadn't died alone while I slept a few feet away. I would've liked to have held him in my arms, his head on my lap or against my chest, and to have been able to express the extreme love I had for him. I would've also implored him not to leave me—to stay here with me. Told him that I couldn't live without him and reminded him that I was supposed to die first.

I looked at my son as he guided me downstairs while the funeral parlor attendees arrived. All were dressed appropriately in black and looking somber. There were three of them, and only one spoke to me and offered me his condolences while I sat at the table…empty…a vacant and broken shell of me. This was all too familiar as I'd experienced it when Pops had died the previous year. The people would arrive—all dressed in black—offer their condolences, and, with the utmost respect and tenderness, tend to the body. In death, they treated my father, mother, and husband extremely respectfully. I have always been grateful for the reverence they received.

"I SWEAR" "I WILL": GONE TWENTY-THREE YEARS EARLY

Everything that night was jumbled in my mind. I found out months later that trauma—as well as grief—totally messes up one's brain chemistry. Suddenly, this once vibrant woman—retired elementary schoolteacher, joint decision-maker for our household, and person who oversaw her parents' care and estate for eight years—could no longer remember anything. My brain had turned to mush. Not only was my memory faulty, but I also couldn't make decisions. This was so uncharacteristic of me. I was always a take-charge person and a problem solver. It felt like my brain had shut down and that I was living in a fog.

I thought that the police officer could provide some real answers, but he couldn't. The officer was very gentle, patiently answered my queries, and tried to be a calming influence. However, all I could do when Nick and Leah got there was sob and collapse onto Nick's chest. Everything was so surreal, and I was unaware that I was in a state of shock. How could my husband be dead? We'd had a party that afternoon for our daughter's birthday. Bono had been treating his chiropractic patients at the office and swinging kettlebells with his gym members. He had looked great, and there had been no indication that something was amiss.

I had always felt that I'd die at an earlier age—before seventy-two, if I lived that long. Carl had wanted to live a healthy and robust life until he was ninety, which didn't interest me. I'd seen my parents age and then die at ninety-five (Pops) and ninety (Mom): living to that age was unappealing to me. For my entire marriage, I'd assumed that I'd die first and then my husband. Yet, that didn't happen. He died twenty-three years too soon and broke his promise. I was left here. Broken. Void of life. Wanting to die and join my parents and husband. What the eff was I supposed to do with my life without my three most prominent and beloved family members?

SPIRIT BOX #3: IN THE NICK OF TIME

"I've left my family behind—I'm dead in their eyes. Guess it was just my time. Even so, I've never felt more alive and loved. I wish I could go back, but I can't. Reminds me of the Stones' song, *You Can't Always Get What You Want*.

"Look at my son: stepping up as head of the family, taking care of his mother, sheltering her from the choices she'll have to make, and putting up signs at the clinic that we're closed for a family emergency. I'm so proud of my son. Nick is weathering the storm through his own grief, and being the man that I always knew he was a caring protector like his mom and me. Rock on!"

Nick took it upon himself to stop by Carl's clinic and gym to put up an announcement for his patients and gym members. He ran into a coach at the gym, Rey, and informed him of Bono's passing. Slowly, the ripples were starting to spread; they later became a tsunami, as the ripples were shocking and affected so many. My husband was a gregarious man. He was full of life and laughter, made friends easily, yet was the most humble and loving man I've ever known. He never had a disparaging word about anyone, and he'd touched so many people's hearts.

I have a huge tribe of friends on Facebook, and many were mutual friends of ours. I felt the need to announce Bono's death via phone calls, emails, and an announcement on social media. Below is the announcement I posted on Facebook the next day along with his picture.

Little did I know back then, but my husband had to die in order for me to live. We would've given our lives for each other, and he'd just done that for me. My husband's death would be my rebirth: a rebirth into someone I'd never imagined—someone I'd never even dreamt of. Yet, before any of this could happen, my journey into Hell was just beginning.

As I mentioned in the Introduction, you'll find Facebook posts at the end of many chapters throughout this book. During this tumultuous time, I turned to my friends on Facebook and started sharing my journey of grief and trauma with them. Each post is labeled with the date it was created, and this sub-section serves as a good example of the grieving process and all of its ups and downs in real time.

FACEBOOK POST
NOVEMBER 9, 2020

See this man? My husband...he always put me first ahead of himself and cared about my well-being before his own. We had planned on moving onto a couple of acres within the next year and just living out our lives together with the pups.

That will not happen, as God called him home last night. I imagine he was thrilled to see his mom, and all of his family members, as they shared a deep love, and he is with our animals that left before him—he also got to see Mom and Pops. My emotions range between complete disbelief, devastation, grief, and anger for him leaving me so soon. I keep expecting to see him sitting in his chair or walking up the driveway with a grin on his face. Damn it. I just want to curl into a ball and die. Thankfully, I have my kids already standing by my side.

I am glad we always had a nighttime ritual and expressed our love for and kissed each other. He truly was a good man, gone too soon. Until we meet again.

No responses will be forthcoming.

Life truly is so precious.

Forever in Touch:
Unbroken Connection and Loving Encounters with Bono

My husband's death ushered in a new and exciting form of After Death Communication with him, even though he'd physically died and was on the other side of the Veil. This communication came in various forms, but I always knew when it was him. I'll share some of these encounters throughout this book, and they may be found both at the ends of chapters and in Appendix III.

One of my first after-death encounters with my husband: I laid my husband's pajamas on the bed the day that he left, and they are still there today. It is comforting for me to lie on them, cry, and talk to him. When I lay on his jammies the first time, even though I was crying, I could feel him laying on top of me. I didn't move. I wanted to feel his weight on my body. My crying stopped, and I was taken aback.

Chapter 2
JOURNEY TO HELL

"Bleeding Love" "Always on My Mind"

Macmillan Dictionary for Children (Halsey, 1975) defines Hell (noun) as:

1. In Christian theology, the abode of Satan and the fallen angels, where the wicked will be punished after death
2. In various religions, the abode of the dead; hades
3. Any place or conditions of great evil, torment, or misery

"IF YOU'RE GOING THROUGH HELL"

I had now entered "Hell"—except I hadn't died. I was going to live and breathe Hell, and experience evil and suffering in my life. I was going to be punished, while I continued to draw breath here on Earth. I knew my husband wasn't in Hell. I knew my mom and dad weren't occupying space there either; they all were now in the Heavenly Realms without a care in the world. Free to appear however they desired. Free to jet around wherever they pleased and to create whatever they wished. Throw parties. Whatever they wanted, it would be theirs.

Hell—this space was reserved for me, one of the living. What had I done to deserve this in my life? Jesus supposedly "died for my sins," which I have never understood as the sins I have perpetrated in this life are not worthy of him dying a horrible death on the cross for.

The pain I was experiencing was a full body, excruciating torture that was continuous throughout every waking moment of my day and night—pure Hell. The only escape from Hell was when I slept. Hell couldn't knock that barrier down. I did find that I could take a respite from all this pain. I could sleep and everything would retreat. My body did not have to feel this suffocating grief and emptiness. I had a reprieve from feeling broken and shattered. In my sleep, I received visits from the Heavenly Realm. I experienced numerous visits from my husband and father—it was a beautiful, comforting break from my tumultuous life. I could fall into their arms, be held and comforted, and cry tears of joy instead of wretched sorrow. When I slept, my husband would visit me feverishly. It was one of the first ways he started contacting me from behind the Veil. In the dream/visitation I could feel myself again—I could feel his body, and it was so comforting. He held me against his chest and held me in his arms, touching me in an intimate way that was reserved for him.

I would also awaken with songs playing in my head, which I would write down in a log. They were beautiful songs from my husband that spoke of his undying love for me, how special I was to him, and how loved, cherished, and adored. There were even songs apologizing for him leaving too soon and for the pain due to his departure. Bono reached me in every way possible to hold me up, to lift me from my depths of sorrow, and to let me know that he was still with me.

SPIRIT BOX #4
SOME HELL-PING HANDS FROM BEHIND THE VEIL

"In life, I was known as, 'Dad,' 'Pops,' 'Bops,' 'Bapu,' 'Ted,' and 'Theodore'—if you ever called me Teddy, I would put you in your place.

"I am here today in Spiritual form with Carl, my son-in-law, visiting my daughter, Karen. My daughter never believed in the traditional concept of 'Hell,' which is found in some religions. She always had a mind of her own, and being punished beneath the Earth in fire where the wicked are tortured after death was something she didn't embrace. However, my daughter is now going to enter her own personal Hell. But she did nothing to deserve this Hell; she's not being punished, and her mother, husband, and I will continue to cross the Veil and be here by her side as she navigates life without us. She wants to joins us, but it isn't her turn yet."

"Bono here (though you should already know me by now). Karen and I incorporated music into our marriage whenever possible. I'm going to flood her mind with some kickin' tunes, so this way she'll know I've never left her."

My waking Hell consisted of stumbling from room to room and up and down the stairs, unending sobbing, tears running down my face, and eyes so puffy I could barely see, while trying to take care of my doggies and myself. Life was meaningless—I didn't care if I lived or died, and, quite frankly, I wanted to die. It didn't matter that I had two grown children—they had partners, were successful, and had good moral character. My husband and I had raised them in the best manner possible, and they were magnificent, intelligent, and caring people. They would survive without me. (When I look back at the possibility of leaving my children, I didn't realize that they then would have experienced the death of four influential and beloved people—four anchors—in their lives. That would have been a huge burden for them to bear. Yet, in this primal part of my mind, I could not see what the impact of my death would do to them. I just knew that my dying would release me from this brutal pain).

THE ORIGIN OF MY RELIGIOUS AND SPIRITUAL BELIEFS

My parents raised me in an all-affirming church—even before this became popular in later years. An all-affirming church accepts everyone—whether you are black, brown, pink or polka dotted. It honors all lifestyles—straight, gay, no matter how you identify and live—and you also have the choice of your path to God. My church, Bethel Congregational Church of Christ, chose Jesus and his teachings, but you were free to choose Muhammad, Yahweh, Vishnu, or others. This church embraced whichever path led you to spiritual growth.

Bethel was not a "fire and brimstone" church where you were banished to live in eternal damnation. In fact, most congregants—and even the minister—did not believe in Hell. My own family actually embraced the philosophy of reincarnation. We were never damned forever for one effed-up life; instead, we each got to experience hundreds—or even thousands—of lifetimes for our own personal growth toward becoming one with God. I believe that before we enter our current lives, we make choices and plans in the Heavenly Realm for our growth—to grow our souls and become closer to God. Our lives are full of lessons we plan for ourselves, in addition to planning with our "Heavenly Team." I must have planned my own lessons with gusto, because my life has been full of peaks, valleys, lost love, pain, strife, losing my power, and much more.

In growing up in this open-minded church, and nurtured by accepting parents, my opinions of Hell were formed. I do not believe that Hell is a physical place one goes to for all eternity for all of the sins committed in a lifetime. I do not think that God gives you one chance to live here on Earth to perfect your life. I believe that Hell is attained by our choices here during this lifetime and how those choices affect us and others. We make our own Hell on Earth, and it need not be permanent. Humans always have the choice to create their perfect lives or not.

Strange—some choices were made earlier in my life that were not the best for my spiritual growth, but that also would not deem me worthy of a lifetime spent in Hell. Sneaking out of the house in the middle of the night with a bottle of wine to meet friends was not worthy of damnation. Lying to my parents about my whereabouts was not Hell-worthy. Smoking weed before it was legal should not have sent me off to the netherworld. While here on Earth, I would pay penance for these digressions—not enter a place full of fire and evil demons upon my death.

If I did believe in Hell, then I should be redeemed anyway as I had paid penance for anything Hell-worthy in my life. Prior to my husband passing, I'd given freely of myself to my parents and taken care of them as they aged. I put my life on hold, put my parents first, and took care of them daily for eight years. The love and bond we had was incredible—they'd do anything for me, and I for them. I love liberally and fiercely, and I definitely gave of myself freely.

HELLZ BELLZ! "LOOKS LIKE HELL"

My father had been in hospice for six months, and he took God's hand on October 18, 2019 at the age of ninety-five. Mom was devastated, as they'd been married for seventy-two years and she wanted to join him. However, God wasn't ready for her, so I took care of her. I moved her into a foster care home after she'd had a bout with pneumonia, and she loved the small community feel with four other ladies and home cooked meals. Covid came into the picture, and I had to visit her from outside on the patio, but we made it through. On October 17, 2020, at the age of ninety, she left to be with Dad. She died one day short of his death date the previous year.

I'd never been able to mourn my father's death as my time had become wrapped up with Mom. I was just starting to breathe, and three weeks later my husband died and joined them both. I'd lost my mother and father, and now I had lost my husband. Compounded grief was beckoning me, and now entered my life. It was going to hit me hard, brutally, and furiously.

"Let's see what we can do to her. Can we take her down? Is she going to get this lesson, or experience it in another lifetime? She wanted it: let's give her all we've got."

Finding my husband laying on the rug was a defining moment. It didn't matter how I'd lived for sixty-five years before that day. None of my accomplishments or good deeds—not my career as a teacher, raising two magnificent kids, or taking care of my parents until the end—had any bearing on the downward spiral I was now entering: a gateway into my own personal Hell.

Living in this personal Hell was taking a toll on me and kicking my butt. I had no more zest for life, and just went through the motions. I found no pleasure or happiness. The world continued, while I sat rooted in my grief. For me, I had to let the grief wash over me and take me down. Since it is such a dark and unforgiving place to be, I had to reach out to others for help during this experience. I found help through my doctor, my counselor, reaching out to other widows, being vulnerable on Facebook, and finding solace in my friends. Everyone wanted to help, but I had to be ready to receive it—and that came slowly.

Forever in Touch:
Unbroken Connection and Loving Encounters with Bono

- I was saying grace at breakfast, and—at the end of my prayer—I always say what I am thankful for. I heard Bono say, "my wife." We have said grace like this for years. It was wonderful hearing that he was thankful for me.
- After saying my prayers, I talk to Bono—this is one of my nightly routines. One night, I looked up and saw his face, and he looked into my eyes. I was awestruck. His hair was black, like when we'd met; he looked younger and healthier and wore no glasses. He was above me while I was in the bed, looking down right into my face. The love was overwhelming and incredible.

My husband woke me with the song "Bleeding Love." While sitting at the breakfast table, Bono gave me a full, tingly body hug for a good five minutes. I cried tears of joy.

Chapter 3
"ALL MY LOVING"

The Good: "Good Morning Starshine"

On September 8, 1955, in Berkeley, California, a second baby daughter was born to Ruth Joy and Theodore Fieldbrave Jr. This young couple was deeply and madly in love, and they'd created a family to complete their partnership. They only lived in Berkeley for the first three years of the baby's life. Afterward, Beaverton, Oregon, became their home, as her father transferred to the Western Kraft Company. That baby, Karen Joyce Fieldbrave, grew up into me.

I have never remembered that baby's life in California. I do remember many events from my life growing up in Oregon, and I will share some of those with you here. However, my beloved Aunt Helen and Uncle Walter lived in Menlo Park, and my Grandmas Alice and Mae also lived in California, so we made frequent trips to visit there over the years.

I was supposed to be the "son" to complete this family; alas, I was not. Nevertheless, I was a rough-and-tumble tomboy, so I effectively became the son my father never had. Pops took me under his wing at a time when the wife normally stayed home, took care of the children, and did not work. My sister, Susan, became very close to my mom, and I to my father. Pops always remarked that he had two daughters, and that they were as different as night and day. From the onset, my sister did not want a baby sister and we had a tenuous relationship. She was content to be an only child, but she didn't get her wish.

My sister passed away a year after my husband transitioned. I was shocked that she'd died, as it was just as unexpected as my husband's death. The night she died, her Spiritual form came and sat at the end of my bed, and I talked to her. I told her I was sorry that she was gone and about how things hadn't worked out between us as sisters. She didn't say anything, but instead just looked at me. My sister was drop-dead gorgeous in life, and when she came for her Spiritual visit, she looked like she did in her thirties. I once compared her to Barbi Benton, a model who was quite striking. Sitting there, she looked lovely, serene, and happy. There is not much more to say about our fraught relationship in life, so from here on I'll mainly talk about Mom and Pops.

Regardless of that relationship, growing up was a lot of fun. I enjoyed my childhood, surviving the teen years, and flourishing as a young adult. The first twenty years of my life was stellar. However, when I got married and moved to Salem, that life would change drastically.

MY CHILDHOOD GROWING UP: ELEMENTARY AND MIDDLE SCHOOL YEARS

I was born at a time before computers, cell phones, fax machines, video games, and the rest of modern conveniences. We had a TV that received four channels, and our phone was on the wall of the house with a very long cord attached to it. Have you ever heard of a party line? That is what we had back in those days. Perhaps three or four different families would share a phone line. You may have gone to use it, but the other people were currently talking on the party line. They would politely end their conversation, so you could make your call. How antiquated does all of this sound? Very old. Yet, one of the best times to be a child.

Pops was the breadwinner, and Mom took care of the household and children. I worked by my father's side outdoors, while my mother and sister worked in the house. Pops taught me everything he knew about tending to a yard. Initially, I learned how to rake leaves, edge a lawn with a push edger, and how to plant; as time evolved, so did my skills. I could rototill like a champ, prune an orchard, lay barkdust, plant a large garden, and everything in between. When we finished, we would proudly stand there and look over everything. Dad was instrumental in developing my work ethic and in my being proud of a job well done.

I remember once asking Pops if I could go to the coast with a couple of friends the following day. He responded that I could go "as long as the front flower bed was weeded" before I left. That is a lifelong lesson I carry: my chores are done first before any pleasure. As an adult, it still stays with me, but occasionally I break that rule which is always in the back of my mind.

During these years, we became closer and closer. I became his favorite. I was always a rebel—questioning so much and often outspoken—and I secretly knew he was proud of me for it. He gave me several nicknames: Kare Kare; monkey, as I liked to climb trees; and Little Girl, which he called me until his dying breath. I was so close to my father. I idolized him. He made me feel so loved. Pops was the first man who stole my heart, and my love for him runs deep.

Mom and Dad were shepherds in our all-affirming church; Pops sang in the choir, and Mom taught Sunday School. Both Susan and I attended church school. If my friend Toni came along to church, I would try to cut class with her. I didn't know that she secretly craved going to Sunday School until I found out later in our adulthood.

One of the assistant ministers, Reverend Ann, dubbed me "a rebel." I was one of those polite, well-mannered children, but I'd also question authority (not always the most welcome action at church) and had a fun-loving, wild side. My sister did too; she just never got caught.

But mischief making wasn't my only specialty; sometimes, I also used my wild side for good. At an early age, I had a strong love for the creatures of the earth. One day, three kids came into "our" field. They were from a different area, and my friends and I talked to them. Later, we saw one of the boys take a huge rock and crush a snake to death. I was so upset at his appalling disregard for life and murder that I chased that boy through the field, but I could never catch him. I didn't know what I would do to him if I did, but my anger drove me forward. Dad used to say that "Karen has the fastest legs on the block." I wish I'd been even faster that day.

A love of animals was deeply ingrained in my family. We always had cats and dogs, which still holds true for me today. My cat days were over once my children moved out, but dogs continue to be ever-present in my life. When I was little, we also had an incubator and hatched duck eggs. I had two ducks who thought I was their mother and followed me everywhere. This was especially fun while I cut the lawn, as they'd follow me up and down the yard, quacking behind me. I loved Dagmar and Elliot; ducks are my favorite birds to this day.

We lived in a suburban American neighborhood that was surrounded by trees, fields, and a park. I had many good friends in that area. I fondly remember us spending a lot of time during my elementary school days exploring, catching crawdads (but releasing them), playing in the large fields, building forts, exploring, climbing trees, riding bikes, horseback riding in local stables, and walking to school together. We also played games like dodgeball, "Red Light, Green Light," and "Red Rover." We did not fear leaving the house during the day, coming home for lunch, or returning when the streetlights went on. You could tell where your child was, because their bike would be outside a neighbor's house—and if there was a gathering, you could always tell which house the kids were at by the number of bikes in the yard. It was an idyllic childhood.

As we grew, we all started noticing boys. All of a sudden, we all acted weird around them. Our bodies were changing and so were we. Then, in sixth grade, I was introduced to "Spin the bottle." Have you ever played that? We'd go to a house where no parents were home, sit in a circle of boys and girls, take turns spinning a bottle in the center, and whoever the bottle landed on would get to choose who they'd kiss. This was so foreign to me, yet also tantalizing. My friends were cuter than me and were getting picked more for kisses, but it was still fun. For some strange reason, when we kissed, we went into a closet with that person to make out. Some stayed there longer than others. I was confused at the time, but as an adult I now know what was going on during those prolonged visits to the closet. I believe this is where I got my first kiss.

In middle school, boys and girls started "going steady," and the girls were given a ring by the fella. Boys would call you on the phone, and then not talk. I usually let the boy take charge, and he would say a little something and then…silence. When I look back, it was all just some silly stuff while learning about the opposite sex.

I look back on my childhood with very happy memories; life was much simpler then. I had such a loving and nurturing bond with my parents—especially with Pops. Since he was the first man in my life, I learned early on what it meant to be loved, respected as a person, and valued. The strong love of animals my family held, and the joy, love, and bonds which we formed with them, also affected my conception of a loving relationship. Even at my age now, I cannot image my life without an animal. The love one shares with an animal is all-encompassing, and you have complete mutual devotion and an unbreakable connection.

When my friends and I played, "Spin the bottle," it was an interesting first experience with boys. Why were we going in the closet? Why so secretive? Was this somehow forbidden and shameful? Did we just want privacy? I wonder if this small act had an impact on me as an adult. When things got rough in my first two marriages, I did not share my problems with my parents. Why didn't I tell my parents? Had I learned at an early age that matters concerning relations with men were shameful and should be kept hidden? Or was I just too embarrassed to admit they were correct in their judgements regarding my ex-husbands? Did this "innocent" game help shape my feelings about love and relationships in the future? It is hard to say.

If I could, I'd erase middle school from my memory: begone kids with rampant hormones and all the elementary schools converging into one school. Life was so foreign, and we were ruled by lockers and having to get to the next class. I had a frightful time. Thankfully, I loved most of my teachers and was a "good student." However, I did continue being rebellious and adventurous. One time, I got caught throwing spit wads in class. My punishment was humiliating. I didn't have to write sentences or stay in at recess; instead, I had to lay down in the back of the classroom—on the cold floor. What? So strange. Kids would sneak a look back at me and I knew that my face was burning red. I learned to be more discreet in my escapades.

I had a math teacher who terrified the class. His class was at the end of the school day. He would make us sit with our heads down until not a sound was made, and we had to scramble outside to catch the bus. He was a horrible teacher; I couldn't learn anything, and I was scared of him. One of my friends bent over to pick up his pencil, and the teacher grabbed him and shoved him up against the wall. I told Mom, and she got me out of that teacher's class. (On a side note, I saw that math teacher again when I was flying to Hawaii with my parents and first husband. He was so excited to see me, and I could hardly engage with him. It seems he'd become a dentist, which made sense as he seemed to enjoy inflicting discomfort and pain.)

The new math class I moved into was amazing. I walked in on the first day, and no math was being taught. Kids were hanging around talking to each other and sitting on the tops of their desks. One popular girl was sitting on a stoner boy's lap, and the teacher was just chatting with the students. What a relief this class was to me. Talk about things "adding up": because little did I know, but my first two marriages would be like having a "relationship" similar to that with my first math teacher, while finding Bono—my true love—would be like finding that second math class and teacher all over again. Both (or all three) were men. Polar opposites. Night and Day.

School in general came very easy for me. I remember loving to write and my teachers complimenting me on my stories and creations. However, I was so glad when I was finally heading off to high school. As for extracurriculars, I don't remember sports being offered before high school, or perhaps my parents simply neglected to mention them. Instead, I was a Brownie, later became a Girl Scout, and took piano lessons for a good nine years (I was quite accomplished and regret quitting). Summers ushered in church camp and traveling. While I didn't have a ton of friends, I had several close, genuine friendships.

In 1969, while I was still in middle school, our family bought a couple of acres, and I moved further out into the country. It was heavenly. We were surrounded by fields and farms. Our neighbor was Guy Carr, owner of Carr Chevrolet, and everyone in the area knew everyone. What a delightful turn of events.

During my childhood, prior to our move, Toni and I had spent numerous hours at the stable riding horses. We'd both loved horses and horseback riding and had said that "nothing is better than being on the back of a horse." It is very freeing. She'd eventually moved a short distance away, though, and we'd quit riding together.

However, my new neighbors, the Speer kids, each had ponies, and their father had a spirited mustang named Apache. He also had "a bad back" and couldn't ride her, so I was given the "task" to do so until I went to college. Mr. Speer said I had to clean the barn in exchange. I cleaned it once, and I must have proven my merit as I was never asked to clean it again.

I loved riding this horse. So much of my time was spent on the back of her. Back then, I rode bareback or with a Western Saddle. The only attire I wore were cowboy boots and jeans—no other gear like they have nowadays. It feels like you and the horse become one.

Where we'd moved to, there was a forest just down the road, and open fields for miles. The feeling of being on horseback there was indescribable. Nothing was better than this. I was very happy there. I was still in the city, but it was like living in the country. Our house backed up to our neighbor's pasture, which had cows and a horse. As a teen, riding was a refuge for me—a way to escape the angst of youth, and to engage in something I loved without a care in the world.

Like her rider, Apache could also be a troublemaker. She didn't have a bit in her mouth, but rather a hackamore bridle. Whenever we came home through the woods, 99 percent of the time she'd grab the side of the hackamore into her mouth so I couldn't stop her. She'd run full tilt up a path in the woods and try to buck me off. It was a game she played with me, and I didn't enjoy it. I usually stayed on her, but she liked to try to fling me off.

Before I had moved to the country, I'd had a very spiritual experience while riding. I'd been alone, and my horse and I had climbed up to the top of a small mountain. I sat on the steed's back, and the wind blew back my hair and the horse's mane. The reeds and grasses bent down in the wind. The sky was cloudy with different shades of gray. The horse and I were mesmerized. Something spiritual was taking place for the both of us, but I couldn't put my finger on it. We were transfixed by the beauty of the land and all we were experiencing. Surely, we were being visited, but I wasn't in tune to Spirit yet. We hadn't moved for quite a long time, and we'd simply stared off into the distance over the valley. When I've thought about that experience, I've still succeeded in conjuring up the same feelings and all the details.

I was a child who had a zest for life. If I was told not to cross this line, I would point to the line, step over it, and ask, "this one?" I wasn't a troublemaker, but I was always up for a good time. In middle school, I started sneaking out of the house at night and meeting up with my friends. Wine and laughter were usually included. We would drink this god-awful Annie Green Springs Wine and Mad Dog 20/20. There were the likes of "Mickey Big Mouth Beer," and we thought if we drank it out of a straw we would get drunk faster—not true.

When I snuck out at night, it was like I entered a different world—and it was my oyster while everyone slept. We snuck over to boys' houses and threw rocks at the windows to wake them up, but we were never successful. One time, Toni and I were at the Oregon Zoo for a nighttime event. We snuck back into the animal enclosures and rode the donkeys. I just pushed the envelope a little bit, and I really enjoyed life. My parents tried to keep a tight rein on me.

I had a strict curfew, which I'd follow so as to avoid getting grounded. I don't think my parents ever caught on that I was sneaking out of the house at night. Frankly, this surprised me, but it was always for the purpose of good, clean fun and never meant to be malicious. These escapades definitely prepared me well for my high school years; they also helped ready me for my later immersion into other entirely different worlds—like college and the Spiritual Realms.

HIGH SCHOOL YEARS: "KAREN"

I attended Aloha High School, and at that time it was an open campus. This was not a good thing for people my age, as we were always leaving campus. You may have had a science class at 8 a.m., and a math class at 1 p.m. Students weren't prone to staying on campus to attend the next class. We weren't skipping school, but we had free reign of our time while at school.

I was a child who grew up with sex, drugs, and rock and roll. I did two out of three, and sex wasn't one of them. In high school, I was introduced to weed, LSD, psilocybin, blotter acid, Thai Sticks, and more. The music was superior too. It was a fun time of life. We left school often to go get high, and we also left enough time before going home so that the high would wear off.

One time, I'd taken some acid, and had to go home on the bus. Acid causes your pupils to dilate. Mom noticed my eyes, and she went to stand by the window. She wanted me to come and look at her hair color in the light to see if I liked the shade. I knew she just wanted to see if my pupils had shrunk, and I hightailed it to my room until the high started wearing off.

Taking hallucinatory drugs can expand your mind in ways unimaginable. However, later in my life, my expansion into an extraordinary sensory experience was through connecting with the Spiritual Realm. This is hands down, by far, THE BEST experience.

High school was easy for me, and I didn't have to study until I got into college. I received a "C" on one of my report cards; Mom was upset with me, and she gave me one term to clear that grade. I told her a C was average, and she told me that I was not an average kid. Those words made an impact on me. I never got a C again in any class through high school or college.

I only needed one credit to graduate when I was a senior, and I decided to go to Portland Community College to get that credit and to do undergrad work. I also think Mom wanted me out of high school so that I wouldn't have too much free time on my hands.

COLLEGE YEARS AND THE PATH CHOSEN

Talk about a new world. I had lived in a bubble throughout my schooling, and now I was being thrown into an ocean of different people of varying ages, lifestyles, and backgrounds. It was so eye-opening. Also, "streaking" was a thing back then, and naked people (usually guys) would run through the school commons. My world was certainly opening up.

I LOVED community college. The professors wanted us to THINK, learn, and discern. They wanted us to debate and discuss—it was exciting. It was also where I met my first husband when I was seventeen. We wed when I was twenty, and a couple of months afterward I turned twenty-one and started my teaching career. Ironically, it seems that Carl—whom I wouldn't meet until I turned thirty-nine—also attended Portland Community College at the same time I did. We never met then; it wasn't meant to happen yet. I've always wondered about what would've happened if we had, though. How different would my life have been then?

Around this time, I decided I wanted to study education and become a teacher. People on campus were talking about computers as "the thing of the future." At that time, computers took up the space of a room and were huge. I couldn't see myself sitting in a room working with a machine, and Intel was non-existent. This was another fork in the road for me: What if I'd decided to enter the realm of computers instead? I'd be on a totally different trajectory. While grieving, I've asked similar "what-if" questions regarding the timing of loved ones' deaths.

The University of Portland is located on the bluff in north Portland. It has outstanding schools of education, business, and nursing. It is a

Catholic University, and it has small classes. I decided that I wanted to go to U of P. Mom and I visited the campus, and I fell in love with it. We met with the Dean of Education, and he planned classes to take me through my two years there. U of P was on a two-semester system. Mom went to write a check for the school. When they told her the amount, she asked if that was for the entire year—but she was told it was for the first semester. Mom decided she had to go back to work to pay for my schooling. She knew the quality of the education I would receive, and she freely gave of herself. I learned to do so too.

Before I started classes, Dad came to visit. I showed him where I'd take public buses to the two schools where I'd be a student teacher. Pops was not okay with his young daughter waiting on the corner alone, so he gave me the VW Bug and a credit card. Gotta love my dad. He always took care of his little girl. Truth be told, the areas for catching the buses were sketchy.

As previously mentioned, math has never been my forte. In community college, I took a class that "got you ready" for a real math class. While I was at U of P., there was another math teacher who terrorized the students. (What is up with math teachers?) He made us work at the board, and he'd throw things at us if we got the problems wrong.

I went to inform the Dean and to change my math class, but there were no others available. He reviewed my transcripts and noted that I'd had a math class in community college. I held my breath, knowing the nature of that class, but he considered it valid. With the swipe of his pen, I'd suddenly completed my math requirement. Wow. Even at that age, I learned to avoid abuse and what I disliked, as well as to reach out to people for help when necessary. These are skills I would definitely need when it came to my first two marriages and later for the grieving process.

I did learn to greet the priests by calling them "Father," and I made many adjustments. Just like community college, U of P was highly diverse. I got one of the best educations possible there. I had some of the best teachers throughout my education, from elementary school through college. I can recall many of them by names and see their faces and the impressions they left on me. They impacted my life incredibly, and I can easily see why I chose to become a teacher.

STARTING MY TEACHING CAREER

Immediately after graduating in 1976 with a B.S. in Elementary Education, I was invited to interview for three teaching positions: in Milton Freewater, Aumsville, and at a local Catholic school. Dad and I drove together to Milton Freewater. There was no way Pops would let me drive across the state alone; my parents always took care of me. My family is very liberal and open-minded, and we were greeted by "Reagan for President" posted all over town when the Vietnam War had ended the year before. Upon checking into the hotel, the clerk declared:

"Oh, you must be the new school marm."

Dad and I exchanged looks; this town was definitely too small for me, and I knew it wouldn't be a good fit for me to start my career. The philosophies didn't match mine, everyone knew everyone's business, and I was alone and far from my family. I declined this offer.

St. Cecilia's Catholic School was a beautiful school in downtown Beaverton, where I lived. However, their faith differed markedly from mine, and they also didn't have my preferred retirement plan. These were major drawbacks. I thanked them for their interest but declined.

Off to Aumsville I drove. The school was just 45 minutes from my home in Beaverton. At that time, Aumsville was a sleepy farming community outside of Salem. I loved the school and the community. The Board consisted of the principal and local farmers. The principal was pleasant and interviewed me, and the farmers sat there stoically; they didn't talk to me at all. In the end, they offered me the job of teaching third grade, and I was over the moon. Third grade was my favorite, and everything had come together so nicely. It was a public-school system, offered the insurance, was close to home, and I loved the feel of the place. It was just right.

My life up to this new chapter had been welcoming. Powered by the love and strength of my parents, I was molded into a compassionate, smart, empowered, and independent woman with the world at my feet. I could take on anything. I had no idea that a new side of reality would hit me upside the head through my twenties and into my thirties. My power would be taken, and I'd become unrecognizable. It was the hardest of realities I could face—it almost caused me to end my life. The school of hard knocks was the biggest growth and expansion point of my life.

THE "BAD": "DON'T WORRY BABY"

(Trigger Warning: The following two sections describe my life and my soul in a downward spiral as I battled spousal abuse and the ensuing depression. It is not a pretty picture. If you are entrenched in grief, you may want to skip these two sections.)

In 1976, I had just graduated college, had gotten married for the first time, was offered my first teaching position, and moved to Salem. So many changes in a short time. I was just a "baby" when I look back. As a recent grad, I thought I knew it all. In fact, I had heaps more to learn. I could spend chapters on this part of my life, but I'll only chat about the pertinent issues.

During this time, I was trying to figure out how I fit in and how to integrate myself without losing myself. I was married and living with a man—a new experience. Prior to that, I'd lived with my parents and then in a dorm for two years. Living with someone presents many challenges: you must learn to give and to acclimate yourself to each other. We lived in an apartment complex with many young married couples, and it was a blast. We all partied together, had barbecues, and created our own fun community. I was able to notice how other men treated their wives—with some more caring, always respectful, and working as a team.

As our marriage progressed, I found that I'd given away my voice to my husband. His wants and needs were always met, while mine only were at times. My husband also had a wandering eye, and he cheated on me throughout our marriage. He had this same disrespect before we were married, but I thought that surely, he would change afterward. One of my first lessons: a leopard doesn't change its spots. My parents had not blessed this marriage and had tried to discourage me—but as a headstrong, twenty-year-old woman, I didn't listen.

I'd never spoken of this to my parents or friends, but I thought this husband was going to kill me. He didn't like the fact that I wanted a divorce. Allegedly, "in his culture," the man would cheat on the wife, and the wife would take him back. That wasn't *my* culture, and I'd finally had enough. He was a skilled marksman. I thought I'd be working in the kitchen, a shot would ring out, and I'd crumple to the floor. Looking back, I realize that this feeling came from my gut—where the truth resides. I should've listened to it right away, and maybe I could've avoided much heartache.

However, my first marriage did produce my son. He's such a blessing from this time in my life, and so it is difficult to regret it. Eventually, I moved back home—with Nick in tow—and later filed for divorce. Further dragging my ex-husband through the dirt won't serve any purpose but suffice it to say he showed me what not to accept in a marriage—or so I thought.

THE UGLY: "HIGHWAY STAR"

I met my second husband while still married to my first. This caused a huge problem for my father, who considered it adultery, but my mother was pushing me to date as she didn't want me to return to my first husband. Thus, man number two came into the picture. He was, I thought, a complete turnaround from my first husband. He owned a home, had a successful job at Nike, was a sharp dresser, and was attentive to my every need. I had someone now who put me first and fawned over me. So romantic. So caring. So thoughtful. I remember one friend being very jealous of the way I was treated as she did not receive the same from her husband.

Little by little, my husband became critical of my parents and friends. He thought very highly of himself, believed that my friends and family were inferior, and had very little empathy. I had to dress a certain way, act a certain way, my panties and bra had to match, and he kept track of my movements. My parents did not want me to marry him. Did I listen? No. I had entered two extremely different marriages, but both had resulted in my giving away my voice and the men making all the choices. How could I have allowed this to happen? My parents had embraced my rebelliousness, and had raised a strong, assertive woman.

My second husband decided to divorce me when I started to push back, and he traded me in for a newer, younger model with a young son the same age as Nick. I left the house, and he moved them in and put that boy in my son's bedroom. This was a horrendous time in my life. Again, the details could fill pages, but that is not the intent of this book.

During this time, I felt like a failure. I'd gone through two marriages, and I couldn't make either of them work. I felt worthless. I tried to be a stable influence in my children's lives, and to maintain a semblance of calm at work. However, I'd sunk into a deep depression. My hopes and dreams had been destroyed. Looking from the outside in, it looked like man number two and I'd had a perfect marriage and that he doted upon me. That was simply the illusion he portrayed.

My doctor was fabulous and supported me, but he also put me on antidepressants. This was back in the '80s, and I wasn't told that antidepressants can promote suicidal thoughts. I don't even know if the medical community knew this yet. When I started contemplating suicide, the pain was unbearable. I had no will to live. I felt hopeless and unloved, and it seemed like the only way out of the pain was to kill myself. Even better, I knew exactly how I was going to do it.

I'd purchase a gun when I was feeling "okay," and I'd climb up a trail at Mt. Hood and shoot myself. That's all. I would put the gun in my mouth and pull the trigger. My family would not find my body. I was hurting so much; I just wanted the pain to end. I felt worthless. I had nothing to offer the world. The world would be better off without me.

One day, my daughter and I were playing, and we fell to the ground. Her head rested on my forearm, and her blonde hair spread onto the carpet. I looked into her eyes. She was not looking back. An inner light shined through from the depths of her soul. I knew right then that I would not kill myself, and I became a fighter again. I was not going to be a defeated, powerless woman. An Angel, or some helpful Spiritual form, had been able to reach me through my pain.

Later, I returned Victoria to her father's house, and he started digging at me. Even though Victoria was present, I picked up a broom and was going to throttle him to death—I truly was. I'd had enough. I could see in his terrified eyes that he recognized what had happened and he backed off. He had lost all his power over me. Thank God for divine intervention.

I look back on this time and think how horrible it would've been if I'd committed suicide. My parents would have been devastated, my children would've had no mom and would have lived with two different men, and everyone's lives would've been destroyed. My friends and students would have been shocked. I would've set the course of a tidal wave of bad ripples.

It took me two marriages and twelve years, to finally chart the course back to the person I'd been twenty years previously. But I had survived, and there was nowhere to go but up.

"TILL THERE WAS YOU," BONO: MY PRINCE CHARMING AND THE "NEVER ENDING SONG OF LOVE"

My Prince Charming did not ride in on a steed with a coat of armor. That giant of a man came in with a beat-up BMW, a rat tail in his hair, a huge grin, and mischievous eyes. He wore suspenders and fancied striped shirts. Carl had a booming laugh, and he never held that back.

He entered my life just as I was regaining my foothold and power. As my power returned, so did my hopes, dreams, and happiness. Carl would help me to rediscover and cultivate the person I used to be, and he'd help me learn to thrive. The sparkle and light returned to my eyes, the laughter to my lips, and joy to my soul. Karen was finding her way back to the world.

However, in dating me, he got the package deal: I came with two young children (three and eight years old) and two ex-husbands. Unbelievably, he stayed and didn't run for the hills. At one point in time, my son offered him an out. He told Carl:

"You've seen the menu; you know what's on your plate. I don't blame you if you leave."

But he stayed. He was just right.

Forever in Touch:
Unbroken Connection and Loving Encounters with Bono

Bono often gives me chills and full body shakes to let me know he is still with me. That is his main way to come to me. I have learned to stop whatever I am doing and chat with him when he does this. His chills and shakes feel different than others. He has a special way of reaching out to me, so there is no guesswork when he makes his presence known.

I was outside with the pups, and Bono gave me chills. Later that night, I was crying about selling his car. When I experience grief, I can't think straight or make decisions. I was just spiraling, and I didn't know if I was making the correct decision about selling it. Bono told me to "rip the Band-Aid off" and to sell the car.

While getting cleaned up in the bathroom, I was thinking about my life. Bono put this song and phrase into my head: "Someday my Prince Will Come."

whoever dies first wins

chapter 4
SPARKS FLEW

When I met you in "Fields of Gold"

1995 was the magical year I met my future husband, and two years later we wed. At that time, I had another chiropractor, and Mom freaked out when she saw how poorly my neck had been adjusted. She kept telling me to go and see her chiropractor, Dr. Bonofiglio. Anyone who knew Mom knows that she was relentless—like a dog with a bone—so I finally made an appointment. She had said he was a great doctor, but she hadn't mentioned that he was also handsome and hot. That appointment was one of the best things to ever happen to me in my life. It was meant to be, and it gives me great pleasure to tell you the story of how Carl and I first connected.

"THE FIRST TIME IT HAPPENS": "CAN'T TAKE MY EYES OFF YOU"

It was one of those times in my life when I lacked money. I'd been married twice, and I was a single mother raising two children. One father didn't pay any child support, while the funds from the other were meager. I was never one of those rich divorcees where the exes always helped out. Dr. Carl Louis Bonofiglio Jr. had a toy drive for Christmas at his office, and he offered a free exam for a toy. I purchased a toy that I could afford and went in for my free evaluation. The toy I purchased was embarrassing as I'd usually spend more.

Upon entering his office, I turned to see him sitting at his desk and froze in my tracks…Oh. My. God. I was speechless. He also froze, looking up from his paperwork. All I could utter was "hi," which was all I received in return. These words may sound like one of those corny romance novels or something out of a soap opera, but here and now these words are valid: sparks flew between us. You could feel the shift in energy: it was strong and electrifying. It was like we'd known each other for years and were reunited. Never had I experienced this in my life, and I couldn't move. I broke the spell by tossing the cheap toy under the tree, hoping that he wouldn't notice its inferiority. On the contrary, he came around from his desk, sat down, picked up the toy, and began *admiring* it. He ran his hands over it in appreciation—he was not pretending but was actually enjoying the toy. I found out later that he collected toys and had a love for them. I was struck by how kind and gentle his demeanor was.

The spell was not completely broken, however, and I could not take my eyes off of him. He was tall, dark, and gorgeous. Sporting thick black hair, a cleft in his chin, and dancing and mischievous eyes, he towered above me by a foot. My heart was leaping out of my chest, but we kept everything professional until months later. I had no idea that not only was he *my* type, but I was *his*. I was short in stature, had long, curly, dark hair, and I later learned he loved my eyes.

SPIRIT BOX #5: "ADDICTED TO LOVE": "BREATHLESS" BONO

"*Man, oh, Man.* Who is this lady who just came into my office? She walked through the door, and I can't move from my chair—she's mesmerizing. Long dark hair, beautiful eyes, and a smile from ear to ear. Wait. She's a patient. I must treat her as one… but if I didn't, I could see myself being with her for the rest of my life…and putting a ring on her finger. She's 'The One,' even though I swore off marriage again…"

After all these years, I can still conjure up the feelings I had upon meeting my "knight in shining armor." I met him when I was thirty-nine, and—even now at sixty-seven—he still makes my heart go pitter-patter. We locked eyes. How could I not fall head over heels for this man? With his grin, gusto, and laughter, I was putty in his hand. I'd found my soulmate, and I'd never believed in them before and was certainly not looking for one. Damn. I was in for the most phenomenal ride of my life.

CARL AND KAREN, A BUDDING ROMANCE: "I WANT YOU TO WANT ME"

He became my doctor, and I became his patient. He had a girlfriend, and I had a boyfriend. However, Doc started coming over to my house and hanging out with my kids and a girlfriend of mine, Vivi, who lived with us. We would cook together and play racquetball and games. He never won a single match—ever. He was too tall. He was a good foot or so taller than me, and I could get the ball down, really close to the ground. We were both highly competitive, and I enjoyed beating this big, tall, handsome doctor.

We built a strong friendship first: I think this was key to our relationship. We formed bonds between him and me and between us and the children. Nick and Victoria were eight and three years old at the time, respectively. I wasn't bringing another man over who was a love interest, but rather my doctor and a friend. We did things together—all four of us.

One day, I was lying on Bono's chiro table—my eyes closed, his hands under my neck cupping my head. He asked about my boyfriend, and he was told that we had broken up. A single tear slid down my cheek, and he wiped my tear away. It was such a tender moment that it is etched in my memory. That was the turning point in our relationship. Once we started being together and touching, we never stopped until he left this world. This connection led to plenty of decadent and loving behavior. We were adventurous and had a fun life together. You can see our shared physical and playful natures in most photos—we're always intertwined.

Before we started dating, I asked him why he didn't marry his girlfriend. He replied:

"Why ruin a good thing?"

I just stared at him quizzically as it was such a strange and shocking answer. I remember the first time I told him I loved him. There was fear in his eyes, and this was something I didn't expect to see. He looked scared and apprehensive, and his eyes shifted away from me as he processed what I'd said. I was taken aback, and inquired if he was okay. He said that he was fine. I had no idea until later that he'd been married before, and it must've left a bad taste in his mouth. Luckily, he sure felt differently about that soon enough, and we eventually got married.

I've never felt more loved, cherished, respected, and adored by anyone—other than Pops, of course. Carl and I both shared these emotions. Our love was palpable. He took care of me, and I took care of him. Like I said, I'd always pooh-poohed the term "soulmate," but—honestly—we were soulmates, as true as could be. The love and devotion we felt were incredible.

He was the first of my husbands who honored my being. He didn't try to control me. He let me…be me. I didn't have to look like arm candy, act a certain way, have a certain look, weigh a certain weight, present myself properly, or acquiesce to his voice and wishes. He let me be the crazy, flamboyant, outspoken, powerful wife whose voice had been stifled by two other marriages. That voice was silenced when I was twenty and married my first husband, and it didn't reappear until I was in my late thirties. Bono unconditionally accepted my flaws, missteps, frailties, and quirkiness, and he loved me just the same (or even partially because of them). I know many were in awe of our marriage—our love truly was that impressive.

CUTTING-EDGE CARL, CORRECT THE CURVE IN MY LIFE: "YOU'RE THE INSPIRATION"

My husband was one of the most dynamic, creative, and forward-thinking men I have ever met. He was always striving to become a better person. Let me share with you some more of Bono's attributes and the many hats he wore that made him such a beloved and inspiring man, and you'll see exactly why his death was so exceptionally unnerving to me and many others who knew him.

"DOC" BONOFIGLIO

Carl kept talking about the need for a scoliosis doctor in the area. He went above and beyond with his practice and used cutting-edge methods—for example, he became the only CLEAR Certified chiropractor on the West Coast at the time, and he was able to treat his patients with nonsurgical, structural changes to their spinal formation. Patients flew in from Hawaii and Palm Springs seeking his services. Many patients and friends lovingly called him Doc.

Due to several car accidents and getting bucked off horses throughout my life, I had an S-curve instead of the proper C-curve in my neck. This used to give me migraines so painful that I'd go to the hospital and get shots of Demerol for relief. Carl corrected all of the angles in my neck, and I was relieved of migraines for the first time in years. What a doc I had found.

Attached to the clinic was a space that he'd converted into a kettlebell gym, and he'd become a certified kettlebell instructor. The gym was fully equipped, with tons of kettlebells of varying weights, and he used the gym to rehabilitate his patients and to teach classes. He had so many passions in life. I never had the drive and ambition he possessed. I floated down the river of life, while he was always planning and living full steam ahead.

SPIRIT BOX #6: CHIROPRACTIC CORRECTION AND A HEAVENLY WORKOUT

"My wife's neck is so messed up; no wonder she gets migraines. A perfect neck, while supporting the head, forms a C-shape. Karen's neck is shaped like an S. The spinal cord runs through the spinal column all the way to the brain; it's a nice messaging center. If it's properly shaped, the communication runs smoothly through the body. Think about a hose: if it gets cricks in it, the water doesn't flow properly; the same can happen with a person's neck. Thankfully, due to my training, I can get Karen's neck back in working order.

"I am so pleased I can offer Karen, and my other patients, kettlebell training once they're ready. Kettlebells look like cannon balls with handles on them, and they come in various weights. They work incredibly well for improving strength and balance. They also improve your core strength, shape up body posture, and can create a better range of motion. Incorporating kettlebells into my patients' care has been paramount, and they get hooked on swing bells. Do you like the name of my clinic? *Hellz Bellz Kettlebells.* It's quite a conversation starter. Now, would you like to join me for a Heavenly workout?"

"DAD" BONOFIGLIO: CARL, KAREN, AND THE KIDS FIND A FAMILY

My husband never had a chance once we met. Not only was I his type, but he was also enticed by my ability to cook. We had a love like not many others seem to experience, which is baffling to me. We loved, cherished, and took care of each other totally and completely. I know my family felt he spoiled me, and he did—no argument here—but I reciprocated in kind. I can honestly say that I only changed a lightbulb once in the twenty-six years we were together. I only did that because he was out of town, and I couldn't see in the closet. I could tell you story after story of what he'd do for me, but then you'd know how much I was spoiled. He rarely told me no.

I wonder if my husband knew what he was getting into when he decided that we should be together. We started dating, and the kids came along with the territory: my kids can be quite outspoken and have no filters. Both of my children had strong personalities, and there were two ex-husbands in the background as well. I'm surprised he didn't run for the hills. I explained to my husband, early on, that blood was thicker than water and that my kids would always come first. He accepted that. What a wild ride we had as a family.

There was something that I could never explain, and I feel that it had to do with him losing his father at an early age in life. He could say the words "I love you" only to me. He couldn't say it to my children or to my parents, and our family spoke those words freely. I would ask him for an explanation, but he never answered. Victoria said one time:

"It's okay Mom, we know that he loves us."

I never questioned him again. He did love the kids. He called them his "son" and his "daughter" and was instrumental in their care and in raising them. He showed them both the qualities of a phenomenal father as their fathers were both complete failures in that role. He not only gave his heart and soul to me, but to my children and parents as well. His humbleness and kindness were overpowering. I wasn't the only one honored by this man.

Nick was a Boy Scout and later became an Eagle Scout, and Bono became part of the troop. He was gladly accepted among Nick's friends and the parents. They used to go on campouts. When they returned from one, Bono let me know that Nick would scream in his sleep. Nick never screamed in his sleep at home, but rather only on his campouts. Bono only came running once; after that, he let Nick scream on all the rest of the outings. Nick had to work something out that came through to his subconscious in his dreams.

SPIRIT BOX #7: BONO FINDS A FAMILY

"I found a woman whom I fell madly in love with, and then I had an instant family. At first, I didn't try to be the kids' father. I was there to love and support them. As we grew as a family, we came to have a great love for each other. I was excited to be included in Son's Boy Scout activities, to take him fishing, and to teach him to play the guitar. I loved having an instant son. I'd lost my father at an early age, and now I embraced filling that same role.

"Having a girl was a different experience for me. Victoria was so different than Nick; she 'hung back' more. But once we settled in as a family, she was very comfortable. She liked to ride on my back like I was a horsey, and to get special treats like coffee cake before school. She was a girly girl and my little

> princess. Teaching her to ride a bike, and seeing her zip around the neighborhood, was fun and exciting.
>
> "I called them my son and daughter. I loved them and our wonderful family completely."

My whole family eats off each other's plates. Even my parents and sister always did so. If we were all at a restaurant, we would sample each other's dishes and it was not a big deal. We still do this to this day. This was new for Bono, but he started sampling with gusto. I remember one time when he took a bite from my hamburger and only about ¼ was left. We had a proper etiquette about it: it was a small sample, and he had to learn.

Once, when we were eating at home, Bono had prepared a shrimp and pasta dish for us all. I was saving some shrimp, and—out of the corner of my eye—I could see my son's fork coming for my plate. I was not going to share as we were eating the same food. The chairs were on wheels, and Nick and I struggled over the shrimp. We were pushing each other around the room and grasping at the food. Carl and Victoria just stared at us. He may have "seen the menu," but this was certainly new to him. Yet, he stayed. I think we left him speechless many times.

Victoria was another story. She may have seemed quiet growing up, but she had definite opinions and let them be known. She would ride Carl around like a horsey, but—thankfully—she didn't kick him. One time, he was driving with her, and she matter-of-factly told him:

"You're not the boss of me."

My husband is not a curser, but he told her: "Knock that shit off."

I think that was the last of that.

He'd drive Victoria to school, and occasionally stop at Starbucks to get her a crumbly coffee cake. He always remarked that a great deal was left on the table and less in Binky's mouth. Binks loved her coffee cake.

SPIRIT BOX #8: THE VICTORIAN EARS

"My daughter, Victoria. She was such a shy, energetic, and entertaining child growing up. From putting tights over her head and pretending the legs were her ears, she made an outfit by sticking her legs into a plastic bag. She was a very creative daughter. Victoria grew into a very outspoken, intelligent woman, and my heart burst with pride at every new milestone in her life. I'm so proud of her. I am especially happy that she never kicked me when we played, 'horsey'."

I was not the only one in this package deal—he had an instant family. Yet, he loved them like they were his own. He loved and was proud of his family, and we all grew together and overcame any obstacles we faced. I felt so honored to be his wife. Even though he jokingly called me "Crazy Woman," I knew he loved me with every breath.

"DARINGLY DIVERSE" BONOFIGLIO: THE AMAZING BONO'S HOBBIES AND PURSUITS

My husband was an amazing man in his personal pursuits too. I was content with teaching school, but he was always extending himself outward. He had a thirst for knowledge, experience, and adventure. Always learning. Always growing. Always being the best version of himself.

He was so adventurous. He introduced me to body shots. We would belly up to The Gypsy and take body shots off each other. We were never kicked out of the bar.

SPIRIT BOX #9: BODY SHOTS WITH BONO

"Body shots with my woman. Yes. Bartender—a couple of shots of tequila, some lime slices, and a bottle of salt please. Sitting on bar stools made this easy to do; I'd put my legs on either side of Karen's stool, so I had full access to her. Of course, I'd start with her neck and eventually work myself down a little lower with each shot (but I'd always be appropriate). A lick on her skin, followed by a sprinkle of salt, a shot of tequila, and then a suck on the lime. Yes, please. And guess what: she did the same to me in return. Fun times.

"Straddling her with my legs and an arm behind her made me feel very protective of her. I love my woman so much. She had two asshole former husbands, and I won't let her be hurt again. I was her protector: her fireman who would rescue her. Always present, always there. I've never experienced love like this. I was in it from the moment she walked into my clinic."

He introduced me to Dragon Boats and to the phrase "paddle till you puke." Those were such fun days on the river, paddling for different teams in different divisions. Bono sat in the back of the boat, and his reach was so long that he could reach two benches in front of him to stroke the water. I swear, he was the one driving the boat. He was a freaking beast.

In all the time we were together, he was constantly surprising me with what was next. He studied and learned Italian for when we were going to travel to Italy—it was beautiful hearing him say those words. He decided that he was going to get his motorcycle license, and he ended up buying a Harley. He would ride his Harley out to my school and stride upstairs in his leathers, holding his helmet out in front of him. The kids were always happy to see him, and I wanted to jump on the back of the motorcycle and leave with him.

SPIRIT BOX #10: BIKER BONO

"I loved the freedom of my Harley. I had great respect for that motorcycle. My wife never bought the appropriate gear to ride—helmet, leathers, and boots—but I'd put her on the back of the bike for short jaunts around the neighborhood. I liked to

> gun the bike and hear her scream behind me. This action made her hug me tighter, and I liked her arms around me. She was never in peril, but I could cause her to have an adrenaline rush. She was fun to play with."

We cooked side by side in the kitchen. Those were some of my favorite times together. He became quite the grill-master, and we ate many racks of ribs until he perfected his recipes. He loved when I cooked Indian food, and I loved when he cooked Thai. He could never understand why Victoria and I would make three hundred Christmas cookies and then give them away. He always got more than his fair share, and then he started joining us in making cookies—with "fruitcake cookies" being his specialty.

He was always bettering himself by expanding his horizons beyond his work, fun, and family time, as well. He never stopped. He played over a dozen instruments, including bass guitar, both twelve- and six-string acoustic guitars, different types of saxes, piano, drums, flute, and keyboard. He joined a band, and Tracy and I became his devotees, following him from bar to bar. Later, he started his own band, and he enjoyed his Friday nights with his bandmates.

"DEPRIVED OF" BONOFIGLIO

My husband was awe-inspiring—he was freaking amazing. He was so well-rounded. Not only was he always a fun spirit, full of adventures, and constantly growing and learning, but he was also the most tender and humble man I knew. He was always so patient and kind with the kids and me, never raised his voice, and only lifted us up and showered us with love and caring.

My hopes and dreams had been dashed and trampled upon, and I'd almost taken my life because of my first two husbands. I do look back at those marriages and know they provided lessons for me to learn and make me stronger as a human. However, when Bono enthusiastically entered my life, I was able to realize my hopes and dreams that then became my reality.

His death crushed me, and my soul died with him. I didn't care if I lived or died, and—quite frankly, I would've preferred to die. However, once again, he rescued me. His Spiritual form was strong after death and reached out from behind the Veil to contact me and spur me on to live. I was surviving on coffee, tequila, and chocolate—not quite the breakfast of champions.

His Spiritual form moved me almost as much as if he were still alive. I know that he is proud of me and the kids. I know that he is proud that—through my grief—I have embarked on a journey of self-discovery and I'm constantly learning new things, like he had done. I know that he is proud that I wrote a book and have helped many people along the way. I know that he is especially proud that I've made the decision to live.

As I write these words, it's been almost two years since he left this earth. I still cry daily. The tears can be of sorrow, of joy, of longing, or even of anger. I truly can't imagine how I can keep crying, yet they still flow…on and on and on. However, tears are healing and part of the process, and I did not stifle mine.

I know our love will never die, and that he waits for me to come "Home." When my days are done, I will gladly take his hand and go Home with him. Until then, he will live on in my memories and in all the ways that he continues to contact and comfort me. He has never left my side. I love you, husband, more than you can ever imagine.

FACEBOOK POST
DECEMBER 6, 2020

Bono's sister, Esther, is a beautiful soul, and she wrote my husband's obituary—which truly captured his essence. Bono was so beloved and touched many lives—he was one amazing man, and I was blessed to share his life and love. I love and miss him to the very core of my being.

It is hard to imagine a life without him. I know that he watches over me, along with Mom, Pops, and others. When my grief becomes unbearable, I call upon Mom to take it away—just like in my childhood when she made everything "better." Just wait until I am called Home—there is going to be a huge celebration.

Please know that I would love to comment on your posts, but it is so draining. I read them, cry over them, feel the love, and appreciate all the caring. Just know it does not go unnoticed. After Christmas, we will have a beautiful, online memorial page designed for your memories and thoughts about this wonderful man.

Rest in peace, Bono—until we meet again.

FACEBOOK POST
DECEMBER 31, 2021

Our anniversary…

I think I cried at least 10,000 tears yesterday knowing that our wedding anniversary was arriving today. I cried while stumbling around, sobbing, puffy-eyed, and while receiving sad eyes from the puppies as they felt my grief. Know that grief never goes away; it comes up from the depths of the soul. We all do the best we can and soldier on. I have learned the truth of the phrase, "the deeper the love, the deeper the grief."

Sweet, fun, loving husband, I wish to say: "Happy Twenty-Fourth Anniversary."

We were so blessed to have twenty-six years together, and I thank God for our union and for being brought together. Cupid's arrow went straight through my heart, it burst, and you entered my soul. I love you to the depths of my being, Bono, with every beat of my heart and every breath I take. I also know of your overwhelming love for me. Until we meet again, Baby.

Forever in Touch:
Unbroken Connection and Loving Encounters with Bono

- Esther got a message from Bono. She is more intuitive than me but doesn't often share her gift. She was told, "I am with Mom, and it didn't hurt to die." And he'd chuckled.

- I was sobbing angrily at the kitchen table. I was mad at Bono: I was angry because he'd left and upset because our new chapter in life together wouldn't happen. I was mad due to my upcoming birthday without him. I stopped and asked Bono, my Guides, Angels, and deceased family members to lift this heaviness and burden. I immediately relaxed, and Bono put into my head the song, "You're My Inspiration." God Bless him.

chapter 5
"HOLD ME NOW"

Life Before My Husband Died

Before my husband left this earth, I had dedicated eight years of my life to my parents' care. I'd never imagined I would be responsible for their supervision, but I'm so grateful that I had this time with them. Our days were spent doing a combination of the following and so much more: going out to lunch, taking drives in the countryside, stopping for ice cream, visiting friends, taking Dad to the barber, getting Mom's hair done weekly, getting pedicures for both Dad and me while Mom got a manicure, going on special trips, navigating tons of doctors' appointments, and running various errands. I spent each day with them and took over the responsibilities of running their household. I teased Mom that she hadn't done her wash in seventeen years, but it was true. I'd taken over that job once when she was sick, and I had just continued to do it.

"LEAN ON ME"

As they aged, dementia and many other health problems set in, and I became depleted—I gave so much of myself to Mom and Pops that I didn't have a lot left for my husband and me. Many days I'd come home, crawl into bed, pull the covers up under my chin, and watch TV. About two hours later, my energy reserves would return, and I could carry on.

I always tried to make sure I had dinner ready for my hubby when he came home, but sometimes I didn't have the energy. I'd ask him to grab a bite on the way home or give him a suggestion about what he could prepare from what we had on hand. Bono was always my protector; when he saw the toll it all was taking on me, he treaded lightly. He wanted to make it as easy as he could for me. At the same time, I'd update him on my parents and how their health and mental capacities were failing. He couldn't help with this; he could only listen and offer suggestions. When I needed his help, he was always there. For example, he was practicing with his band on a Friday night, and I called to tell him that Mom had had a stroke. He immediately left the practice and came to be at my side.

I remember so many times through the years that I'd call him because either Mom or Dad had fallen, and he'd had to pick them up. There was one time, while Mom and Dad could still get around, that Mom had fallen into a bookcase in the kitchen with all of her cookware on it. Six shelves of supplies had crashed to the floor, and they'd just left for an appointment. I knew they couldn't clean up the mess, so I headed over to their house. When I got there and saw what I had to do, I cried. I was drained. I called up Bono at work as I needed to lean on him. About fifteen minutes later, he showed up to help clean up the fiasco. This man couldn't have been more caring or loving to my family and me. He was perfect.

PREPARING POPS

Pops was in hospice care for six months before he died. He was adamant about not leaving his home for a care facility. He also had dementia, and his personality started changing. He was quick to anger, and he was very mean to me once. My father had never in our entire existence been rude or mean to me, and I was crushed. After I left my parents' house, I was so distraught that I ran into a pole in the parking lot: tears had filled my eyes, Pop's words had cut deeply, and I couldn't think straight. A while later, in one of my psychic readings, Pops apologized for this digression and for being mean to me. He explained that it was the disease, not him, talking. He had so much love for me, and he was sorry that he'd hurt me.

Nurse Beth taught me how to deal with aging, dying, and dementia in parents. I learned to never reason or argue—just to accept and deflect. I used my teaching skills, I'd change my voice to something happy and uplifting, and I would always validate what they were saying. I'd often repeat their words back to them. From there, I could direct the conversation so things wouldn't escalate. I didn't read books about dementia, but rather had Nurse Beth and a psychologist, Betsy, coach me. They were so helpful. They actually threw me many lifelines as I sailed through these turbulent, unpredictable waters.

If you are ever at this crossroads, do some research on how to deal with people with memory loss and dementia as it is an easy skill to learn. I had two other friends who were "taking care of" mothers with dementia, and I was appalled by how they argued about and made light of their mothers' condition. I tried to give these two friends advice, but it fell on deaf ears. I would try to pull in my experiences to help them learn and process, but some people are not receptive.

One morning, I was getting cleaned up so that I could take Mom to the doctor to get a shot in her eye—yep, right in her eyeball, and I could never look. Joan, the caregiver, called me as Dad was quite belligerent and they were arguing. She had never called me for help with Pops, so I knew he was being quite difficult. I arrived at their house, and he was angrily sitting on the bed with the caregiver trying to dress him. In a very light and happy voice, I inquired:

"What's going on, Pops?"

"I want to go home, and this lady won't let me go home." he snapped.

I explained that he had to take this (anxiety) pill, get dressed, and then I'd take him home.

Mom and Dad had rented a living space on the second floor of a retirement center. After getting Dad into his wheelchair, I explained that I'd take him home, but that I needed his help to direct me. Off we went through the halls and floors of the retirement community. He insisted we take the elevator up a floor, so we did. I pushed him down a long corridor to where he thought their room was. That room was exactly one floor up from where he lived.

I put on my happy, teaching voice and pointed out to Pops that a different name was on the nameplate, and not his. I was talking to him like a child. I excitedly commented that I knew where he lived, and off we went. By then, the medicine had kicked in and he was no longer agitated or angry. We went down a floor below to his room, and I eagerly pointed out his name was listed on the Nameplate. We walked through the door, and Mom and Joan were smiling at us. Again, with an exaggerated and excited voice, I exclaimed, "Look, there's Mom." He happily smiled at Mom while I wheeled him into the room. He took her hand, and he told her how "beautiful" she was. My old Pops was back for now.

MOTHERING MOM

After Pops passed, I moved Mom into a beautiful foster care house with four other ladies, and she went through the grieving process of losing her husband of seventy-two years. She, too, was in hospice care with the same nurse as Pop, Nurse Beth. Nurse Beth was my first lifesaver.

Unlike Dad, who had insisted on staying in their apartment with twenty-four-hour caregivers. Mom was more social (like mother, like daughter) and needed to be around other people. However, due to Covid, the dining hall had closed, and meals were delivered to her room. She was unable to interact with her friends, which was paramount for her.

She developed pneumonia and was hospitalized. Boy, did she have problems in the hospital. She never got mean like Dad had, but she was very cross with the people ignoring her at the hospital and not taking care of her properly. I am sure, since she wasn't in her right mind, that her perceived quality of her care may have been somewhat skewed. While she was there, I moved her into a foster care setting. There were four other beautiful ladies living there, as well as an onsite caregiver and her family. Although mom was entrenched in grief, she loved being around these ladies and the homecooked meals. I saw mom go through what I was going to experience: the endless sorrow, unrelenting crying, and hopelessness of losing a spouse.

I wish I could've gotten Mom a counselor, but they weren't seeing patients in person or accepting new ones. Life after Pops was a tragedy for her. She was sequestered in foster care, and for a while I couldn't visit. I'd sit outside in the cold and talk to her as she sat inside, all wrapped in blankets. Later, the owner broke the rule, and let family members come inside. I was gladly welcomed into the fold as I'd bring treats, and I also later had Mom's hairdresser come in through her patio door. Mom always dressed and looked impeccable; this was important to her.

PALLIATIVE AND COMFORT CARE

My life was going to change suddenly and dramatically; I was going to enter the world of death, grief, and trauma. Nurse Beth was the first Angel I was blessed with, as she helped my parents to the end of their lives. I learned so much from her and how she cared for the elderly. She coached me on dealing with dementia, the stages of dying, and the ensuing grief from losing a parent. Nurse Beth had taken care of Pops for six months before he left for Heaven, and she was my Friday "date." I was cautious with my parents and grilled her about their meds and the procedures to follow. She patiently explained things, and I eventually opened up and trusted her.

We developed a very tight friendship. She'd always take my phone calls and offer me advice. She explained to me throughout how the whole process worked. My parents started with palliative care, which later changed to comfort care. They were at the end of their lives and were receiving palliative care that would optimize their quality of life by anticipating, preventing, and treating their suffering ("Explanation of Palliative Care" n.d.). This type of care is not just for the dying, but rather it brings emotional and physical care to anyone with an illness. When used for the dying, medical interventions are still in place for treatment at this stage.

This later changed to comfort care for each of my parents, which is an essential part of medical care that helps, soothes, and makes comfortable a person who is dying. The goals are to prevent or relieve pain and suffering as much as possible, to control symptoms, and to improve the quality of life while respecting the dying person's wishes ("Helping with Comfort Care" 2008). No medical treatments or interventions will ensue for the patient at this point. Comfort care is just that: making the person as comfortable as possible before they transition.

Nurse Beth stayed with me during the last few hours of Mom's life and explained what was happening to her. As Mom lay in her bed, Nurse Beth would point out to me the stages of dying. She remarked that "if you could screen write a peaceful death, then it'd look like your mom's." Mom, in fact, did seem to die very peacefully. She became unresponsive, and Nurse Beth would point out when her breathing patterns would change. At times, her breathing was rapid and shallow and would lead to longer pauses and deep breathing.

Mom grimaced in pain once; from then on, Nurse Beth administered meds (I think Oxycodone and Lorazepam) to make her transition more comfortable and pain-free. She would point out that Mom's hands and feet were cold and when her skin mottled. Mom never moaned; her face was peaceful and relaxed. In my heart, I knew that she wasn't suffering, and that her Spiritual form was likely going in and out of her body, but I didn't mention this to Nurse Beth. I have deep gratitude for this Angel who entered our lives, and now we have a deep friendship.

SPIRIT BOX #12: "TENDER LOVING CARE"

"Looking back in my memory (which is much better again now that I am in the Heavenly Realm), I can see that I am now in hospice. I know what that means: I am at the end of my life. Nurse Beth is my hospice nurse, and she is so bossy; I don't like what she always tells me, but Karen soothes my nerves by explaining why we are doing things. Nurse Beth provides me with medicine and makes sure I am always comfortable and not in a lot of pain. After a while, due to my dementia, I will forget that I didn't really like Nurse Beth, but then I'll be happy when she comes to check on me. She will become my friend, and someone who my wife and I can trust.

"My wife, Ruthie, and I had such a deep love for our daughter Karen throughout our lives on Earth. It is hard to imagine that our love for Karen could be even stronger now as we see her trying to tackle grief on Earth from our new Home in the Heavenly Realm: but it is.

"Karen always helped me in the yard and around the house until she went off to college. Would you believe that even after she married, she would come to help us out at our home. She and her first husband would power wash the house together while I supervised. Afterward, I would take them out to get a burger, but my daughter balked each time. She'd remark, 'Pops, look at me,' and I ignored her work clothes and wild hair. I stated that 'they'll take my money,' and when we went I could see her ravenously devour her food, as she'd worked so hard.

"Karen learned her work ethic from me. If something had to be done, it was completed before she took off with her friends. You could set a clock by me, and my daughter is the same way. Her mom taught her social graces, to be a friend to all, acceptance of others, made sure she kept up with her studies, and taught her how to cook—and bake.

"She became quite an excellent cook and baker. One year, she and her sister, Susan, decided that they were going to perfect how to make pies. Was I happy. Every few days, they'd tackle a new pie—apple, blueberry, lemon meringue, coconut cream, sour cream pear, and more—and, each time, they'd bring me another piece to sample. Such a delicious treat. And they remembered that I liked cheddar cheese on top of my apple pie."

Those eight years of caring for my parents were exceptional, and our love and bond only grew stronger and strengthened. They knew I'd always be there for them and keep their best interests at the forefront. I would never diminish or trade the time I was able to spend with my parents. They took care of me when I was younger, and I was able to give back to them during their waning years. I was able to be with them as they drew their last breaths.

Still, nothing could have prepared me for what was coming.

Forever in Touch:
Unbroken Connection and Loving Encounters with Bono

- On Pop's birthday, I was extremely fatigued and got into bed. Bono came to me to be with me for reassurance. He is always there to help me when I experience such deep grief, and he knows my feelings about my father.
- The week before my 66th birthday arrived, I was worried about my first time without my husband, and I cried so

much. I could feel him, Mom, and Dad holding me up in love all day on my birthday. I felt good all day and was not depressed. They all came to me at the end of the night and showed me their love and support. I cried tears of gratitude.

chapter 6
"MOURNING GIRL"

Numbness, Confusion, Tears, and Disbelief

The first morning of life without my beloved was unbelievable. So many conflicting emotions were spilling over, accompanied by endless tears. I began the unfathomable task of calling and contacting family members, and everyone was in disbelief. Hearing Bono's sister cry out in pain like she'd been stabbed was the worst. It was the guttural cry of a wounded animal, and I could relate. This passionate, healthy, fun-loving, free-spirited, funny, loving man was no longer on this Earth. How could this be? He'd visited his doctor two weeks before, and he'd checked out great. His blood work was terrific. Why was he ripped away from me? It made no sense.

There were no answers, yet everyone had so many questions. I remember crying, crying, and more crying as I was trying to explain what had happened. As trite as it sounds, God has his own plan…and I wanted no part of this at the time. I would never say, "God has his own plan" to anyone who has lost a loved one. There was no peace or solace in this phrase for me. At this point, all I felt was numbness and disbelief.

In the background of all of this, COVID-19 was running rampant. Covid had taken over the entire world at this time. Countries had closed their borders. Many of our daily rituals in life were uprooted. People kept their distance, quit having family gatherings, and closed restaurants or only opened for take-out; the world felt barren. We were not allowed to eat in restaurants, had to constantly wear masks, and had to stand six feet away from people when in a store or in any place that we were allowed to visit. This cold, sterile world just became even more unbearable.

For me, this was brutal. Our souls thrive on connections—my soul in particular. All my life, I have constantly talked to, greeted, made comments to, and interacted with strangers. Now, people started ignoring your existence, and I think it was from fear. We were all scared to catch this disease, which was killing thousands of people daily. Those it's killed may include many of my readers' loved ones, which may even be why you're reading this book right now. It's been a hard time for human connections, and it was especially so at the beginning of the pandemic.

One time, I was in line at an ATM machine. While I was waiting, another man stood a distance from me. We started chatting about him and his family going to Mt. Hood to innertube. It was a delightful conversation. After he finished his transaction, he turned to me and remarked:

"Thank you for being nice."

My mask covered my mouth, so he didn't see it drop open. I was shocked at his words, as we should always be nice to those we meet on our travels. However, Covid had dictated different standards of interaction, and—like grief—these were often difficult to navigate. In fact, it was as if the whole world was grieving, in mourning, and hadn't the slightest idea of how to react.

Such uncertain communication standards also applied to people's reactions to Carl's death. It's funny…people don't know what to say when a spouse dies. It is hard to reach out to provide comfort when you're in disbelief. When my parents died, it was so much easier for my friends to express their condolences, as Mom and Dad had been in hospice before they passed and were elderly. It's a common experience for a lot of people. This was a natural progression of life and death. They had lived long, full lives, and had created such legacies—they were beloved.

But now my husband had died just three weeks after my mom? God. Come on. Could you give me a break? You just took three of my most important family members—the primary support in my life. What the hell? I'd lived a good life, and I felt like I was being punished. I was supposed to die before my husband. That was the agreement. This was not how my "happily ever after" had been planned. I'd taken care of my parents for eight years, and this was meant to be *our* time now. A time to travel and really be with each other—when the kids were grown, and Bono and I could create a life as a couple again. My whole life had been ripped away from me.

BONO GONE-OH: THE IMMEDIATE AFTERMATH

I felt like a crumpled-up piece of paper in the weeks that followed. My life was void of any laughter and love, and the grief was suffocating. Bono's death brought me to my knees, and I was drowning in grief. Heartache, disbelief, anger, and numbness were the first experiences, and they were overpowering. This once effervescent woman was a shadow of her former self and had now tasted a very bitter life through death.

My good friend Tracy came and lived with me for two weeks—what a godsend to have someone there to hold me up in support and love. The ensuing days were a blur, but she helped me immensely with love, kindness, moral backing, and with my doggies—who were also now grieving and trying to make sense out of what'd happened. I can't thank her enough for her love, support, and time. In addition, while aiding me, she was dealing with her own loss and grief for my husband, for he was her good friend too. Whenever something had gone missing or wrong in the house—any kind of glitch—we'd say, "Tracy did it." Even if she'd been nowhere nearby—we'd always blamed her in jest. It was a standard joke, and she'd laughed along with us.

My kids and their partners—Nick, Victoria, Mitch, and Leah—were my lifesavers. I am a control freak, and I had to give control to them. They pretty much did everything and called the shots—once I stopped trying to micromanage. I could not have done this without them. They gave freely of their time and took time off from work to help—plus, they were processing their own sorrow and loss. They were always kind and considerate.

SPIRIT BOX #13: GRIEF IS THE WORD

"In death, just as it was in life, I have a robust sense of humor. Karen and I liked to hide a little toy Mickey Mouse around the house and play hide and seek. I was really good at hiding Mickey. Today, I hid my wife's earrings and 'it just so happened' that Tracy had visited yesterday. She's now blaming Tracy (as usual) for moving them, and I'm not gonna tell her…uh oh. Busted. Tracy denied touching them, and the wife has her hands on her hips, asking me where they are. Should I make her wait, or lead her to them? Hehe

"But seriously, I was just 'taking the mickey' out of the wife and her friend (as they'd say where the Beatles hail from), and giving Tracy some grief. Giving grief: what a funny expression. It's hard to believe anyone would intentionally want to give someone else anything at all related to that word (even if it is an alternate meaning), given how much sadness is associated with it. It makes you wonder where the word 'grief' came from.

"Luckily, I met this intellectual type here in the Heavenly Realm who lived a long, long time ago, and he told me he first read the word 'grief' way back around AD 1200. However, he said he'd heard it originally came from the Latin verb 'gravare,' which meant 'to burden or make heavy,' which itself came from 'gravis,' meaning 'heavy.' This led to other English words, like 'gravity' and 'grave' (as in 'serious,' but clearly also as in its other meaning) ("Definition of Grief | Dictionary.com" n.d.). Wow, it's amazing what you can learn in the Heavenly Realm.

"Grief definitely feels heavy and serious, weighs you down, and burdens you. Just ask Karen or keep reading her book. I guess I see why it's called that. As for the phrase 'taking the mickey,' I'm sure that has nothing to do with any mouse—but we'll save the origins of that one for another day. Now, back to annoying my wife. Maybe she'll say, 'Good grief.' But messing with her further may be a grave mistake, given the gravity of the situation. Ok, I'll stop now."

"GOOD MORNING": CHOCOLATE, COFFEE, AND TEQUILA

During the initial days of my husband's death, chocolate, coffee, and tequila were my life-sustaining substances. People would bring me food—it would often be frozen—and if my friends forgot that I was a vegetarian, Tracy was happy to devour the meat dishes. My housekeeper kept telling me to eat. Unbeknownst to me, she was checking my food—or lack thereof—in the fridge when she came over. Only when my hair started falling out did I begin to eat for nourishment.

For me, life had lost all meaning. I didn't care about anything. I was merely existing in a painful state of angst. My doggies were the only reason I got up each day. Even though they were grieving with me, I knew they needed to see me moving and upright, as well as to get exercised. During this whole time, Tracy was here, and she did a wonderful job of running interference for me and making decisions. My brain chemistry had changed, and I experienced brain fog. I couldn't for the life of me make any decisions or remember any that were made. She and I would talk, and she—through her wisdom and quiet spirit—would help me function.

Tracy only came—as she put it— "to make space" while I was grieving, but she was instrumental in keeping me alive during those two weeks she stayed. I was this blob—moving from room to room, crying, and I felt like a pin ball just bouncing slowly through different parts of the house. I felt like I was in an altered state.

This once determined, take-charge, organized woman was turned into a crying, helpless, incapacitated mess. I mentioned earlier that I felt like a crumpled-up piece of paper—this described me perfectly. When your partner is still alive, you don't even begin to fathom that you can constantly cry and start the process again, and again, and again each day. The brain gets befuddled, and you just can't remember things. I had to start writing down what I had said to people, because I actually couldn't retain the information. I was wondering how I could keep crying throughout each and every day and not run out of tears.

I also lost my laugh. I didn't notice this until close to the end of the first year—that I hadn't laughed. I used to laugh all the time. I was a schoolteacher, and I'd always been amused at the antics of my students and had constantly laughed throughout the day. My laugh had been an integral part of me throughout my life. Do you know how I discovered that I'd lost my laugh? I laughed one day; I heard my laughter. I realized then that I had not laughed in so long. I sat there, amazed at my new knowledge, and pleased that my laugh had come back. Sounds crazy, but those little milestones are huge when I look back at them.

SPIRIT BOX #14: BIG HEARTED BONO

"My sweetheart. My woman. Love of my life. She's on a downward spiral. It's so challenging getting through to her, as her layers of grief are so deep. She's not eating; she doesn't care about living anymore and finds solace in eating chocolate and drinking coffee and tequila.

"We lived a healthy lifestyle. We became vegetarians and exercised. I must bring in the Spiritual forms of her parents and our beloved dogs—Roosevelt, Vinni, and Isabel—so Karen can feel our loving and caring. We all want her to feel vibrant and full of life again, and it's going to take all of us to help her with our energies."

During this time, one of the most important lessons I learned was to "grieve however the hell you want." No one grieves in exactly the same way, and I started cutting myself some slack. If I needed to subsist on coffee, tequila, and chocolate for now—so be it. Whenever I'd be ready to move on, I would. I learned not to question why I cried daily or why I constantly had a dark cloud over my head; my naturopath made no judgments when I told her about my three foods of the day, so why should I? Nevertheless, I'm glad this phase of eating didn't last too long.

FACEBOOK POST
NOVEMBER 15, 2020

It has been a week since my husband passed away unexpectedly. The grief is suffocating, and nothing can ease the pain. To have him ripped away has been unbearable—I had time to ease into Mom and Pop's death, but not Bono's. I am NOT writing this post trying to gain pity or sympathy, but there have been questions asked about my husband and wondering how I am.

My husband was sixty-seven years old and planned to live until he was ninety; I told him I would not stay that long on this earth. Two weeks ago, he saw his MD, bloodwork was drawn, and everything checked out great. Last Friday he saw his ND. His vitals looked good. He'd been tired the last few weeks and had muscle fatigue—those were the only changes he experienced. Since he died at home, and it was not a homicide, there will be no autopsy. He probably had a heart attack. The officer, and Nurse Beth, said he went peacefully. There was absolutely no indication he was going to die.

These words may ring hollow, but know they are true—you don't know how long your time is here. Treat every conversation and action like it's your last: it may be. Let love, compassion, empathy, kindness, and caring be your legacy. I hope Doc [knew] how beloved he was in this life, but he definitely knows now. He was a gentle giant—a king among men. All who knew him had a special bond with him. He will be missed by many.

Our family grieves and cannot honor him in a memorial service at this time due to the situation of the country. My kids are devastated yet trying to rally for me through their searing grief—I don't know what I would do without them. As for myself, I am broken and feel all crumpled up. However, I will get through this and have the support of all my family and friends. All the love from your posts, phone calls, and messages, have lifted me up—thank you. I apologize for not taking your phone calls or replying to the posts and texts—I don't have the energy and strength. If I forgot to thank you for flowers, I am sorry—my brain is mush. I will NOT be able to respond to any comments [here].

Hold your loved ones close, never live in anger, and always show your love and appreciation to everybody. Love to you all.

Little did I know about the journey through Hell on which I was embarking.

FACEBOOK POST
JANUARY 8, 2021

Dinner with my hubby...I think I have hit a milestone, as this is the first meal I have cooked since Bono passed away two months ago. I am pleased I remembered how to cook (seriously), as my hubby used to always cook our stir fry. He loved to take out his wok and smoke up the kitchen.

For the first three weeks after he died, I didn't eat—I had no appetite and didn't care. However, I started losing my hair and made myself eat. I tell you—it is sad dining by yourself—so many adjustments for me.

I still cry daily, many times, but find I have more energy and strength. Naps are still my best friend.

Two days ago, I ran into a fellow teacher who I have not seen in over a year. It was so lovely and heartwarming running into her, but I couldn't stop crying to carry on a decent conversation. I was overwhelmed, but so happy to see a close friend. I hope this isn't what happens every time I initially reconnect with my friends.

I muster on. Be well, stay safe and sane, and keep loving on your loved ones.

Forever in Touch:
Unbroken Connection and Loving Encounters with Bono

- I went to the storage unit to start going through Carl's stuff, and I was amazed at how much I still had to move out and incorporate into my house. I got angry at this never-ending process. I had to liquidate the clinic and gym, and now I had to empty his storage unit. The work was insurmountable, and being engulfed in grief was agonizing.

- Later in the evening, I apologized for getting mad at him. I am sure that if he had had any indication he was going to leave, then he would have made this process a lot easier on me. After apologizing, he brought me the lyrics to "I Swear" as sung by John Michael Montgomery. I stood and faced Carl; and was held in his arms.

Chapter 7
"BABY ELEPHANT WALK"

Unconditional Love and The Grieving Of Pets

Pets are of the Angelic Realm, and only offer pure love to humans. I am an avid lover of animals. I have fed squirrels and crows for years in our backyard. Since I was a child, I've had doggies and kitties. At one point, I had ducks and hamsters. Animals have been an integral part of my life. It is so gratifying sharing unconditionally with an animal that you've adopted to be a part of your family, and to look into their eyes and see their souls looking back into yours.

SOME IMPORTANT INSTANCES OF GRIEVING PETS IN MY LIFE: APACHE THE MUSTANG: "BROWN-EYED GIRL"

As I've mentioned, in my teens, I was lucky enough to have the pleasure of riding my neighbor's mustang, Apache. We had such fun times together, riding through fields and forests. It was one of the best times of my life. Apache had a mind of her own. I didn't know at an early age how to communicate with animals as I do now. I wish I would've known, because she was constantly trying to buck me off on one trail—I thought it was a game for her. She would try to nip at my foot while I was on her back, and my neighbor told me to kick her in the face. I couldn't do that.

Apache was a strawberry, roan mustang, about sixteen hands high. Because she was a larger horse, her joints had taken a beating during her life. She developed arthritis and had constant pain and discomfort in her joints. She was just a teen when she passed. Veterinary medicine has evolved greatly, and today she would have been kept more comfortable before she passed.

I was not informed when Apache died. I was in college at the time, and I was no longer riding her. When I returned home, I went to see her. I was informed that she was no longer alive. I was sucker punched. I lost my breath and could not respond. I had so many questions, but I did not ask; I didn't want to distress her owners as they'd lost their beloved horse. I was heartbroken.

The horse I had ridden was no longer next door for me to visit. I couldn't provide her tasty oats mixed with molasses (her favorite treat), couldn't hear her crunch on apples or carrots, and couldn't tenderly stroke her face. Gone were the days of saddling her, and riding into the forest under the shade from the trees. No more of her trying to buck me off when she ran up the last trail before going back to the barn. It was a hard loss, and it left me feeling quite empty.

ROOSEVELT AND STREAK

Animals were also a part of my life with Bono. When he met me, I had a miniature schnauzer named Roosevelt—we called him Rosie for short. We also had two rescue kitties, Sam and Streak. Rosie and Streak welcomed Bono fully into their lives, while Sam was a bit reserved.

Streak became sickly later in life. When I arrived home one day, she came out from the trees and welcomed me. Her eyes shone like the bluest stars I'd ever seen—they had a heavenly light to them. I picked her up and snuggled her, and she walked back toward the trees. I had a feeling she was saying goodbye—and she was. It still makes me sad, but she was ready to go off and die. I look back and wish I would've taken her into the house, but I wasn't as in tune with animals then as I am now. I didn't listen to my intuition. The heavenly light in her eyes is etched in my memory. She looked bright and lighter—she knew what was happening and welcomed it.

Later, during the family's life together, Rosie got into some slug bait and died. His death was a tragedy, and we raced to save him. It was so hard on the whole family, and we grieved him deeply. I didn't go to work the next day, and I just lay in bed and cried. He was so beloved.

When we'd all leave for the day, Roosevelt would remain outside and have a nice yard to himself along with shelter and blankets. I usually arrived home first, and he'd come to the gate and loudly bark his happiness that I'd returned. He was an exuberant doggy.

When I returned from work two days after he died, I heard him on the other side of the gate BARKING at me. I sat in the car astounded. I'd never heard a spiritual voice like that before. I went over to the gate and talked to him. I went to the back door of the house to see if he was there. I hadn't yet fine-tuned my abilities, so I didn't feel his energy or hear him anymore.

VINNI "MR. VIN" AND ISABEL

Soon after Rosie died, I knew we needed to get another pet. Our son was at college, and our daughter was very sad without her doggy. Vinni, a mutt, and Isabel, a beagle, entered the picture. Vinni became my doggy, and Isabel was my daughter and husband's. The two became fast friends and played continuously in the house and yard; they were always full of antics. They were well loved, and eventually died of old age.

We were able to have both doggies put to sleep in the house. Not too unlike my parents, Vinni passed first in October, and Isabel died of a broken heart six months later. Isabel aged incredibly after Vinni died: she'd lost her brother who she loved deeply. It was then that I started noticing signs from my dogs—lots of them. I kept a record of all the times they visited and how, but I no longer have that folder. Two of those times are still in my head. Right after Vinni was put to sleep, Victoria, Carl, and I were sitting at the kitchen table. Something came crashing down in the garage, and we all looked at each other—we knew it was Vin letting us know that he was okay. Carl went out to the garage to see what had fallen, and everything was still in its place.

Once Vinni passed, Isabel went to work with my husband daily. She was grieving, and we didn't want to leave her alone. One day, I ran into the house between errands to use the restroom. Upon trying to leave the restroom, I could physically feel Vinni's strong energy, and he was standing right in front of me. I was paralyzed and couldn't move. His energy encompassed me, and I started talking to him. I had a huge shift come over me from behind the Veil, and I was starting to feel and open myself up to Spirit. When I say this, I am referring to God. To Source. To Divinity. For me, these words are synonymous. This is in contrast to Spiritual form, which refers to heavenly family members, animals and others who come to visit once they've crossed.

My body felt Vin's energy, and it was energetic and happy—I think he was pleased that I was able to feel it. As Vinni had aged, he'd become blind, and I'd taken care of him like a baby. I'd read about how to take care of a blind dog—how to put rugs down on the carpet so he would have markers, move things out of the way, and to have a special spot for him that Isabel could not lie. Our already strong bond had become tighter.

DEFINITION DOGGY BOX 1
DUTIFUL DOGGIES

"Hi, I am Roosevelt. But my hooman family usually calls me Rosie. That's a girl's name, but I think it is cute."

"And we are Vinni (or Mr. Vin: my Mommy calls me that) and Isabel, two more of Mommy's doggies who were family to her, her children, and Dr. Bonofiglio."

"We miss our mommy, Karen, but we are still by her side watching over her. Her doggies who are with her now, Maddy and Bean, can see us, and they keep a watchful eye on us and on our mommy. We all want Mommy to feel good. Dr. Bonofiglio got a message to us and said that Mommy is sad and misses all of us, so the three of us will be jumping in (because, you know, dogs love to jump) here occasionally to provide better understanding to key concepts in the book.

"Mommy said that animals are from the Angelic Realm, a part of the Heavenly Realm, and we are. Animals are beings of light and are from a higher dimension. We come to our humans to show them unconditional love. The only reason we are here is to form a synergistic bond and love between a pet and its owner; we teach them the lesson of our souls connecting and forming a loving friendship. We feel Mommy's grief like it is our own. Whenever she was sad, we used to follow her wherever she went and hope she could feel the loving energy we sent her. She can't hide her feelings from us—we see in her body and eyes what she's experiencing—happiness, sadness, pain, and so forth. Our eyes are sad

> when she is sad, and our ears droop. Our eyes are happy when she is, and our ears and tails perk up. We will take care of her—we kept her safe while on Earth and continue now as we watch over her. We wuv our mommy."

THE GRIEF AND SPIRITUALITY OF PETS: LOSS IS NOT UNIQUELY HUMAN

About three years before Bono left for the Heavenly Kingdom, we got two Mini Australian Shepherds which he named Maddy and Bean. Our previous doggies, Isabel and Vinni, had passed a year or two before, and I wanted to get more. Dogs are pack animals, and they do better when in a pair; it seems like it'd be more work, but it's actually easier when they have one of their own in the doggy partner. They can have adventures, play together, and teach each other.

I thought I was getting Maddy and Bean for me, but in all actuality, it was for my husband. Unbeknownst to me, he was under a lot of stress at work (remember, he always tried to protect and shield me) and needed the love of an animal. He selected Maddy and I chose Bean to be our respective dogs. Maddy turned out to be a hyper, outspoken, and barky dog. She was extremely smart and demanded attention. Her sister—they were from the same litter—was sweet, kind, sensitive, and gentle. Maddy chose me as her owner, and Bean chose Bono.

My son once said, "That makes sense, due to your personalities."

I was a bit offended, but I could see the truth in his words.

About a year later, after Bono died, I was sitting on the hassock in front of my husband's big red chair. I was rocking back and forth crying, and my doggy Maddy jumped up into the chair. I stopped and watched her. Her head did not move, but her eyes were moving all around the room, looking up, behind me, and to the side of me. Then she would look to the other side of me and repeat this pattern. I know she was looking at all the Spiritual forms in the room, because we all have many who come to visit us. She was fortunate enough to see them, but not I.

There was so much silence in the house when Bono died, except for my sobs and cries of anguish—looking back, when I found Bono's body on the floor, the dogs were nowhere to be found. They had left the room and had just watched from afar. When the police and my children came into the house, the dogs were reticent and absent—always in their beds, just watching. I've often wondered what was running through their minds when they lost their daddy. Bean was Bono's baby, and I know her heart was especially broken.

Animals feel and feed off your energy. They can feel your happiness, pain, grief, anger, and all your emotions. If Bono and I ever got cross with each other, we'd stop and settle down because it upset the pups. When I'd get amped up and happy, the dogs would start barking to join in the fracas—all animals feel your energy. Ever wonder why a dog doesn't like a certain person? Pay attention because they're aware of something about that person you may not be.

Unfortunately, the pups experienced the deepest levels of my grief with me. When all I could do was stumble around the house and go back to bed to cry, they never wavered from my side—laying in their beds, silently watching their Mommy, yet experiencing our grief at the same time. There was a softness in their eyes, body, and demeanor. I tried to stifle my grief and hide my tears at times to help them, but then I couldn't honor the feelings that needed to be expressed. We all grieved together.

In Chapter 1, I described the nightly ritual sharing of our daily activities and expression of our love that Bono and I performed on the couch with the dogs beside us. Dogs like routines, and I wanted to keep them in a pattern. After he passed, I adapted our nighttime routine, telling them what we'd be doing the next day while petting and loving them. I'd always say, "Mommy and Daddy love you." Carl was always included in our conversations.

The pups also helped me heal. All they offered was love. There is a synergistic energy between a pet and their human. Do you know what it is like to wake up each morning and look into the face of an animal that loves you? They are happy that you are awake and ready to start a new day. The girls wanted me to heal and return to being the Mom they had known previously. I would hold them, pet them, and cry—they accepted all my feelings, and we healed together.

We'd take walks in the field and forest to calm ourselves down. I had no clue these walks would evolve into a spiritual quest. This, too, became a ritual. Little by little, I was opening myself up spiritually to the realm behind the Veil—the Heavenly Realm, where you could communicate with your Birth Angels, Guides, and people and pets who'd passed and were behind the very thin curtain (see Chapters 11-16 for an in-depth discussion of my spiritual awakening). My life would take so many twists and turns. I found that I'd fully embrace all the connections that I have with my family and friends, while bettering my heart and soul and seeking a deeper connection with how the universe works—and I was in for the ride of my life.

FACEBOOK POST
OCTOBER 15, 2021

Last night, as I was kissing my husband's picture goodnight, I thought how lovely it would be to wake up from this bad dream and find Bono sitting in his big, red chair.

Maddy, my brown puppy, has really soft eyes for me when I sob. I used to compare grief to a sneaker wave, but now it feels like I'm on a rollercoaster.

Forever in Touch:
Unbroken Connection and Loving Encounters with Bono

- As I was walking in a muddy field, I kicked a ball for one of the doggies and slipped. Bono kept me upright. I was falling when I felt myself being pulled up from behind. He always had my back.

- One morning I awoke feeling extremely peaceful, happy, and serene. I knew my husband was there and felt nothing but love. Love permeated every space in the room. Bean ran to his side of the bed and started frantically pawing the bed to try to get to him. She, too, had felt him and knew he was there. Animals are very fortunate, as they can see Spiritual forms. Bean was my husband's favorite dog, and she'd seen him.

- Although Bono loved both of our doggies, Maddy and Bean, he had a soft spot in his heart for Bean. I had been working with the dogs trying to curtail all their barking, thinking how quickly Mad had picked up on her training, and Bean—not so much. I thought, "Bean is not the sharpest tool in the shed." Bono quickly came to me because I talked disparagingly about his dog. He was so intense and kept giving me shakes and body chills. I think I was in trouble with my hubby.

- I was on the couch with the pups and called out Bono's name. I turned and saw him sitting in his big red chair with his cap on and smiling. He looked like he did later in life.

chapter 8
"DOWNTOWN"

FEELINGS OF GRIEF

It would be impossible to truly capture all of the swirling feelings that come with grief and loss, but it's important to identify the impact that these feelings have on you while you're trying to heal. I have found that everyone processes their grief in different ways, and that there is no "right way" or "wrong way." There is just your own way, and honoring those feelings and how you process them. I would recommend that you allow yourself to feel all of these feelings. If you tend to stuff them down inside, compartmentalize, and not allow yourself time to grieve and heal, it is all going to come back to you tenfold at another point in time. And not just once: it will hit you like a ton of bricks again and again. There is no easy way of getting around your feelings.

DEFINITION DOGGY BOX 2:
CONCERNED CANINES

"Bark! Bark!

"It's me, Mr. Vin!"

"And me, Isabel! I'm so glad mommy acknowledges and works through her grief. I'm so happy she does not compartmentalize her grief, and stuff it away. If she did that, it would come back to her time and time again—and even harder."

"You are so right, Isabel. She is wise in honoring her feelings. If you don't face your feelings, and if you avoid them, you will go barking mad."

"Mommy will not go barking mad. She has taken steps to help her live through this merciless time. Poor mommy now suffers from panic attacks and will take a 'chill pill' to help calm her down. Her panic attacks hit her like a tsunami of intense physical symptoms. She'll be fine one minute, and then, suddenly, her heart starts to race, she has trouble breathing, she can feel cold and sweaty at the same time, and she often sobs uncontrollably and feels trapped. Mommy feels the need to flee. I am glad Mommy shares her attacks with her doctor, and that she is seeing a grief counselor. Both of these people help her out so much in understanding what is physically and psychologically taken place within her."

"Too true, Isabel. I hope Mommy feels better soon."

"Me too, Vinni. But hoomans need a long time to process these things. They're like us dogs in that way. And Mommy is getting stronger every day. I'm sure she'll be just fine."

"Bark! Bark!"

I've had friends who couldn't function for years after losing their spouses. They'd give themselves time, and not pressure themselves to move forward until they were ready. Other friends have returned to work immediately and stuffed those feeling of grief down or aside; that grief was compartmentalized. Most of my friends have found ways to honor their loved one while going through grief. Their loved one is still incorporated into their lives.

When my parents and husband died, I threw myself into experiencing all the feelings. It's draining, and I later learned coping strategies so as not to sink to the lowest levels of grief and depression. Deciding to live generated an internal shift in me—a turning point in my life—through expanding my heart and connecting with the world and my friends on a deeper level. I was exposed to Spiritual forms from behind the Veil, and hungered to understand the intricacies of how the universe operates. This takes you into living in a space of vulnerability, as your heart is open. It's not easy, but it's one of the ways my personal connections with others have been enhanced and have thrived. I live with one foot in this world, and another in the spiritual.

Making that shift to operating in two different worlds was savage for me. It certainly was much more complicated than the two different worlds created by sneaking out of my parents' house at night in my youth or the "different world" of attending college. I believe the Universe wanted me to experience a raw depth of emotions through loss in preparation for the changes in myself that were forthcoming. Let me give you a little taste of what grief may feel like.

LIKE YOU'RE SUFFOCATING

Imagine you can't breathe. Imagine you have a heavy weight compressing your chest. What do you do? You start sucking air fervently into your lungs so that you can breathe again and sustain your life. You feel like you're going to die. You may start to hyperventilate. This feeling has been very common with my widow friends and me. It will subside, but it can be very scary while it's happening. I've found some strategies that have helped me with it, as it's not pleasant.

I'd now entered the realm of having panic attacks, which I'd never before experienced. At first, I took an anti-anxiety prescription. I refused to go on antidepressants, as they had made me suicidal at another point in my life. I never abused the anti-anxiety prescription, and it was closely monitored by my doctor. I also called friends on the phone, crying and telling them what was happening. They "talked me down": it is good to find friends who will do that for you.

Everyone wants to help the grief-stricken, but they may not know how to do so. Showing them "how to help" benefits not only you, but them as well. I had four friends I primarily would call. They would answer the phone while I struggled to speak and help reassure me that everything was going to be alright; just having someone be there for me was comforting. It is now two years later, and I still reach out to my friends when the grief is too hard to cope with.

LIKE IT'S ALL SO OVERBEARING

When your loved one dies, you have the weight of the world on your shoulders. All of a sudden, the responsibility of running the household, decision-making, doing EVERYTHING falls on you. Your partner is not there to bear the load. I cannot stress this enough, but please do whatever you can not to have to make any major decisions in the first year.

I did not have this luxury, as I had to close my husband's clinic and kettlebell gym and liquidate all of his items. I look back, and I would have done so much differently had I not had to make all of these decisions so soon. You really can't make good decisions when you are enmeshed in grief. Even if you chat with others and get advice, you may regret later making these decisions. Take your time: if nothing has to be done immediately, then let it ride. Later, you will be stronger and can make decisions and still discuss them with your friends and family.

My husband did everything for me. He was my fireman, and he was constantly rescuing me. My friends and family helped me continually after he died. They still do nearly three years later. Suddenly, you're taking care of everything in the household; it can be very overbearing. Learn to delegate, and to ask for help and advice. You'll get stronger, and this weight will begin to lift. It really will—I promise—although it may not seem like it while you're experiencing it.

LIKE A CRUMPLED-UP PIECE OF PAPER

You may feel all crumpled up like you have been discarded. Just trash. Blowing around in the wind and taken wherever the wind decides to deposit you. This was very hard for me to experience. I am a Virgo, and everything is always planned: I knew my direction in life, and my life ran like clockwork. My father used to use the expression "you could set a clock by him," and I had always carried that trait. My life had had a routine, and now—all of a sudden—it didn't.

Not only was there no more routine, but I also had no energy, drive, or ambition to enter life again. I was just being blown from place to place with no direction. This aspect of grief took a lot of time to overcome. I wasn't ready to engage with others again for a *long* time. It was hard to be with people I'd known for twenty – thirty years; I didn't want to be pitied. Little by little, I learned to re-enter life and take back my power. I'd be standing outside someone's house—deep breathing—getting up the courage to walk through the door, or I'd be crying on my way to meet someone. However, slowly I learned to find my power again and not feel worthless or discarded.

NO LAUGHTER OR JOY AND LIKE CONSTANTLY CRYING

These feelings are non-existent. They are unable to break through the pain or angst. There is no joy in the soul. You may smile, or give a quick laugh, but it is not felt in the soul. It was hard for me to re-enter life, so I had been told to watch TV shows or movies that would bring me laughter and happiness. For myself, I think it would have been better to be around younger children. I taught school for thirty-one years, and I loved the spontaneity and joy from being with kids. This may have worked for me, but I couldn't get out of my pain to explore that option.

Worse still, I couldn't understand how I could cry day after day. Surely, I'd run out of tears. Surely, the grief would subside. I became used to tears streaking down my cheeks, and quite versed in driving while crying. I had to pull over if tears became sobs. Carl's been gone for nearly three years, and the tears still haven't stopped. I read tears are cleansing and a means of release; I quit asking when they'd stop and learned to accept them as a part of my life and value their benefits. I still cry at a moment's notice when reminded of my loss, or when grief sneaks in.

LIKE YOUR WHOLE LIFE HAS BEEN RIPPED OUT FROM UNDER YOU

This is HUGE. EVERYTHING in your life changes. I was no longer Carl and Karen. I was now a widow. I lost my identity. Making phone calls to get bills and such was so hard. People were extremely understanding and considerate once I explained. One service agent talked to me for nearly thirty minutes about loss and grief as I sat there crying and listening to her words. You are now flying solo. You do everything in the household—all the things your husband used to do or help you with. There's no one else to help on a regular basis: you learn to do it all on your own.

I didn't want pity when Carl died, but I found that friends want to help you out. They just need to be told what is needed. I know the "call me if you need anything" rings hollow. Unless you tell someone that you need help, you may not get any. I started turning to my friends for help, and they were grateful that they could assist me during this time.

Don't let this paralyze you. You'll eventually reach a new normal. I've grown a lot, but I'm still finding mine. I'm constantly adjusting to my new life. I know I'm destined for many things before I'm called Home. Writing this book will lead to greater growth down the road.

AS THOUGH ANIMALS CAN FEEL YOUR PAIN

Let me preface this: always honor your pain and sorrow. Don't suppress your anger, angst, or tears—let them come. If you suppress them, then they will come back to you later tenfold. I tried to hide my sorrow from my doggies, but it didn't work. Those loving animals are in tune with you and feel your energy. Let them grieve together with you. They miss their mommy/father as much as you do. Guess what. They still see them. Don't you wish that you could?

Animals are far more tuned in to Spirit than most humans. I can tell when Maddy is watching and tracking the Spiritual forms with me at that moment. You'll heal together with your animals: you'll heal each other. They offer you unconditional love—isn't that wonderful?

LIKE YOUR BRAIN HAS TURNED TO MUSH

This drove my family crazy. I couldn't remember things I'd said or promises I'd made, and my memory was non-existent. My friends were understanding and gave me grace. I started taking notes in a tablet to remember what I'd said to whom, agreements I'd made, and other important info. This helped immensely: I liked having a reference point for when I talked to people. Little by little, your mind will return. Do I still get mixed up? Sure do. Yet, I've made huge strides.

NO ENERGY AND EMPTY INSIDE

For me, lack of energy was huge. I struggled getting up and down the stairs, and I napped constantly. I found the latter extremely beneficial to getting my strength back, but it was also a pain-free experience. Since I was opening myself up psychically, sleeping allowed my husband and parents to come visit me. I've kept track of their dream visits, and of how I felt upon waking.

Give yourself grace, and don't make yourself fill the time. You only need your own permission to rest. You're in charge of yourself. Don't feel you *should* be "doing something." Not doing something *is* doing something. Get your reserves back up. Put yourself first in life.

Moreover, unless you have experienced any kind of loss, feeling completely empty inside is a hard thing to explain. Whether this loss be from a death, a divorce, or a traumatic event, you feel like a ship being tossed around in the waves—void of all feelings. I felt like an empty vessel. There is nothing inside you. I found that I couldn't do anything to make the emptiness go away. I eventually started finding myself again and anew, and this empty feeling vanished.

ANGER

Yep. Very natural. I was so angry my husband died twenty-three years early. I was mad that he left me. I was angry at God. Why me? This wasn't fair. I threatened God. If you take my kids, that will be my undoing. Luckily, the anger left me relatively quickly. However, if you've lost someone to murder or a horrific tragedy, it may stay longer and eat you up from the inside out.

I determined that finding a good counselor was what I needed. I was lucky and found a therapist who helped me process my grief, and later also found a coach who became an anchor in my life to help me deal with challenges and anger. Looking outside myself was beneficial.

DISBELIEF

The shock of losing your beloved, especially when unexpected, is unbelievable. Wait? What? I went to bed with you, and only I got up? No. This can't be true. This can be very traumatic.

When a loved one dies, you also expect to see them. My husband should be coming home now. Oh, that's right, he can't come home. Your mind is just in a daze. I remember falling asleep on the couch, and awakening at 7:30 p.m. and thinking, "Oh, Bono will be home in a few minutes": only to remember he was not coming home. For me, this lasted for just a few months.

LIKE A VICTIM OR HELPLESS

This was really hard for me. I was a powerful, dynamic, take-charge woman, and—all of a sudden—I felt helpless. Bono took such good care of me, and I was so spoiled. Yet, I also took care of him. I felt so incapable—just drifting around in my life. I didn't want to accept help or be pitied. But friends and family DO want to help and make everything easier; you just have to ask.

I started asking for help and learning from whoever was available and had expertise. One time, Farley Cat asked me to hand her a ratchet. I replied, "Sure. What's a ratchet?" In addition to learning this, I found they came in various sizes. This happened all the time. While asking for help, I was finding my strength. I was starting to get my power back, and it felt good.

ALTERNATING BETWEEN FEELING LIKE SCREAMING OR WAILING AND FEELING NUMB

Find a place to let it go. These emotions need to get out. Scream into a pillow, or wail to your heart's content. It is extremely cathartic to let these emotions out in a loud voice. The strength, intensity, and volume of your own voice and grief may scare—or at least surprise—you.

At other times, you may become totally numb. You are actually shell-shocked. Your body is experiencing a part of trauma when you become numb. Nothing matters. You care about nothing. You just wander about your house, your life, and all around in a state of not caring.

LIKE YOU'RE MEANDERING IN AND OUT OF THE STAGES OF GRIEF

Grief is not linear. It doesn't extend in a straight line where you move from one phase to the next. Nope. Nothing that easy. You will experience the different stages of grief multiple times and in various ways. I found my anger didn't last long, but the crying hasn't stopped yet. I don't dwell on the past, but it does seep down my face at times in longing for and missing my family.

GRIEF IS AS INEVITABLE AS DEATH: BUT SO IS LIFE

Death is a part of life; we don't get out of this life without death. With death, comes grief. In life, people will experience opposites, such as life and death. What is the opposite of grief? I dare say joy, bliss, happiness, and ecstasy, among other emotions. Even though you may wear your grief like a big overcoat, the opposite of grief awaits you. Life can be beautiful and joyful again.

FACEBOOK POST
JANUARY 13, 2021

Today I awoke happy—the second time since my husband passed. The "river of rain" from yesterday has left, and the pups and I had a nice, long walk in the sunshine.

The government decided I was worthy of $600, and—as I waited at the bank to cash out—a fellow struck up a conversation with me. I have always loved to talk to people, but, once COVID-19 struck, people quit talking and would avert their eyes when waiting in line. We had a nice chat about snow, inner-tubing, and such. When he left, he thanked me for being nice to him. Sadly, we have lost this connection, and I will start greeting everyone when I am out and about. It was a delightful morning.

Upon coming home and turning onto my street, I saw my husband's SUV and everything came crashing down on me. The tears flowed as I remembered how happy I felt when he would come home, walking up the driveway, a grin on his face, and a cap on his head. Fricking grief. As I cried in the car so the dogs wouldn't feel my grief, "Hold Me Now" played on the radio. Hold me now…Warm my heart…

Forever in Touch:
Unbroken Connection and Loving Encounters with Bono

- In one dream, Bono came walking to me in all his glory with a massive smile on his face. In other dreams, I have seen him walking toward me, with a huge grin on his face, or driving up in his SUV—window rolled down, hat on, and grinning. That man was always smiling—not just at me, but at everyone. He made such a huge impression in everyone's lives. I was so lucky to have him as a husband, and to be the recipient of his smiles and love. Dreams are such an easy way for Spiritual forms to communicate, and I always feel fortunate when I remember these encounters while dreaming.

Chapter 9
"FEELIN' ALRIGHT"

LOSSES, GAINS, AND GROWTH OUT OF GRIEF

When Bono died, I didn't want to read books about widows or grief. The world had opened up a bit from Covid, but I didn't want to go out and couldn't be around people. Phone calls were exhausting, and so was just about everything else. It was hard to see friends—the pain they felt for me was clearly visible in their eyes. You can't disguise or hide that pain from the person experiencing it. It wasn't pity, but their faces radiated caring for me and wanting to be gentle.

I ran into a dear friend while out shopping for photo frames. Having photos in every room of the house brought me comfort and made me feel closer to Bono. I saw him at different stages of our life together: his hunky self at the beach, the beast as he was crossing the finish line of the STP Seattle to Portland bike race, his arm around me at his niece's wedding, and more.

SPIRIT BOX #15: BONO'S PHOTOS

"Karen took so many pictures of our family as we grew together. She has two picture frames of the children, and within each frame there is a school picture from kindergarten through high school. It's cool to lay out the pictures, and to see how the kids have grown and changed.

"Keeping photos of loved ones, is similar to having water during a bike race; the longer the race or life lasts, the more necessary the water or photographic memorabilia becomes for survival when you begin to lose willpower."

I hadn't seen my friend, Jan, in over a year, and I was just amazed to see her. However, I couldn't string words together to carry a coherent conversation. I couldn't stop crying. Tears, tears, tears. I tried to talk, but it wasn't working. She tried to fill in the conversation gaps with her warmth and kindness—I will never forget that. We parted, and I couldn't drive as my tears had turned to sobs. Unbeknownst to me, she was touched at the depth of my grief, and she sat in her car crying for a long time before leaving the parking lot—as did I.

My husband was a very dynamic and beloved man. I don't know if he knew how he impacted the people in his life while he was living. He always remarked on *my* "tribe" of friends, but *his* friendships ran deep—all the way back to his childhood. I know that, once he passed, he understood from beyond the Veil the deep friendships and love others felt for him. He truly touched everyone he came into contact with, usually through a combination of his amiable nature, his laugh, his thoughtfulness, his gentleness, and his kindness all rolled into one.

So many of our friends knew us as a couple, and having to tell people was excruciatingly painful. One method was through Facebook. EVERYONE was in disbelief. He was such a healthy and enthusiastic man—nothing would've led anyone to believe he would die so suddenly. I know my friends had questions they wouldn't ask out of privacy and respect for me. Later on, I was asked if he'd died from Covid. No. How did he die? I couldn't answer this; I could only describe how I'd found him, and what Nurse Beth and the police officer had said. I knew my friends wanted answers, and it took me quite some time to be able to talk about it.

Facebook became cathartic for me. People gave me constant support, and I made friends with many other widows. They were my saving grace, as they truly understood what it was like to lose a spouse. I wish I could copy all of their posts, messages, and texts—I still receive caring posts from my friends even today. I'd never opened myself up to being this vulnerable in a public forum. I was a very private person, and my rule for Facebook had been to "never complain," because people had enough of their own shit to handle. My posts had been light, fluffy, and uncontroversial, but I'd shared snippets of my life and people had learned about me.

That all changed when Bono passed. My soul cried out in despair and pain. I shared everything that was happening to me and all my experiences. I held nothing back. I'd never engaged in this type of expression in my life. It opened up my vulnerability. It opened up my heart. I shared things on Facebook that I would've previously kept to myself or only shared with close loved ones. Now, the world that I knew—and who knew me—was exposed to every detail.

I can't return to the state of "who I was" before I started sharing. Once my heart opened up, so did I. I became forthright, a realist, and very honest about situations. My intuition was cracked wide open. I could now see dead people, talk to the dead, and more. It was mind-blowing, and I embraced this gift with every part of my being. I'd had to suffer a huge price to expand the gift we all have. My personal growth and connections with others were phenomenal.

I discussed this in a post, and others also became forthright and opened their hearts in their responses. When I discussed my brush with suicide, my wall filled with people responding that they, too, had had the same experience and describing what they'd gone through. It was magnificent sharing heart to heart, with nothing held back. We opened up parts of our souls that had hidden things, and we were able to express ourselves in a safe place. It truly was wonderful.

Think about that—all of the comments that I received back. They were all written with loving, caring thoughts. Many people kept me in their thoughts. Many prayed for me, and this went on for months. Just think how much healing energy was sent my way. It was phenomenal. This process truly helped me to regain my strength. I know my posts were raw and full of emotion, but they depicted precisely what was happening to me. I want to think that my posts not only helped me, but also others. And all that love and support—those words that were written and expressed by others—helped me feel better. We all shared a symbiotic healing relationship.

FACEBOOK POST
OCTOBER 17, 2021

On October 18, 2019, Pops let go and took God's hand to return home. Mom joined him one year later, one day short of his death, on October 17, 2020. They were reunited, and the Heavens rang out in celebration.

Three weeks later, on November 8, 2020, my husband joined my folks and his family. Losing my three most prominent, beloved family members changed my life forever and all but broke me, but I am still walking this Earth.

Yesterday, the family gathered, and we raised our glasses and toasted them to "lives well lived." My parents and husband impacted so many in their lives and have left imprints on many hearts—especially mine. How blessed was I to have all of them in my life? Incredibly. I miss them all with every part of my being, and my heart will be jubilant when we are all reunited.

Forever in Touch:
Unbroken Connection and Loving Encounters with Bono

- While opening packages that I didn't remember ordering, Bono told me, "No more drunk shopping." How right he was. This had happened when he was alive. Tracy and I had ordered a whole bunch of stuff while drunk, and we didn't remember doing so. At that time, he made the same remark: he was still giving me advice while in Spiritual form.

> You don't just lose someone once,
> you lose them every time you open your
> eyes to a new dawn,
> and as you awaken,
> so does your memory,
> so does the jolting bolt of lightning
> that rips into your heart,
> they are gone.
>
> — (Ashworth 2022)*

*This is such a sad yet true realization of loss... With time, we progressively heal more and more...then, suddenly, back to day one of our experience of loss.

SECTION II

FOR YOUR GROWTH

"YOU ARE THE REASON"

chapter 10
"FOR YOUR GROWTH"

"There is no energy higher than love. All energy in the Universe responds positively to love.*

— DANA MCQUIRE

I made a wonderful friend on Facebook. These beautiful words that she shared about love and transformation resonate with me, so I share them with you here.

After losing my beloved father, mother, and husband in just thirteen months, I knew this was a lesson for me: I was to experience all this grief, loss, and trauma for my spiritual growth. It didn't matter that I was suffocating in misery, feeling like a helpless victim, or that I was constantly crying and angry at Bono for leaving. When he died, I was numb and a shell of my former self; an empty vessel with no energy for anything but tears. Yet, I had to soldier on and deal with everything that occurs when a loved one dies. Your life stops, but the world carries on.

Everyone has their own opinion on life, death, and the afterlife. I grew up in a very accepting household, and I hope that you can accept my view too. As I've mentioned previously, I believe in reincarnation: God doesn't only give us one chance to get life right, but rather we have numerous, or even thousands, of lives to expand our souls and learn. We have soul groups that we make contracts with before we come to earth to help us complete our lessons and growth.

Since the '80s, I've visited psychics and/or mediums for advice. When my husband passed, I visited my favorite psychic, Thea Strom, and I was told that one of my main lessons in this life was to experience deep grief and trauma. When she said those words, I knew in my heart they were true. I believe we work with a team of Heavenly Guides to map out our lessons before incarnating on Earth. I'd mapped out this lesson prior to this lifetime (I'd been avoiding it for previous lifetimes), and now was the time for my soul to grow through this experience. Unbelievably, I'd wanted to get it over with and had planned this grief I was now experiencing. My Guides had advised against this burden, but I was stubborn and wouldn't listen. I wanted it over with. Ironically, I'm stubborn in this life too—it must be a trait I carry throughout lifetimes.

When Carl died, I left things as is in the house. I've still not gone through many of his belongings. The jammies he wore on his last night are still on his side of the bed. I've lain on them and felt his presence on me, talked to him, and cried into them. Early on, I was so angry with him for leaving. I asked him *"Why?"*

I reminded him he'd promised to live to ninety—our life was just restarting after my parents transitioned, and he would've had my complete focus—and damn if he didn't give me an answer. My husband's answer for dying and leaving me was "simply" this: *"For your growth."*

SPIRIT BOX #16: MAKING THE BEST OF WHAT'S PASSED AND WHAT'S TO COME

"I died early in my life. When I'd written my plan with my Spiritual Team for this lifetime—before I met the love of my life, Karen—I'd chosen to leave early. However, no matter when we leave this existence, we can always try to make the best of the circumstances. For me, making the best of it involved getting to see Karen grow and develop her spirituality and independence as the strong, capable, and mystical woman she was always meant to be. Of course, I already knew she was all that. If I were still of the material world, I'd like to have a drink and make a toast to Karen's expansion. Whiskey, please."

This answer was unacceptable to me. I could still "grow" with him alive. I was stunned and angry at the response. I could become a better, complete person with him around. He didn't have to leave. Little did I know how valid his words would turn out to be. His death unearthed and cracked open my spirituality, and it fostered my growth as a "child of God" (or a child of the Divine, Source, Creator, Supreme Being, Divinity, Almighty, Yahweh, Buddha, Lord, Jehovah, etc.). We all hail from one Source, and we will return to that Source when our walk here is done.

For my growth, you said, husband? You were so incredibly right. However, I had to be torn down and put back together again for my growth. My spirituality was put at the forefront. Although he was a Spiritual form, suddenly, I could physically see my husband. He looked young—perhaps in his late thirties. He put messages in my mind: he left me coins, feathers, and personal messages to let me know he was around. It has been two years since his death as I write this page, and I've grown tenfold as a soul and as a human being. My growth and spiritual connections will be revealed as you continue reading the next section of this book. If spiritual development isn't your cup of tea, and you simply want more general advice about coping with grief, please feel free to skim or skip that part of Chapter 12 and Chapters 13-16.

FACEBOOK POST
FEBRUARY 26, 2021

I don't believe in happenstance or coincidences, and I feel there is a reason for everything—all part of a greater and divine plan. Losing my dad, mom, and husband in thirteen months has all but broken me. Yet, there is a lesson in this great loss, as there were with other challenges in my life—challenges we all face and that are personal for us. I will "get" this lesson, and it is my daily focus—learning from my loss and grief.

The gut-wrenching sobbing and grief have lessened, and when I cry, sometimes the tears are of joy with memories of my hubby. I miss my husband with every beat of my heart, but I also know we will be rejoined.

During this time, whether it be due to my broken heart or open spirit, the outpouring of love and caring from my friends near, far, and on Facebook has been instrumental in my healing process—true story. I have never experienced such an outpouring of true love and caring. So many offers of help, so many people checking in with me—it has taken me aback in its magnitude. I want to thank you ALL for being in my life, for lifting me up, and for all of your support.

The love has opened me up more as a person and made me want to become a better human. I am going to "amp up" the love I spread in the world...

chapter 11
"SUNSHINE" AND SPIRITUAL AWAKENINGS

"You Are The Reason" For A
New Chapter In Life

When my husband left "for my growth," I had no idea what he meant. Dammit. I could still grow if you were still here. As the year progressed, though, I began to understand.

Years prior, I had joined Facebook to connect with my children: Victoria was attending University of Oregon, and Nick had graduated and lived in Manhattan. Over the years on there, I found I was making quite a few friends worldwide. I enjoyed connecting with different people from around the globe and the United States—we shared our lives, adventures, and struggles.

When my husband died, I announced his death on Facebook so that people would be aware of what had happened. Everyone was shocked. He had been in good health, fit as a fiddle, gregarious, and had still possessed a passion for life. I've learned that God calls you Home when it is your time—not according to your schedule. There is a divine plan for all of us on Earth. I'd grown up in an "all-affirming church" that accepted the different walks to God, lifestyles, and choices of each individual. After college, the church had become history, but I'd embraced a spiritual way of life. I'd tried to live a good, fulfilling life as a teacher, wife, and mother. I knew in my heart that God didn't care if I walked through those church doors—what truly mattered was how I was leading my life and if I thought I was doing a good job. Apparently, I wasn't.

I found that, before all the deaths, I'd been mainly just living life—going through the motions. I'd done what needed to be done. I'd raised my children—most of the time as a single mom until Carl and I had married. I'd had an extremely fulfilling life as a schoolteacher. However, I needed to *experience* life—not just live it.

When I started experiencing my life—not just muddling through—it changed in astronomical ways. My heart and soul lived in a state of vulnerability. It felt like I led a bipolar lifestyle without the disorder. I could be dancing while preparing breakfast yet start sobbing when I sat down to eat. My soul wanted to burst out of my body—it couldn't be contained. The highest of highs and the lowest of lows were prevalent and often coexisted. I became more in tune with others, and I could feel their pain. An entire new world opened up for me.

I started sharing my vulnerable soul on Facebook with my friends. I was raw with the emotional expression of my experiences. I had so much support. Those who were widows could understand my grief; those who weren't learned how to treat a grieving widow as well as words of advice on what to do and say and how to help. It seems people are more at ease reaching out when a parent dies than when a spouse does. My friends were always supportive and found the right words to say after Mom and Dad passed; when Bono died, they were often tongue-tied. There were no words they felt comfortable expressing—especially if they knew you as a couple.

There was an uncomfortableness about what to say or do and regarding how to act. I was able to provide answers to their questions. Showing my raw grief and vulnerability was divinely inspired. I never would have done this before. I would not have shown my soul and nakedness.

Now, I'd present a message to others, and this was a way to be of service—to help others in grief. I was going to become a different sort of teacher. I had a new mission in life: I was going to be a helper and a healer. People would reach out to me privately with their pain and losses and for advice and help. We were able to walk this path together and to hold each other up. When someone died, I knew what it felt like and hopefully said something comforting for those left behind. I was experiencing their grief.

As this progressed, my mission in life became clear: to make the world a better place, to have a life well-lived, to help others, and to live in compassion, love, and empathy. I started praying and talking to God, the Archangels, my Birth Angels and Guides, and my family in Heaven. I asked God daily, "How can I be of service?" At the end of the day, I would again pray and see if I accomplished my mission. Everyone is born with intuition—a sixth sense—but it is lost early in childhood. It is like a muscle and must be used to be developed. Boy, was I ever developing my intuition and sixth sense.

DEFINITION DOGGY BOX :
DAZZLED DOGGY

"Holy Dog Bones. I have such a hard time pulling something over on Mommy, because she uses something called a sixth sense. Mommy can sometimes feel, or know, something is going to happen before it does. I heard her tell a friend that people can learn to develop this sense. Wouldn't it be cool to know about things before others or to know things others don't know?" (Collins English Dictionary)

Essentially, I was on a personal quest to be the best human and to be of service in this lifetime. I tried to keep friends and connections strong and made new friends. Reaching out to others and trying to do the "right thing" were paramount. I had an internal shift in my perception of others and came from a place of love and acceptance. I lived in both the physical and spiritual worlds, which helped my soul's evolution. I wanted to live the best life I could and to make a positive impact. When I die, I want to look back on my life and be proud of my accomplishments and their impact on others. I want to arrive at Heaven's Gate and be told "well done." Below are some of the ways in which I've grown, and in which I've balanced my own personal growth and living my best life with helping others to also grow and expand their horizons.

THE NEW AND IMPROVED KAREN: EXPERIENCING MY BEST LIFE

Sports and Social Inclusion

I've never been that much of a sports fan. My husband was a huge Niners Fan. Oh, how he loved football. I didn't like all the background noise, and never understood what was going on, so I let him enjoy it by himself. He always made sure I knew who was going to the Super Bowl and World Series so that I wouldn't appear too unknowledgeable.

In the summer of 2023, a longtime friend, Richard, invited me to watch The Portland Thorns play professional women's soccer. I normally would've said no, as I had no interest in sports, but I decided to accompany him. I had a blast. I didn't understand what was happening, so Richard explained the plays and players to me. I loved standing up and yelling, booing, waving my scarf, and getting excited with 20,000 other fans. It was very cathartic.

While Richard's wife indulged her love of travel, I became Richard's alternate soccer buddy. I attended the playoffs, and they won; they went on to the championship round and were triumphant. When season tickets became available, I decided to purchase some. I have another friend who loves soccer, and she also bought some so that we could sit together. We are right next to Richard and his wife, Linda, for games now. The first game night, I went into one of the stores on the concourse and purchased Thorns attire: I became an official fan. Before then, I'd never have worn team athletic gear other than a dragon boat shirt from the team I paddled with.

It's so odd: at the age of sixty-seven, I've started to embrace sports. I'd never been part of a large, unified crowd urging on a team playing any traditional sport. Even in high school, I wasn't up in the bleachers watching teams play; I was off with friends on adventures. Now, here I was, robustly joining the fracas and opening myself up socially. I was even finding new, different, sports-minded friends. This was just one of many ways I've explored personal growth.

I had a psychic reading with Renee. While telling her about my new adventures in life, Bono chimed in and said:

"See now? She is perfect."

Spirituality and Social Networking

Exploring my spirituality has simultaneously led me to new worldwide friendships on social media. It seems that a lot of people thirst for knowledge about existence behind the Veil—I did at one point too. I've made many friends who share the same spiritual philosophies as me, and we support each other. I've become closer to a friend in my area, and we are walking spiritually together. We attend the same channeling and mediumship classes, listen to podcasts together, and share our readings by psychics and mediums as well as our spiritual encounters and stories. It's comforting having friends with whom you can have such mutual understanding.

In addition, as I previously mentioned, I've made new friends through bonding over grief—not only with those grieving a spouse, but also with those grieving a child, parents, pets, or other loved ones. Grief, love, and support are binding agents for friendships. A person who has experienced any sort of loss can understand mine better than someone who has not, just as I can't really understand someone who has cancer as that has not been my experience. I can sympathize with them, but I can't truly empathize.

Finally, through enhancing my spirituality and intuition, I've grown skeptical of coincidences. Nothing is happenstance. Nothing. From the driver in the car in front of you who is driving you crazy by going ten miles per hour under the speed limit, to the friends on social media that you discover and make—we have orchestrated and drawn these experiences to us. Pay attention to everything in your life; it has not occurred by happenstance.

House and Feeling at Home

My husband has never left me, and he has now become one of my Guides on the journey left for us to experience. There was divine intervention when I purchased my house, and I knew that Bono and my Heavenly Helpers had brought this new home to me. I'd made a checklist of what would be acceptable for me in an abode, the area, and the amount of money I was going to spend; quite frankly, it was a tall order, and one not easily attainable. However, my new house was meant to be mine, and it came to fruition.

I was able to secure one above what I was approved for, in a wonderful neighborhood, and that checked off all my boxes. In addition, working with the seller was like a dream come true. They never said no, and they picked up many of the associated costs. My house was twenty years newer than those I'd been looking at in my price range: it was structurally sound; the roof was two years old; it came with a new AC and furnace; and it had a remodeled kitchen and bathroom. I wasn't going to spend a lot of money fixing up this house, which was beneficial to me. I know Bono and my Heavenly Helpers had worked hard to make this happen—especially because I'd almost overlooked it as it had been out of my price range.

Courageous Karen

I no longer recognize who I am sometimes. I've told this to my friends countless times, but I can tell they don't understand what I mean. I am the same person at my core, but I have also grown exponentially. I am constantly adjusting to this "New Karen."

I'd never lived alone. Ever. I now like being "Ruler of my own Kingdom," and only having to answer to myself and my doggies. After the first year, once I lost the panic attacks, I started stretching my wings. I began taking adventures, and it surprised me just how much I extended myself. I've tried things I always used to avoid. Engaging in spectator sports was just one of them. I put myself out there. I drove to the beach to meet up with my family. I also soared above the Earth in a hot air balloon. I should mention that I'm afraid of heights. I climbed into a woven basket with two other ladies, and we flew over the land. It was breathtaking and beautiful.

While driving toward the coast, I saw gliders flying in the air before the Coast Range. I decided I wanted to go hang gliding. A hang glider is a motorless plane that is taken into the air through a tow line by an aircraft. Once a certain altitude is reached, you release yourself from the airplane. The pilot let me release from the plane and fly. I was white-knuckled, and my hands were sweating, but I flew for about ten minutes. I was happy to relinquish my control to the pilot, and he flew and gave me the ride of my life—all while I was ooowweeeiiiinnnggg and aawwwwiiiinnnngg and crying out when he did something that scared me. I liked flying the hang glider even more than in the hot air balloon.

These two adventures had always been out of my reach since I was afraid of heights. I never thought I would attempt any of this, but I reached into myself and started doing things that were so unlike me—and I enjoyed them. Through embracing my fears, I opened my wings and flew. And I inspired many of my friends along the way.

Calm Karen

I'm way mellower than I've ever been before. Things don't bother me as much as they used to. I have a different understanding of why things happen, and I don't get bent out of shape as much.

My children have noticed this in me. They are shocked at the relaxed version of Mom they see and at how I react to things now. Upon leaving my new house, Nick and Leah had an in-depth conversation about how "chill" I was.

New Karen

I liked the old me, but I prefer the new me. It took me a long time to understand and accept my husband's death. It took me a long time to understand my three most beloved family members dying within thirteen months. Acceptance beats resistance. Resistance is a fight against yourself. I've heard it said that a fight against anything is a fight against everything. Now, I understand.

FACEBOOK POST
MAY 7, 2021

A few of my friends do not understand why, since I am retired, I awaken at five o'clock in the morning. They tell me to turn over and go back to sleep, which doesn't work. I bask in the glory of an early morning sunrise, out in nature, with the pups. It is a spiritual time for me, where I have my morning prayer and chats. It usually gets my day off to a good start, and the pups get to run free and herd crows. It's a beautiful time of day.

Forever in Touch:
Unbroken Connection and Loving Encounters with Bono

- Upon waking up in bed, I heard Bono call out to me. I heard his voice. He called out, "Honey!" It was such a nice way to start my day.

SECTION III

TACKLING GRIEF

SOCIAL, FAMILIAL, SPIRITUAL, AND PERSONAL COMFORTS AND TOOLS TO HELP NAVIGATE AND COPE WITH THE PAIN.

chapter 12
HONORING GRIEF EACH DAY

You will survive and you will find purpose in the chaos. Moving on doesn't mean letting go.

—MARY VANHAUTE

"ALONG THE NAVAJO TRAIL"

Grief swallowed me whole. Grief is an entire body experience, felt also in the soul and the mind.

I honored every feeling that came to me—every wail from my body, and each tear that ran down my face. I found it beneficial to honor and recognize my grief. It didn't have to be my friend, but it did become my teacher. I found strategies for coping with trauma, loss, and grief.

I learned from riding Apache, and other horses in my life, that if you get bucked off and fall, it hurts. It can be downright painful, but you keep getting back on the horse. No matter how painful the trail of living may get, no matter how much you're aching, you keep getting back in the saddle and riding that horse again. It's the only way you'll ever return to a stable life.

Here I provide an overview of some of the different types of coping strategies I've used throughout my grieving process. I discuss spiritual, social, and personal supports and comforts. These and similar coping strategies will be discussed in further detail throughout Sections III and IV, with Chapters 13-16 focusing heavily on spiritual supports and comforts and Chapters 17-24 focusing more on social and personal supports. Of course, these three broad forms of coping strategies are largely intertwined and often overlap. I encourage you to use any of the methods discussed that you think would work for you, personally—whatever helps you grieve and grow.

SPIRITUAL SUPPORTS AND COMFORTS

I opened myself up to communicating with the Heavenly Realm. I disagree with people telling others how to pray. You must offer up these words, face these directions, God will hear these words, and so on. God listens, and you don't have to be in a church to express those words. God cares how you live your life—not what you offer from your lips to Him—but how you live your life. I have read prayers from books which were not my words, and the verbiage rang empty to my ears. I suppose some of you think I am speaking blasphemy, and I am okay with that. I know God wants to hear my words—what comes from my heart to my lips.

These words and prayers that I speak are mine. Don't simply make them yours. Don't pray to these ascended masters just because I do. Do so only if it rings right in your soul. These are who I find comfort in speaking with now, and it may change in the future. The beauty of life can be that we are always evolving and changing. Lord knows, I have changed so much since all of this grief and trauma made a grand entrance into my life.

On my morning walks with the pups, and in the evenings before going to sleep, I speak to Divinity, Mother Mary, Father Jesus, Archangel Michael, Archangel Ariel, Archangel Raphael, Archangel Uriel, my Birth Angels, my Guides, Bono, my parents, Aunt Helen, Uncle Walter, Grandma Alice, and Grandma Mae. I choose to speak with those individuals or entities for certain reasons. When I pray, I do not ask only for myself: I ask for everyone in the world. My prayers encompass all of humanity. We all suffer, and we all need guidance and help.

DAILY PRAYERS AND OTHER SPIRITUAL EXPERIENCES: DIVINITY/SOURCE/THE CREATOR OF ALL THINGS, FATHER JESUS, AND MOTHER MARY

I started by thanking God on a daily basis for giving me another day on this Earth, and another breath of life in my body. I wanted to help others, to be of service, and to grow as a soul. If I could help anyone with grief or trauma, I was ecstatic. If I could be of service this was paramount, and I started looking daily to see how I could do so. It took me out of myself and my own needs, while at the same time elevating others.

It is my belief that Mother Mary and Father Jesus are the epitome of love. I asked them to reign love into my heart and into everyone's on Earth. I asked these two ascended Masters to wrap the world in love and help us find our way back to our true selves and to Source. Love is the answer. Love is always the answer.

DEFINITION DOGGY BOX 4:
ANAGRAM OF DOG

"Bark! Bark! Why does Mommy call God 'Source'?

"For her, Source and God are interchangeable, but other hoomans will argue about that. If that's confusing, wait until I tell you about Archangels.

"Some hoomans suggest there are nine levels in the 'Hierarchy of Angels.' It seems that Angels can have different ranks, with some higher and some lower, and these Angels are treated differently in some religions. Their wings can even look different. I never knew this. Mommy talks to 'The Archangels,' who are God's Emissaries—God's special representatives. She finds great comfort in speaking to them, and knowing they listen to and can assist her. Bark! Bark!"

ARCHANGELS MICHAEL, RAPHAEL, URIEL, AND ARIEL

I thanked Michael, as he is the keeper of all the Archangels and the most powerful. I would ask him to use his formidable sword of blue light to cut all of the negative, earthly cords tethering me to my existence. Cut those cords, and release them into the ether. Let me live a full, unencumbered life. Archangel Michael can also offer a shield of protection. When I drive, I ask him to put my car in a protective bubble and for me not to get into any accidents, harm anyone, or get any tickets. I can have a heavy foot on the car's accelerator at times. If I am ever fearful, I reach out to this Archangel. He is extremely powerful, and I always express my gratitude toward and love of him. I express that to each Archangel as I pray and talk.

Raphael is the healing Angel. I would thank him for my waking up pain free and being able to walk and move freely and unfettered, and for his keeping all of us on this Earthly Plane wrapped in a bubble of green healing energy according to their plans. I'd thank him for allowing us to live our best version of ourselves in a healthy body. I immersed myself in gratitude daily.

Archangel Uriel helps with the divine connection we as people have with the divine power and Spiritual Helpers. He is the embodiment of wisdom and light. I call upon him while I am meditating, and when I am connecting with my loved one and my Guides.

Ariel is the keeper of all the animals, creepy crawlies, and vegetation on Earth. That's a tall order. I am so in love with Mother Earth and the animals that inhabit this planet. I would thank her for keeping all the animals safe, protected, and provided with shelter, food, and water. My doggies mean the world to me, and I would thank Ariel daily for my pups. When my puppies are not doing well, I reach out to this Archangel for help. For example, if Bean is feeling anxious, I ask Ariel to help calm her down. I ask for wisdom in finding and providing the best treatment for my puppies when they suffer. As for bugs…not my favorite creations on the Earth, yet I would have gratitude for their existence too. Gratitude! Gratitude! Gratitude!

BIRTH ANGELS

I believe when we come into each lifetime, we have a team of Angels that watches over us. They prevent us from leaving when it's not our time. Have you read—or seen stories on TV—about people who were saved by "Angels," people upon whom miracles were performed, those who can't explain why they were saved, sole survivors of plane crashes, and so on and so forth? This happens because it wasn't their time to die. My coach and mentor, Jeff Tolley, tried to take his own life and overdosed on sleeping pills. He had a Near-Death Experience. He went to Heaven, and he immediately returned as he knew what he wanted to do and help accomplish during this lifetime: he wanted to be of service to others. It wasn't his time, so his Birth Angels intervened.

Everything has an order progression. Although we are all here with free choice, if it not yet our time to die—if we are not supposed to have this exit point—then we will stay here. Exit points are written into our earthly contracts while we are in Heaven working with our Team. They are "outs" that can be taken, or not.

My Birth Angels (I have two in this current life) have been very busy keeping me alive. I am so happy that they've intervened. I almost died three times in this lifetime, and they've kept me from taking an inappropriate exit point. I will share details of these brushes with death with you a few chapters from now. I talk to and joke with my Birth Angels, as I would with friends, about having to make them work so hard to preserve my life, but I also always have extreme gratitude that they've done their jobs and intervened to keep me alive.

I tell them, "Job well done. You've certainly had your work cut out for you. Thank you for making sure that I have lived."

MY GUIDES

Have you ever heard the expression, "You never walk alone?" Usually that is in reference to God; yet I also attribute this to our Guides who work with us. This is a spiritual team from the Heavenly Realm that you can access while you live your life. Guides help you to manifest—ask them for help in this area. I have six Spiritual Guides that I have been told about. They have helped me at different times during my lifetime. These include my:

1. Health Guide
2. Healing Guide
3. Trauma Guide
4. Business and Financial Guide
5. Two Native American Guides; a Path Finder and a Ritualistic Healer

DEFINITION DOGGY BOX

GUIDED GRRROWTH

"Mommy knew that she was taking on a lot of growth and evolution in this lifetime, and that her Guides reflect her thinking. Mommy has mentioned that all humans have Spiritual Guides, and that she has six Guides helping her in this lifetime. All the Guides and Mommy agreed to their help before she came to Earth. They step in when needed, and especially if you ask for help.

Mommy has said that grief has different cycles of intensity. She's able to manifest (make evident) and receive messages that help her cope with the ensuing grief. She calls upon her Guides in this way to help her when she's traumatized.

"Her Health Guide protects her and helps her with health challenges. I am thankful for this Guide, cuz I want Mommy to remain healthy. The Healing and Trauma Guides can work hand in hand, or separately. Mommy married some men who were not very nice to her, and her healing and trauma guides worked overtime. When she's beaten down by grief in general, they may step forward to help. I've heard Mommy cry out and ask for help when she's sobbing about Daddy, and

> they help her calm down. So, gratifying that we all work as a team. Right Isabel?"
>
> "That's right, Vinni! When Mommy's family died, those two Guides were constantly helping her heal; they get doggy brownie points for working so hard. The Business/Financial Guide helps her make financial decisions that will support her, so that she can also support us. All hoomans come to Earth with things they wish to experience and learn from. Mommy's Path Finder Guide helps her not to deviate from what she had previously planned. The Ritualistic Healer Guide has learned rituals and alternative practices like ceremonies, animal or mineral based medicines, energetic work, or hands-on techniques to help heal the hooman body."
>
> "That's some exciting stuff Isabel! It sounds like these Guides help Mommy when things get ruff. Ruff Ruff!"

Look at the types of Guides that were chosen for me in the Heavenly Realm. Their choices made sense, since I would require this team to help me fulfill my purpose in this life. Every single one of them has been accessed, and all will be helping me until I leave this planet.

Since I made it a spiritual commitment after my family members passed, I've continued talking and praying to all of the above Heavenly Helpers to this day. In addition, I talk to and pray to my loved ones who are behind the Veil, including: my husband, my parents, Aunt Helen and Uncle Walter, and Grandma Alice and Grand Mae. From this list, the people who I've seen in their Spiritual forms—and many of whom have otherwise made themselves known—include Bono, Mom and Dad, Aunt Helen, Uncle Walter, and Grandma Alice. I know these Spiritual forms come and go, but they are always looking out for me and giving me guidance.

As you can see, we never really walk alone. We all have a team. I encourage you to discover yours. In case you need some assistance in doing so, a highly gifted psychic told me all about my Birth Angels and Heavenly Guides. Maybe one could help you as well.

SPIRITUAL TOOLS

There are other tools that you can use to get answers from your Spiritual Guides. Currently, I am using a pendulum, and I also have a dowsing rod and tarot cards. Both a pendulum and a dowsing rod achieve the same outcome. With the help of your Guides, they will provide answers to a "yes" or "no" question. I have a friend who does not utilize any tools such as these. Instead, she stops whatever she is doing and asks her inner self—her soul—and waits for the answer. There is no right or wrong way: simply find the best way that works for you.

PENDULUM

The pendulum is used to gain a good working relationship with your Guides. I keep mine in a pouch on my table, and—when I remove it—I "clean" it. I don't physically clean it. Instead, I pray to Divinity to give me a divine connection. You can cup the pendulum in your hands and clean it by thinking of cleaning colors—indigo, ice blue, and white colors—you can sage the pendulum before its use, use sounds from a Himalayan Bowl, use a crystal bowl, beat a drum, or various other methods. As you can see, there are many ways to clean items and their energy.

Do you think, "Geeze, Karen. This is crazy." I don't blame you. At one point in my life, I was that way too, until I opened myself up and accepted. There are many, many things that we don't know about or haven't experienced. The key is to remain open. It's like in the song "Free Your Mind" by En Vogue, which refers to being color blind and accepting in dealing with people. I find the words quite appropriate in this vein too. Check it out. It's great.

In reference to the swinging of the pendulum, you can read it in the following manner:

1. Clockwise movement means "GOOD"
2. Counterclockwise movement means "BAD"
3. Vertical movement means "POSITIVE" or "YES"
4. Horizontal movement means "NEGATIVE" or "NO"
5. Hesitation or random motions means "DOUBTFUL"

("Ho'oponopono Course Certification by Joe Vitale and Dr. Ihaleakala Hew Len")

When you're finished using the pendulum, thank your Guides for blessing you with answers and express gratitude to Spiritual Helpers who have helped you before putting it back into the pouch.

DOWSING ROD

Repeat the same cleaning techniques that you used for the pendulum. The dowsing rod will give you a "yes" or "no" answer. Ask your Guides for assistance. For me, if the rod swings to the right, then the answer to my question is yes. If it swings to the left, then the answer is no. When you're finished with the dowsing rod, again, thank your Guides and express gratitude to any Spiritual Helpers who have assisted you.

TAROT CARDS

I personally love tarot cards and use them daily. I've found them to be more accurate for me than using a pendulum or a dowsing rod. Tarot cards have been around since the fifteenth century, and hail from Italy. It's been said they were "divinely inspired" and "blessed." Tarot cards can be used to answer questions one may have, or to gain insight into the past, present, and future.

There are many different "spreads" in Tarot. You can start with a one-card spread and work your way up to multiple-card spreads. Vivi and Tracy got me using cards in the '90s. They are superior at reading the "spread" and the messages from the cards, but I'm learning quickly.

Since Bono passed, I have not stopped using them. I started with just choosing one card. I prayed and asked my Guides and Divinity to tell me what they wanted me to know, and I'd get a one-card answer. There is always a book in the tarot deck that explains the symbols on each card, the definitions of the Major Arcana cards, and what the different suits mean (Cups, Pentacles, Wands, and Swords.) Most decks do not provide a simple "yes" or "no" answer; you must interpret the card, and you can do so with practice and with the help of a tarot book.

I currently pull three cards for my readings and use them to interpret a story. It's so cool. It's enlightening and enjoyable. I've started doing it for a friend; he finds the info "fascinating."

SOCIAL SUPPORTS AND COMFORTS

Once I healed enough to be around my friends, I started leaning on them for support. I had a huge core of friends who wanted to help me with my loss. I felt weak, and didn't want to ask for help, but that is when I should have asked my friends the most. Perhaps I might have sent out a text, had a conversation, or called for a chat. I remember many times calling a friend, and—when they answered—I couldn't formulate a sentence. My voice just cracked, and the tears would stream down my face while they patiently waited for me to speak. Experiencing love and compassion from others strengthened these attributes in me. Their voices were always soft and tender, and I was told to call "any time, day or night." So, I did.

PERSONAL COMFORTS

Vocalizing Grief

I found out that vocalizing my grief was so beneficial. While I was at my husband's clinic, and no one was around, I would scream and wail. Sobbing uncontrollably and immersing myself in my grief was a relief. It felt so much better than pushing it aside. Some of you will understand the depth of this trauma, and we all have different ways of coping. Yet, screaming and wailing can be so cathartic. Sometimes my screams, and the strength of my voice, scared me.

If you don't have a place to scream, it works just as well to scream into a pillow. There's a field near my house that provides a place to vocalize my grief. That may work for you too. I also found out some communities have "Screaming Circles." People gather and scream it out together. The idea of "physical venting" has been around for decades and can be very purifying.

I didn't carry on my screaming for an extended period: only when my grief was so savage in the early months. It was saved for the times when I felt I had no control, or that the grief was overtaking me, and I was in desperate need of relief. Upon feeling the need to scream lessen, I started focusing on deep breathing—where you breathe from your diaphragm and not from the top part of the lungs. I still use this strategy today, and it is very calming for me. Stopping what I am doing, closing my eyes, and focusing on my breathing has a very calming influence.

Journaling

Another way in which I tried to "honor my grief" was by journaling daily to my Birth Angels, my Guides, and my husband. I thusly opened the door for communication. If you want to open yourself up to your intuition, and this is not normally prevalent in your life, then working on journaling will help that part of your mind. It is like a muscle that needs to be worked on.

I found journaling very purifying. Reading back, I can tell my earlier stages of grief apart from now. As I grew and began to tackle grief, my perspective changed. After breakfast, I would open my journal and invite my Guides in to speak with me. I would ask them,

"What do you want me to know?"

I allowed answers to come. Whatever came to me, I wrote it down. After I finished with my Guides, I did the same with Bono. Many times, I received surprising answers. I did question myself, which I think is very common. Was I making this up in my head? Yet, I kept at it.

I found that, by flexing this muscle and opening myself up to Spirit, I am able to receive messages when not at the table journaling. I hear things that sound like someone talking in my mind—this is known in spiritual circles as clairaudience. The tone of this voice is almost always the same: even and calm. I'd receive messages from my Guides when I was in a quiet state.

Remember how I've mentioned that your brain is lost in a fog due to grief? Journaling is also a great way to keep those memories and other important things in your head. I look back at my journal from the first year after Bono died, and at my thoughts from that time, and I can see how they've changed over the years. I was reminded both of the good times, and of the long trail of grief. I've truly come so far in my life. I've accomplished more than I ever could've imagined.

I've kept track in a different journal, and on the computer, of how my husband and other Spiritual forms have reached out to me since all of this death occurred. I am surprised by how many things I've seen and experienced which lay dormant in my memory. Journaling is cathartic, and it's a reminder of what has happened in the past.

I've journaled enough to fill a book, and it has developed into more. I've used the assistance of tarot cards and a pendulum to ask questions and get answers. Tracy has given me numerous tarot decks, and I use one daily. I ask my Guides, "What do you want me to know?" I pull a card and read my answer in the book. I am becoming more proficient with the cards now, and I know most of their meanings without using the book. Some people have "the knowing" without even having to practice. For others (like me), the muscle needs to be flexed, and the doors will open. I like peeking on the other side of the Veil.

SPIRIT BOX #17: GROWING PRAISE TO RESIST GROWING PAINS

"My freaking wife is so incredible. She was so angry at me when I told her the reason I died. However, her soul has exceeded expectations that even she knew she was capable of. Her pain and vulnerability have connected her to so many people that are also suffering, and she has often been referred to as someone who can provide comfort and relief. Many of her friends now are open to the spiritual side of life and are more receptive of reincarnation. She has offered hope to so many people. I'm so proud of her that I am bursting my buttons. She has made a difference in the world; she has been a beacon of hope by surviving and thriving after the darkest of times."

Forever in Touch:
Unbroken Connection and Loving Encounters with Bono

- At dusk, I was sitting in the swing. My husband was standing in the doorway looking at me and letting me know how "proud of me" he was. He was so pleased with how I was surviving and handling everything that I had to experience.

chapter 13
"TIPTOEING THROUGH THE TULIPS"

"Across The Universe": Clarifying The Six Clairs

Everyone has intuitive abilities, but some people are more in tune to theirs than others. If you want to fine tune your abilities, find a reputable psychic, medium, or psychic/medium in your area or online, and work with them independently and perhaps through classes. (For differences between types of spiritualists, please see Section V) Your abilities are lying dormant and waiting to be accessed. We are like antennas: we can pick up subtle energies (Carlos The Medium 2022).

    I started my own spiritual journey over thirty years ago, but my spirituality cracked open when Bono died. In the past, I "knew" things or heard them in my head; now, I was receiving smells and seeing apparitions, fleeting shadows, orbs, and more. There is a whole new universe right at our fingertips.

There are six clair senses that utilize psychic abilities. You may be very strong in one and have tendencies in the others (Carlos The Medium 2022). These Six Clairs include:

- Clairvoyance (Clear Seeing)
- Clairaudience (Clear Hearing)
- Clairsentience (Clear Feeling)
- Claircognizance (Clear Knowing)
- Clairalience (Clear Smelling)
- Clairgustance (Clear Tasting)

CLAIRVOYANCE: CLEAR SEEING

A person with this clair-sense ability can see things in their "mind's eye" (also called "inner eye" or "third-eye") in a way similar to daydreaming. Visions often happen suddenly and may include striking detail or be quite simple in nature. The person may see signs that are significant for them and can then interpret their meaning. I know one psychic who will see a bunny, which is her sign for new things coming. A clairvoyant may see colors, shapes, have visions, and may see flashes out of the corner of their eye. They can both connect with and receive messages from Spirit (Carlos The Medium 2022).

I remember—from years before my spirituality blossomed—going into the bathroom late one night. I "knew" that someone was standing outside my door, and I also knew who it was—a friend of the family who had passed. It scared me half to death, and I asked God to take that ability from me. (I asked for it back later when my husband died and received that gift again.) I was scared to see the dead, but now I find it calming and welcome their presence.

Another time, my husband, daughter, and I were home during the day. My husband was laying on the bed watching TV, and my daughter and I heard something in my son's room. There should have been no noise coming from there, as he was away at college. Victoria and I went in to investigate, and we saw an elderly gentleman with gray hair sitting at Nick's desk. He was a solid figure—nothing translucent. It was as if a man was sitting there in physical form working at the desk. She and I looked at each other, and we ran to where Carl was lying on the bed and jumped into bed and under the covers. It seems covers have the magical ability to protect you. I find it rather interesting and cool that we BOTH saw the same ghost.

CLAIRAUDIENCE: CLEAR HEARING

A person strong in this clair-sense can hear messages from their Spiritual Team and loved ones in Heaven. Such messages are sometimes repetitive and are usually heard inside of the head as sounds, music, or jibber-jabber: however, at times, they can also be audible. Usually, the sounds and messages are from a spiritual source and not a physical one. Yet, hearing actual sounds or voices from Spiritual forms is rare, although possible. Clairaudient people generally hear things out of the blue and receive messages in their mind (Carlos The Medium 2022).

Oh, to hear voices in your head and know that you're not going looney tunes is comforting. However, I hear the voices speaking directly more than hearing them in my head. I always question myself when this happens, as I'm hearing impaired. I've heard conversations and have gone to investigate only to find that no one was there, or a TV wasn't playing.

One time, I was in the waiting room at Toyota, and I clearly heard "Karen" called out. I looked around, and no one had paid any attention—which is not unusual if you're only waiting to hear your own name called from the service area. I finally went to investigate and ended up feeling rather silly when I asked; the attendant joked that I was hearing voices in my head. Uh…no. I was reading a book, engrossed in the content, and I clearly heard my name called out. I didn't say these words to the agent; I was not going to go down that road with him. I returned to my seat and asked Spirit, "What's going on? Why did you call me?" But I didn't get an answer.

There have been occasions when I've heard the voices inside my head too, but these are not as prevalent. I was riding Apache one time, and I was told to "STOP!" I didn't listen, and I moved the horse forward even though she didn't want to go down the trail. I had stumbled upon a wasps' nest, and she had walked over it with her feet. She took off running, and I clamped my legs to her tightly as we ran away from the danger I could have so easily avoided.

Since I've started meditating daily, and connecting with my guides each morning, this ability has now become very strong. My Spiritual Team will put an answer in my head before I can even finish my thought or question. I love that. I get the answer before fully stating the question. Talk about mind reading.

CLAIRSENTIENCE: CLEAR FEELING

This is probably one of the most prevalent of the psychic clair senses: the ability to feel. Clairsentients can feel someone's energy, and they can pick up information from that energy. This energy does not have to be a person; it can also be a place or thing. One can feel in their "gut" if something is "good," "bad," or more nuanced, though it goes beyond mere instinct. Clairsentience is thought to be highly intuitive. A clairsentient, who is also often a highly sensitive person with a great deal of empathy, makes decisions based on emotions, feelings, and sensations instead of primarily depending on logic. They can tell why someone is having a problem without that person saying anything at all, for example (Carlos The Medium 2022).

Like many people, I can feel another person's energy. I can tell if we are going to vibe or not. I also process from my gut, and I listen to my gut and rely on my feelings and emotions more heavily than on my rational mind. You've probably heard the saying, "Always listen to your gut." I can feel someone's sadness, anger, joy, and other moods, but I can't explain "why" on a deeper level like a true Clairsentient.

CLAIRCOGNIZANCE: CLEAR KNOWING

I find this to be a cool clair sense. You just very clearly and precisely know things, without knowing exactly how you know. The knowing can be about people, places, and things, but without having any feelings or emotions tied into the mix. It may happen seemingly randomly and very suddenly. The information comes as very strong impressions; this clair can make one aware of another person's character, and the claircognizant person can also know the outcomes of situations before they happen (Carlos The Medium 2022).

This is probably one of my stronger psychic abilities—knowing. Spirit puts a thought into my head. One just knows. I would bet that at some point in time in your life, you "knew" something that later turned out to be true. That was your psychic muscle flexing itself and giving you a message. I can think back throughout my life having the ability to know.

CLAIRALIENCE: CLEAR SMELLING

This psychic gift allows a person to have an extrasensory experience through their sense of smell. Spiritual forms may present smells associated with them, to try to reach out. It would be a smell that would remind you of that person, such as the odor of their favorite food, perfume, cigarettes, flowers, etc. I've heard in the past that animals can be clairalient, and this is illustrated when dogs or cats can smell diseases in the body, such as cancer. The dog or cat may lick or sniff the area of that body. This clair sense provides an interesting way to connect with Spiritual forms that are there with you. It is not as common as some of the other clairs, but it is still an important means of contact for spiritual encounters (Carlos The Medium 2022).

I'd never accessed this ability in myself until after my mother died. While living, Mom had wanted to give me a "smell" so that I'd recognize that she was nearby. We discussed many options, and we came up with the smell of coffee as it's so distinct and we both love to drink it. Since her death, there have been times when she has brought me the smell of coffee. She has also brought me other smells. One time, when I was sitting in the office, I smelled the aroma of freshly baked cinnamon rolls. This brought back childhood memories. Keep in mind, I am the only one who lives in this house, and I was not baking anything at the time. Mom has also done this with floral scents—sweet smelling flowers. This is one way in which mom makes her presence known. She has diversified the types of aromas she uses to reach me in this way.

A couple of my spiritual friends have told me how they smell perfume when their mothers come around. Several have also smelled cigarettes when their moms and dads have visited. It is a way for the Spiritual form to give verification that they are visiting you.

CLAIRGUSTANCE: CLEAR TASTING

Imagine tasting something in your mouth that is not physically there. If this happens to you, you may have tendencies of being this type of clair. The taste comes randomly and may bring a memory or emotion with it at the same time. It doesn't have to be food. You may be provided with the taste of rust, plastic, alcohol, tobacco, or anything with a sense of flavor. If you strongly taste foods even when you're not eating, you may have this. Have you ever seen someone eating pizza on TV, and suddenly you can taste pizza? That's clairgustance (Carlos The Medium 2022).

Clairgustance works like clairalience, except it involves taste. It's also much less common. Both of these clairs create bridges to behind the veil, connecting you with the Spiritual forms of those who've passed. My friends and I have never received messages in this way. I wonder what it'd be like to suddenly taste chocolate or something else pleasurable in my mouth.

CLAIRIFYING YOUR ABILITIES

Which clair resonates with you? Do more than one? Which are you currently using?

As Albert Einstein pointed out to us, energy cannot be destroyed. We are all energetic beings, and we can use this energy for communication.

SPIRIT BOX #18: CLAIR AS DAY

"I am Karen's Mom, Ruth Joy; she is my second-born daughter, and we shared the ability of being psychic. I always encouraged Karen along this road, and we visited psychics together too. I love that I can reach out to her, and that she's receptive to me. I love to put images and memories into her thoughts for comfort; when I do this, she recognizes that I am with her and gets excited.

"Karen also has 'seen' the image of her father and me when we accompany her in Spiritual form in the car. Ted will put songs into her head that we used to sing while driving, such as 'Anchors Aweigh' and 'Off We Go into The Wild Blue Yonder.' Karen will get very happy and excited, and she will start singing; we will join in, but she cannot hear us.

"When Karen sits on the couch and pets the pups, she can sense her father sitting in one nearby chair and me in the other. We smile at her when she talks to us, as we know she feels our energy. We are so pleased with how our daughter has so bravely weathered the storm of grief."

Forever in Touch:
Unbroken Connection and Loving Encounters with Bono

- I was in a dream state in Bono's big, red chair. I could see him coming through the entryway from the garage toward me. He had a big smile on his face. The Veil was thin, and I could experience him. His hair was blacker than the more recent gray. I saw him from the chest up. He was smiling so huge, and I was full of joy. He knew that I could see him. He looked radiant, healthy, happy, and at ease. This image is etched in my mind.

- I took an afternoon nap. As I was awakening, I heard, "Karen, I have some bad news to tell you." I never found out the bad news.

chapter 14
"FREE YOUR MIND"

Flexing My Psychic Muscle In Mysterious Ways

I mentioned earlier that all of us are born with psychic medium capabilities, but, unfortunately, we begin to lose those abilities around four or five years of age. This loss of being in tune to Spirit and its abilities does not happen to all of us, but most of us are out of luck. However, this capability is like a muscle, and it can be used for our spiritual growth. The more you use it, the stronger it becomes. What is that old saying? "Use it or lose it."

MY "MAGNIFICENT" EARLY PSYCHIC EXPERIENCES

My mom always encouraged my psychic ability. However, when I was growing up, there were no schools or informational resources on how to grow your psychic knowledge, so I never really flexed my psychic muscle. My friends and I played with the Ouija board, but we usually scared ourselves while doing this. When we placed our hands on the disc, it would give us weird answers or move crazily around the board. We also met in darkened rooms to have seances, which always scared the bejeezus out of us.

I remember, as a young girl, laying in my bed at night and seeing colors swirl around and above my head. I didn't understand where these colors came from, but they were beautiful. I am still not sure what I was seeing as a child, but it was some sort of energy. I vividly remember going to my mom, who was sewing, and telling her what I had seen. I needed validation or an explanation. She didn't look up from her sewing, but she validated what I had seen and didn't discourage or negate my experience. She gave me a soft piece of fabric that I could rub to bring me comfort when in bed.

At night, I can still see these colors swirling above my head and bed. I can also close my eyes and see them. They are beautiful to watch, and also make me very sleepy. I've always been anxious to see what type of colors I'll see each night before they magically appear above my bed.

When I was nineteen, Mom, Susan, my aunt, and I all went to see a palm reader. During the reading, she told me that I would marry a man with blonde hair. I discounted this prediction, as I was currently engaged to a Cuban gentleman with very black hair. I didn't put much credence in what she had told me, and she didn't flinch at me being skeptical. She had a knowing about herself, and she was secure in her knowledge. She offered no explanation: just what she had read in my hand. The marriage to the Cuban man lasted nine years, and guess what. After we divorced, I later married a Finnish man with blonde hair. The palm reader was correct after all.

When my aunt had her palm read, the palm reader asked her about a child that she didn't carry to term. We all stopped breathing in the room, as my aunt had never shared this tragedy, and she confirmed to the palm reader that it had happened. I was blown away that someone could ascertain these pieces of information by reading our palms. She had seen that my aunt had a miscarriage, and none of us had known this information beforehand. I am sure that my aunt was taken aback, but she didn't blink an eye when she heard the information—yet we were all in shock. We were polite and did not ask my aunt about her miscarriage.

"EVERY" PSYCHIC'S "WAVE"LENGTH

It wasn't until ten years later that I would venture out to see psychics. I frequently visited a prominent one in Portland. Along with seeing clients, she also assisted the police with crimes that had occurred. She was a brusque lady who didn't mince words. I saw her many times and took some classes with her. I was just beginning to flex my psychic muscle.

She was one of the first psychics who I frequented. In one reading, she told me that I would be writing a book, and then numerous books. I sat thinking:

"Lady, I am a schoolteacher. There is no way that I am going to write a book. I don't have the time, energy, or desire to write a book."

Yet, here I am now, penning a book forty years later. Since my husband died, I have had three different psychics tell me that I would be writing two or three books, and that I'd be talking to people about their grief and trauma and flying around the country to do so. Let's see what happens. Let me finish this book and see where my life is going to lead. I know I made a plan that is larger than I could have conceived of while writing my spiritual contract.

I started reading books written by James Van Praagh, Dr. Brian Weiss, Dr. Michael Newton, Anita Morjani, Sylvia Browne, and many others, which all opened up and expanded my mind into different realms. In addition, I took classes from the Portland psychic until she left the area. After that, I took a hiatus from classes for a number of years. However, I started studying again more recently. I took classes in my area and on Zoom that dealt with mediumship, developing your mediumship and psychic abilities, communicating with animals, and more. In turn, I brought people into my life that had the same thirst for knowledge, and we all took classes together, recommended books to each other, and opened ourselves up to more new experiences.

HOLY HOLISTIC HEALING! "YOU MIGHT THINK" THAT'S SOME CRAZY SHIT!

I know that I'm off on a new spiritual adventure. Spirit is moving in and through me and helping me to develop my gifts. I know that many will travel the same road. It is a road into the unknown with no map—only trust. Trust that there is more out there than what we experience physically. Each person's spiritual journey is unique, and—through our journey—we meet others who are either learning from us or teaching us something. Developing the sixth sense is exciting.

I did have some bizarre incidents at the beginning of this adventure. My husband melding with me was a major one (see Bono Encounter at the end of this chapter). I had never felt a Spiritual form in my body before that. Since I knew that it was only my husband, it did not cause me any fear—only comfort and love. That man has consistently reached out from the other side of the Veil to help me on my new quest, and he is always by my side. I know that, wherever I go, I am together with a room full of Spiritual Helpers—whether they be my Guides, my Birth Angels, or my family members. Know that YOU ARE NEVER ALONE. You always have a team that is gently nudging you back onto your path, whether you recognize it or not.

THE "MYSTERIOUS WAYS" OF CHANNELING

I believe that I have experienced attempts by my Guides to come into me in order to prepare me for channeling. A channel is someone who serves as a medium for a person who has passed. I'd always thought channeling was a "little left of center," and that I wouldn't want a Spiritual form to enter my body. It sounded too bizarre. What if you channeled mischievous energy? One evening, my body was overtaken by one that I believe was one of my six Spiritual Guides (see Chapter 12). My body was shaking out of control, to the point that my teeth were chattering. I'd never had this experience before. I knew it wasn't my husband, as he doesn't contact me in this way. It was so strange not to have control over my own body—which felt electrified.

I experimented some, and I could stop the movement and then also allow it to come back. It was exciting and peculiar. I didn't tell my friend, Tracy, because I thought that she'd say that an evil Spiritual form had possessed me. When I finally told her, she was excited. She said I was starting to channel. I was so excited to start pursuing this avenue of my spirituality. Since this happened to me, I don't find people who do this to be odd. It is strangely exhilarating.

Another incident happened while I was eating lunch with my friend, Marilyn. I felt a pressure in my body. I looked to her side and saw her husband sitting there, looking at me straight in the eyes. I sometimes saw Spiritual forms, but I was surprised that he was there and that we made eye contact. He had on a summer shirt, shorts, and his ankle was crossed upon his knee. I looked away, and—when I looked back—he had vanished. I was taken aback to see him sitting there and staring at me. I did not tell my friend, as she is not on this wavelength. I told her about the visit from her husband a year later, and she accepted that I had seen him.

I went to lunch with another friend, Chris, to celebrate her wedding anniversary. As we talked, her husband entered my body, and I could feel him head to toe. I did not feel the overwhelming love that I did from my husband; I just knew that it was her husband validating his presence to her. I couldn't sit still, and I was wiggling all over. It is rather strange to feel this type of energy, while the person casually sitting across the table does not notice anything.

Jill, a fellow widow, has strong psychic ability, and her sixth sense is highly developed. When we broke bread, her husband entered my energetic field. When I mentioned that I was wiggling all over and that I could "feel" her husband, she commented,

"Isn't he lovely?"

She had total trust, and she knew that her husband was with us and that he was communicating with me.

SPIRIT BOX #19: BEGRUDGING BONO

"Hey, that's my thing! Keep your energy to yourself!"

PSYCHIC SUMMATION

Seeing psychics and mediums throughout my life has been mind-blowing, and they've helped me immensely with processing my husband's death, connecting me with him, helping me move forward, and comforting me. My son is a naysayer, and he wanted me to promise him that I wouldn't visit any psychics or mediums. I made no promises, and his mom is now developing her abilities via these modalities. That will be his road to walk—hopefully, with acceptance.

I want to recognize four psychic mediums: Thea Strom, Kim Carrey of Intuitive View, Renee Terrill, and Joshua-John. Thea lives in my area, and I've been taking classes from her and seeing her for years. Joshua-John and Renee are also in the Portland area: I continue to see them, and I am also taking classes from Renee. Kim is a psychic I found on YouTube. They all helped me retain my sanity during the hellish time of the past several years. I will not review their readings in detail here, but excerpts can be found in Appendix I at the end of this book.

FACEBOOK POST
APRIL 4, 2021

A year or two ago, I put up a video that I had taken of a rain shower in my courtyard, and a floating, clear orb could be seen. Many of you also saw the orb.

That green orb—which looks like a vortex—was not showing when I took the picture, nor was it caused by the light from the sunrise. I have taken many sunrise pictures from the same spot, and I've never had this occur.

We are never alone, even though we may feel separated.

Forever in Touch:
Unbroken Connection and Loving Encounters with Bono

- Incredible. I was watching a girl perform on TV and was touched by her singing. Bono suddenly came to me, and I could feel his Spiritual form on and inside of me. It was indescribably joyful, overwhelming, and loving. I lay there, couldn't move, and just felt his presence while crying tears of joy. This feeling lasted about five minutes. I went into the bathroom and still could feel him with me—merged, but not as strong. I couldn't speak or move, and I just stood there crying and feeling his love for me. This had never happened before. I was breathless and weak in the knees thirty minutes later. My sensors were on overload, and I felt his genuine love for me. The entire experience lasted about an hour. I had never before experienced a Spiritual form melding with me.

- Once, I stepped into my husband's energy and asked him to hug me—he did. I had goosebumps all over. Maddy came over and looked deeply into my eyes and wagged her tail. She rolled onto her back and had a soft face and eyes. I told her, "Daddy loves you so much," for she had also felt him.

chapter 15
IT TAKES A BREAKDOWN TO HAVE A BREAKTHROUGH

"The Rain," The Exit Points,
and "Other" Worldly "Things"

These chapters on spirituality are personally the most important to me. They involve my Angels, Spiritual Guides, and After Death Communication from Carl. These encounters strengthened my knowledge of the afterlife, and helped me to know that he was happy, at peace, learning more lessons in Heaven, yet still with me. My trials with deep grief grabbed my heart and wouldn't let go. Through the losses of my parents and husband, I was trying to find my purpose and become the best human being I possibly could. I was determined to make a difference in this world—to really live a life of value and to help others. Death has a way of making life even more valuable.

One psychic told me we all could connect with the dead (mediumship) and have psychic abilities. It involves a muscle in our brain that gets stronger when it is exercised by connecting with others. He recommended that I keep a journal and talk daily to my Spiritual Guides, and that utilizing this technique would enable me to become more adept at mediumship. I've written in my journal for almost a year, and I've spoken to my Guides and my husband on a daily basis.

I initially wondered if I was creating these thoughts in my head, or if there really was a connection with others behind the Veil. As I continued journaling, I started noticing that the phrasing of the words began to take on a life of its own—one where it wasn't my style of speech. This was fascinating. I learned about my Birth Angels and Spiritual Guides. As I've discussed, Birth Angels serve as protection so that you don't exit too early from this Earth. I'm sure you've read stories or watched movies about people sent back to the world, usually by loved ones, because "it wasn't their time." Birth Angels help avert such brushes with death and keep you here; they even bring you back if it's not yet your time to depart. The latter are called Near-Death Experiences (NDEs), and often involve visions of a tunnel of light or out-of-body experiences. I personally have had three brushes with death, one of which qualifies as an NDE.

DRIVEN OVER THE EDGE AND DRUNK DRIVER

Looking back, my Birth Angels absolutely kept me from leaving this life early a few times. In my early twenties, I was a passenger in a sports car with my then-husband on Mt. Hood. We hit a sudden icy patch and went careening down the road, crashing on top of the buried guardrail in the snow. I looked out my door to the cliff that lay before me. We were inches from going over it. If I'd gotten out of the car using the front passenger door—my life would've ended. If we'd moved, or if we'd rocked the car, we could've gone careering down the mountainside. I carefully moved across the seat to get out on the driver's side. Whew! That was a close call.

A car and truck stopped to help us dig the vehicle out and off of the guardrail. One fellow stood by the roadside directing traffic, while the excavation began. Suddenly, a truck came careening around the corner toward us. I ran for cover, and the man directing traffic jumped out of the way; he had astonishing reflexes. It looked supernatural. The truck hit the guardrail and our helpers' truck—the driver was drunk. It was amazing no one was injured or killed. Our Angels and Guides were busy up on the mountain that day.

DELICATE DIVINE DELIVERY

When I gave birth to Nick, my first child, I had a straightforward pregnancy: I had no complications, and I was huge in the tummy with this baby. Strangers would comment on my size, because the rest of my body had not put on weight—only my stomach area. People would actually come up to me and rub my belly. It was weird, but I got used to the touching and the comments people made. I remember one man remarking on my month of pregnancy and how much bigger I was than his wife. I was in my late twenties teaching Jazzercise when Nick was born. I taught on the day before giving birth to him, and I resumed classes shortly afterward. Within weeks, my pre-pregnancy body returned. It was a super easy process with Nick.

An uncomplicated pregnancy was not the case with Victoria. She was born to a different father, and I suffered throughout this pregnancy. I was massive from the onset—in my tummy and my body. My legs went down straight, and there was no difference between my legs and my ankles. Her pregnancy was hard to bear. Eventually, I developed toxemia, and I was admitted to the hospital. Victoria wasn't due to arrive for another six weeks. Every day, I looked different in the mirror, and sometimes I barely recognized myself due to retaining so much water.

One night, I developed a debilitating headache. My doctor came to the hospital in a tuxedo: he'd left a dinner where he was being honored to check on me. I consequently was transferred to another hospital that specialized in early births and premature babies. The doctor informed my husband there was a good chance we'd lose the baby that night. Apparently, if there were a chance only mother or baby would live, the life of the mother would've been the priority.

While riding in the ambulance, I could hear the attendants cursing back and forth. Evidently, Victoria's heartbeat had ceased and no longer showed on the monitor, and they were lost trying to find the hospital. I wanted to speak about their cursing, as it wasn't comforting, but I wasn't able to get any words out. I believe that Victoria's Spiritual form was so stressed during this time that she left my body only to return later. For the entire ride—which felt like it lasted at least thirty minutes—there was no heartbeat coming from my baby.

Upon arriving in the ER, I was strapped down like I was being crucified—possibly due to emergency care. I wanted to tell one of the attendants to leave because his aftershave was nauseating, but I was unable to speak again. Thankfully, he left the room. My second husband kept stroking my hair and telling me how much he loved me through the entire ordeal. I was finally able to speak, and I said to the doctors:

"Turn down the lights. It's so bright in here."

The room became deadly quiet, and there was no movement or talking. I believe I saw the divine light that takes you when it is your time to leave. I can only imagine the looks they were exchanging. After this, everything was a blur.

My daughter was born healthy, but she weighed less than a five-pound sack of sugar. She has since grown into a remarkable, dynamic, brilliant, and empathetic woman. After her birth, I had a private room at the hospital for about a week or two for my recovery. Many of the staff who'd been in attendance during the delivery would come to my room to visit me. They were astounded that I was alive and usually ended up crying. I didn't remember any of these people, and I had no clue how close I was to death. I saw the light, and was brought back from the brink. This brush with death was a possible NDE, but it wasn't my exit point: my Birth Angels were working very hard to make sure I stayed here on this planet.

My children are my biggest blessings.

DANGEROUS DIVORCE DEPRESSION

(Trigger Warning: This section reiterates my battle with spousal abuse and the ensuing depression. It's not a pretty picture. If you're entrenched in grief, you may want to skip it.)

I had two husbands before Bono. My parents didn't bless either marriage. Each time, once they saw I wasn't going to change my mind, they went along with the union. They knew their headstrong daughter well. In each marriage, I'd given away my voice and control to my husband. Their wants and needs were always met, while mine only were at times.

My first husband had numerous affairs. In my Pollyannaish world, I thought he'd never cheat on me once we were married—but I soon learned many harsh realities about life. I finally got tired of this lifestyle, and we got divorced. I honestly feared for my life during that time, but never spoke up. Aging has taught me to always speak your truth; it's up to the person who receives those words whether or not they listen to and heed them. Be forthright—honest and open about situations. Do you think if I'd told my parents about this, they'd have let me stay where I'd be in harm's way? No way.

Thank God for Nick.

I thought my second husband would be better, as he was quite a catch. Yet, my parents—once again—knew better. I found him to be very attentive to me, which later turned into controlling my every move. He eventually cut me off from my friends and family. Finally, he grew tired of me early on in our marriage and traded me in for a younger, blonde model.

Thank God for Victoria.

I'd spent fifteen years of my life allowing two other people to make decisions for me, to beat and keep me down, and to make me feel worthless. I'd been such a powerful person until I married those two; now, I fell to my lowest of lows. At this point, I felt like a failure—a failure as a mother and as a wife. I was in such pain. My kind and well-meaning doctor prescribed antidepressants, but the side effects led to my having suicidal thoughts.

I'd felt the only way to stop this pain was to die. It was so excruciating to live. I look back at a picture from this time, and I looked lifeless—a shadow of my former self. I decided I was going to kill myself. People, at this point, don't think about others, or how their own actions will impact their family. I didn't think about my parents, children, or friends. I wanted out of my misery. Someone contemplating suicide cannot see beyond the pain, which can be debilitating.

When I had one of my "good days," I'd buy a gun and go to the mountains, where my family would never find my body. Finito. My pain would be gone, and the world would be a better place without me. However, for the third time, divine intervention in the form of my Birth Angels saved my life. I was playing with my daughter one day, and we fell to the floor. Her hair fanned out on my arm, and I looked into her eyes. They were bright and sparkly, and she wasn't looking at me—something else was. I knew instantly I'd never kill myself, and I started changing my life to regain my former self.

BIRTH "ANGELS CALLING"

Three exit points had presented themselves: careening over a cliff, dying while giving birth, and contemplating suicide. My Birth Angels were certainly working overtime during this lifetime to make sure I didn't check out early, and I'm so grateful. I've thanked them frequently, as my life with Bono was yet to unfold—a life I never could've imagined. I had a friend tell me once, "You never know what's around the bend in the river," and I've found that to be so true.

> ## *Forever in Touch*:
> ### Unbroken Connection and Loving Encounters with Bono
>
> - I was watching a video about a boy who came back from Heaven. I could feel a slow-moving and loving body chill coming from my hubby. I was so thankful and felt so loved. He stayed with me for a long time.

chapter 16
"UNCHAINED MELODY"

EXPANDING SPIRITUALITY AND CONTACTING LOVED ONES BEYOND THE VEIL

If you've been diligently reading, you now know more about the following: my spirituality; my Heavenly Helpers; the six main types of clair senses; my history with psychics, mediums, and channeling; and my three potential exit points and brushes with death/NDEs. In this chapter, I'll share with you ways you can further explore your own spirituality, and I'll teach you about After Death Communication (ADC), piercing the Veil, helping loved ones transition when it's their time to leave this Earthly Plane, and considering what's important in life while you're still here.

NO "NIGHTS IN WHITE SATIN": DISCOVERING DEEPER LOVE, APPRECIATION, GRATITUDE, AND SPIRITUALITY THROUGH DEATH

Losing my father, mother, and husband in quick succession damn near killed me, and it was certainly demoralizing. Yet, it took this profound loss to usher in an awakening of my spiritual gifts. I'd asked my husband in anger, "Why did you go?" Who knew from his answer, "for your growth," that this was exactly what had needed to happen for the expansion of my relationship with Divinity? Once he died, my spirituality was ignited.

My parents and husband have continually let their presence be known after they left this Earthly Plane. I want to share some ways in which they've "pierced through the Veil." They've continued to contact me, as well as others, in Spiritual form as I continue my journey down the path of spirituality. I am constantly surprised to see how Spiritual forms contact me. I am not any more special than you—we all have this ability. It took great loss for me to develop my powers.

DEFINITION DOGGY BOX 6:
SPIRITED GOOD-DOGGY ENERGY

"We are such good doggies, aren't we Vin? Mommy always said we were good doggies when we were in physical form, but we have been extra special in Spiritual form. We no longer have physical bodies, but our spiritual souls are very much alive. There is a Veil between the physical and spiritual worlds; the physical world is an illusion. The veil can be penetrated, and we did this when we returned to our real Home. We pierced the Veil with our Spiritual forms and were able to reach Mommy through After Death Communication."

"That's right, Isabel! Do you know what Mommy thinks happens to one's Spiritual form when they die? The soul rises from their body, and they're led Home by their Birth Angels and Archangel Azrael—he's God's Angel of Death, and it's his duty to help bring the soul Home. He gets a bad rep as 'Angel of Death'; there is no death. The soul is energy, and it'll live on."

"I know that Vin! Depending on your beliefs, your entry into the spiritual world will honor that belief. If you believe Jesus will greet you, he will. If you believe your family members will greet you, then that will happen. Mommy is going to be surprised when she comes Home. All the animals she had in this lifetime, and from other lifetimes, are going to beat everyone to see her. We can zip around Heaven and are even faster than Daddy. We will reach her first!"

"I visited Mommy many times. She was always in awe when she felt my presence and energy. I was always the good boy. Isabel was always digging holes, howling at the backyard fence, and raising a ruckus. Mommy always said, 'Who's a good boy?' I knew she meant me."

"There you go again, Vinni. Mommy loved me just as much as you. She could feel my presence too, and I made a loud noise in the garage that Daddy, Mommy, and Victoria heard right after I left my body. See how powerful I was? Vin always wants the credit for being a good boy; I was the good girl. So there."

Would you like to develop your sixth sense? To open yourself up spiritually? Find and explore the gifts you were born with and have not yet discovered? Communicate with the dead? Do you feel that you're not living your purpose? Is there something else? Then perhaps it is time to start awakening these talents that lay dormant in your body. It can be overwhelming to think about. You're entering uncharted territory, but the world offers a wealth of information.

After you've made the choice to explore these realities, the universe will let the experiences unfold for you. However, you can't just sit back and wait— you have to take action. Where to start?

SPIRITUAL BOOKS

Read. Or get audio books. Find those sections at the bookstore and locate books that interest you. There are so many well-known authors on this subject. I will provide a list of some, but it would be much more effective if you first started exploring on your own. You will find authors that resonate with you. As you read, what feels like the truth for you? Your mind will expand into a whole new universe, and it is one wild ride.

SPIRITUAL YOUTUBE AND INTERNET CONTENT

Watch YouTube through Google and find credible psychics and mediums. Find some in your area. Ask your friends for recommendations. Once you start down this road, the universe will provide for you. When I started down my most recent road of grief, the universe brought a great magnitude of people into my life for support. Listen and see how accurate their predictions are. When I started on my spiritual journey, Google was non-existent. We now have a wealth of information at our fingertips with the Internet but be discerning. I started out with one psychic, and it has blossomed into five I know and trust. Two of those can easily be found on YouTube.

SPIRITUAL READINGS

Have a reading from a psychic, medium, or psychic/medium. Know that everyone's abilities are not the same: just like a chef, doctor, or teacher, some are more adept than others. Most of mine have been extremely insightful; others not so much. You will become more discerning with time.

My friend's boyfriend lost his daughter to a drug overdose. He poo-poohed spirituality; however, for a couple of years, I pushed him to go see Thea Strom, and he finally decided to do so. He walked out of there a new man. True psychics don't want to know anything about you because it unfolds in the reading. This is what happened for this fellow. He connected with his daughter along with others in his family who had passed away. He was told things that only he knew. Now, every time his daughter's birthday comes around, he has a reading. This brings him such comfort and joy. He feels like he can talk to her at any time. This initial reading was crucial to his healing. He was stuck in an extremely dark place, and he couldn't move forward until then.

SPIRITUAL CLASSES

Do you want to know how to communicate with animals? Chat with your Angels? Become a medium? Discover which "clair" you are? Credible psychics, mediums, and psychic/mediums offer classes. Again, find someone that resonates with you to work with.

LET GO AND BROADEN YOUR MIND: "LISTEN TO YOUR HEART"

At first you may think you are crazy. Aren't we all a little left of center? I love being left of center. Your mind will broaden. You may be unsure of your abilities, which is perfectly normal. I questioned mine. Was I making this stuff up in my head? Above all, have faith and trust. Let go. Don't try to control. Let your heart lead you, not your mind. Your heart is always right.

Letting go was hard for me to do, as I'm a Virgo and a schoolteacher by trade; this birth sign and career led me to be quite rigid. My life was formed around schedules at school that had to be followed. I am the least spontaneous person I know. I had to learn to let go.

I started attending psychic fairs, and saw different types of tools and consultations used, including tarot cards; pendulums; past life regression sessions; readings; taking aura pictures; numerology; and more. I explored these, bit-by-bit, and decided to partake in past life regression. The psychic had me lie down, and slowly hypnotized me. I was in a light, hypnotic state; I knew what he was doing, and where I physically was, yet I was being drawn to another place.

I saw and felt myself as a Native American bravely riding a horse bareback. During the regression, I could feel how freeing it felt to be on a horse running through the open field, dark black hair flying back over my shoulders. I could see the strong legs of the horse running, and I could FEEL these sensations during the regression. I knew I was male, and that I was responsible for taking care of my family. When the psychic wanted to bring me out of the past life regression, I expressed the desire to stay because it felt so good. I didn't want to leave.

James Van Praagh came to Portland and did a group reading at a church. He'd be drawn to a member of the audience, ask that person questions, and give them a message from their family member. Afterward, he'd sign class members' books. I knelt down so I was at his level while he signed mine. He looked at me indignantly and inquired, "When are you going to start using your gifts?" He was so blunt that I was taken aback. I didn't feel like I had psychic gifts to share, but he was telling me to take action. Yet it took me many more years to nurture these gifts.

I started following James and others through their websites and on YouTube. Most psychics have classes you can take in person, through Zoom, or with downloadable content where you learn at your own rate. I found these to be beneficial for growing both my spirituality and as a person. I've recently taken two classes with Renee: one on channeling, and the other on mediumship. To reiterate, channeling attunes one to receive messages, insight, and energy from Source. Mediumship is the ability to connect with family members from the Heavenly Realm.

What I really found amazing as I opened myself up to Spirit is how I made friends with like-minded people. We took classes and attended events together. A whole new world opened up for me. In letting go, and opening myself up, I truly "found" myself. Isn't that crazy?

AFTER DEATH COMMUNICATION

All my life, I've had "unique" experiences. They started when I was a child, and continued into adulthood, but they became much stronger later in life. Mom was psychic; she'd answer all of my questions and support me through my experiences. Like many, I can feel people's energy—I am psychic and an empath, which is quite helpful when meeting people and in public life.

DEFINITION DOGGY BOX 7:
PSYCHIC EMPATHS, PIERCING THE VEIL, AND ADCS, OH MY!

"Rosie to the rescue! That's my job! Ruff! Ruff!

"Mommy uses words that I do not understand, but I pretend I do. For example, the word psychic: this is a person who has extrasensory perception about the world—one who can detect things with their senses that others cannot. Mommy says she uses her sixth sense when being a psychic. I find my best sense is using my nose—it never lets me down.

"Mommy says I am an empath. She says I have the capacity to feel what she is feeling. I am sad when she cries. I can pick up her vibes instantly. My love is over the top. I feel deeply. I am a good boy—I am an empath.

"As for After Death Communication, or ADC, I am so happy for this. I died, but Mommy can still feel and sense me. I am still with her. I will always watch over Mommy until she comes back to her true Home. I'm still not sure I know the difference between an ADC and piercing the Veil, though. Maybe Grammy can help."

"You are a good boy, Rosie. Did you know I tried to get your Mommy to call you Kennedy, but she wouldn't? I am glad that you go and visit her through ADC, Rosie; I do too.

"I will explain the difference between these ideas. An ADC is a connection with a living person via a person or animal who has died and is in Spiritual form. The two are able to connect with and perceive each other without the use of a medium, psychic, or other tool (like tarot cards or pendulums). The Veil is very thin: if your energies can connect by 'piercing the Veil,' then you can have an ADC with the person on the other side. My daughter works on piercing the Veil so that she can communicate with her Birth Angels, Spiritual Guides, doggies, and all her Heavenly Helpers, including me. As you can see, piercing the Veil and ADC go hand in hand."

This section gives you an idea about some of those "unique" experiences, specifically touching on some of the After Death Communication (ADC) I've encountered. ADCs have been a very significant and helpful part of my grieving process and life after losing my loved ones.

MY DEATH-DEFYING DOGGY, ROOSEVELT

My first vivid ADC was with my miniature schnauzer named Roosevelt, or "Rosie." He, unfortunately, passed away early in his life. Rosie was an extremely vocal dog. He would run along the fence line and bark at anyone passing by. Rosie liked using his voice exuberantly.

Roosevelt would have the run of the backyard when the family had gone to school or work—he was the king. After losing him, upon returning home from work one day and driving up the driveway, *I heard him barking*—welcoming me home. I could hear his barks coming from behind the gate by the garage door. I was thoroughly shocked.

I sat in my car, stunned, and listened to my "dead" dog barking. I didn't have the wherewithal to go talk to him—that developed later in dealing with death. I know Rosie reached out many times after he died, but I wasn't open and in tune yet—this would develop over time.

SPIRIT BOX #20: ROSIE REJOICES

"I did it! I am so happy Mommy heard me bark!"

VINNI AND ISABEL CROSS "THE RAINBOW BRIDGE"

After Rosie crossed the Rainbow Bridge ("The Rainbow Bridge Poem" 2019), we brought in two other doggies to join our family: Vinni (a mutt) and Isabel (a beagle). They brought so much love and joy to our family and lived for fifteen years before transitioning. Vinni left for Heaven first; Isabel died of a broken heart six months later. We were able to be with them at home when they left this world. Saying goodbye to a pet is heartbreaking *and* gut-wrenching. A part of you dies.

During Vinni and Isabel's lives, I was on a spiritual quest. I took seminars, read books, attended classes, went to a spiritual church to help me grow spiritually, and more. I made many new friends who were also in the same vibration, and we were learning as a family.

When Vinni passed, I was able to connect with him. He reached out to me so many times, and his energy was so forceful that he stopped me in my tracks. I learned to document each ADC with Vinni, and I did the same when Isabel decided to join him. I still have those records, and I am re-experiencing each memory as I read back through them. In addition—when I had these experiences—I talked to the doggies as if they were standing right there, because, in actuality, they were. The Veil between our world and Heaven is so sheer.

Everyone can connect, just as I have done, whether it be with a deceased pet or a missed loved one. Many lucky people have this ability firmly ingrained into their being. There are others, like me, who have had to develop their abilities.

Are you willing to learn how to grow psychically?

The day after my husband died in November 2020, he started communicating with me. I have kept a journal of all of the times I remember his communication, and it manifests in a variety of ways—he has come through the Veil and comforted me so much since he left.

THE DOC OF LOVE CARL "BONO" BONOFIGLIO

After Bono passed, one of his ways of communicating with me was through music; music was a huge part of our lives before he transitioned. A playlist of many of those songs can be found in Appendix II in Section V of this book. The titles of my chapters and sections contain some of the songs he's sent me. Some are ones we sang together, others are not, and some I'd never even heard before. It seems he "sees/feels" me from the Heavenly Realm and sends me the perfect song for how I'm feeling. The songs were mostly sent as an affirmation of our love, to cheer me up, to let me know he's still there, and out of concern for my well-being. As you continue reading this book, think of him singing each song to me and to all of you and your lost loves.

Bono also communicates with me in dreams. The first three times he did so, he looked the same age that he was when he'd departed—older and with gray hair. I think that he came to me this way so that I'd clearly recognize him. In one dream, I could actually feel his arms wrapped around me and feel myself being held against his chest—it was unbelievable.

Bono verbally addresses me, as well. During the month after he passed, my daughter, son, my son-in-law, and I were sitting in a very cramped space working in the clinic. I heard my name called, and I looked up at the same time as my daughter. We'd both heard my name—not the others—as clear as day. Binks and I are on a similar vibrational level, and it was such a relief to hear Carl's voice. That was beyond exciting. When Binks and I looked at each other, I asked who'd called out my name. She said that it was Dr. Dan in the other room, and—upon asking him—he hadn't called out to me. It had been my husband.

I understand some of the wording I use can be confusing. Every human, every living thing, has a vibrational level. We are made of energy. If you are open to the spiritual side of life, your vibration changes—as is evident in people being able to see or talk to the dead, receive messages through other means, or possess other spiritual abilities. Victoria and I are psychically in tune; thus, we have the same vibrational level, and are able to hear, see, and perceive things others cannot. It is not good or bad; it is just part of our being. Everyone has the ability to change their vibrational level. Vibrational level can also be indicated when saying "vibration" or "wavelength." You may find this in everyday life—some people will be on the same wavelength as you, and you may become fast friends. Alternatively, someone may not be on the same wavelength, and you do not cultivate their friendship. It's not judging anything—it just *is*.

Moreover, Bono leaves me signs of his presence. On our wedding anniversary, he left me a smiley face that I saw on the paper towel after lifting up my coffee cup. Each time I make coffee, I put it down on a paper towel in case the cup is wet on the bottom. As I lifted up the cup, I could see a perfectly formed smiley face looking at me as if to say,

"HAPPY ANNIVERSARY, BABY."

Bono left me another sign of his presence. I am a Virgo and a neatnik—everything has a place in my house. My house is usually very orderly, and I know where everything is. Upon arising one morning, I found a quarter on the rug in the hall right outside of my bedroom—it had not been there the night before. I know that Spiritual forms will leave coins out, and I was impressed that Bono was able to leave me a quarter.

However, as I reached into the pocket of my robe, I found another quarter which he had placed there. Amazing.

By then, my mouth had dropped open, but my husband was not through yet. As I got ready for the day and to take my pups out for a walk, I opened the car door to put them inside and found two quarters on the seat. The dogs don't carry money, and the quarters had not been on their covers when I took them out of the car the previous day. I frequently walk these areas, and the coins had not been there until the morning.

Quarters denote significant life changes that bring new opportunities your way and enhance your life. They inspire you to have faith, to trust in yourself, and to stay strong. I may have been feeling particularly weak at the time. Bono's death had almost killed me, and I didn't care if I lived or died. Now, he was making me aware of his presence and trying to give me hope and confidence in myself. My husband had been very busy the night before my discoveries.

Finally, I've actually "seen" Bono four times in the house. He looked young, healthy, vibrant, and handsome as hell. These ADCs always bring me tears of joy, as I know this is how he looks now and that he's feeling radiant. His hair is longer with no gray and he looks more like he did when we first met.

In one instance, I was sitting on the patio swing, and—when I looked up—I saw him in the bedroom window looking down at me. It was a solid form, and he had his arms on the windowsill. In a second instance, I was in the family room, and I saw him come in from the garage in his red coat as he'd done on a daily basis while alive. Again, he looked young and vivacious. A third time I saw him; I was changing out some parts in the vacuum and feeling proud of myself. I looked up to see him sitting on the piano bench. I saw his entire body. He had his hands on his knees, and I noticed how long his legs were. He smiled at me and was proud.

One more time that I saw him, I was sitting on the hassock in front of his red chair. His red chair was significant for us. He hadn't wanted the chair, but I'd made him buy it and it had become his favorite seat in the house. Almost daily, I'd move the hassock aside and kneel on the floor and lay against his chest, and he'd hold and embrace me. I'd also sit on the hassock between his long legs and have conversations with him when I really wanted his attention.

One night, I was extremely entrenched in my grief. I sat on the hassock with my head bowed, sobbing, and with tears and snot running down my face. I was rocking back and forth and moving my hands against the seat of his chair—stroking it where his legs would have been. I was so distraught; the pain was so unbearable.

Upon lifting my head, he was sitting there staring at me—looking at me so intensely. His eyes were penetrating, and he looked younger and slimmer with his dark, black hair. He was trying so hard to come through to me and for me to see him. It is very hard for a Spiritual form to come through as an apparition. I was taken aback, yet so grateful to see his presence.

Until my husband died, I had not seen apparitions. Seeing them scared me, and I asked God to take away that gift. After this occurrence, I asked for the gift to be returned, as it was comforting to see my husband. There have been many more styles of ADC from Bono, but I will stop here for now. Some samples of my many different styles of encounters with him can be found in the Encounters Section at the end of most chapters, and a longer list of some more encounters in general is located in Appendix III of Section V at the end of this book.

DEFINITION DOGGY BOX :
APPARITION VIN

"Mister Vin here! Mommy's favorite good boy! Ruff! I was never able to appear to Mommy as an apparition. An apparition is a deceased person or animal that you can see. When Daddy appeared to Mommy as an apparition, he did this in various ways. Sometimes he came to her as an older man, like when he died, and other times he appeared to her looking like when they first met and when Mommy called him an 'Italian Stallion.' (How could Daddy be a horse?)

"An apparition is a Spiritual form that can be seen. A Spiritual form could also reach out to the person in other ways that don't involve them being seen, such as putting thoughts into their heads, giving them a smell to remind them of you, making noises, and more. One day, maybe I'll be able to show the handsome face of this good boy to Mommy again as an apparition."

My mother and father have also reached out to me from behind the Veil, but their communication is a bit different in nature than that of my husband.

POPS FROM THE "WILD BLUE YONDER"

My father seems to connect with me through songs, as we always sang together when I was growing up. He will put songs into my head that I have not thought about or heard in years. I've heard "Anchors Aweigh," and "It Ain't Gonna Rain No Mo'" in my head many times. When I am leaving the garage, I will often hear the U.S. Air Force theme "Wild Blue Yonder," since Mom, Dad, and I would sing that so many times when we went on our daily adventures. These songs always bring a smile to my face and happiness to my heart.

One time, I was standing by the kitchen counter, and I felt his presence standing next to me. I was not facing him, but I could feel him. I bowed my head and started crying. I told Pops:

"It's so hard."

"I know, little girl," he replied.

He always called me "his little girl" even as I became an adult. It was so comforting to have him by my side.

"MAMA ME-AHHH!"

Mom had a really high spiritual energy, and I'm not able to connect with her as much as I am with others. As I've described, we all have different vibrational energy. On the Earthly Plane, you can connect with everyone even if your frequency vibrates higher or lower. However, when someone enters the Heavenly Realm, they are returned to a vibrational energy that can be higher than theirs was here on Earth. It also depends on how many advancements a soul made in its last lifetime. Mom vibrates at a faster and higher frequency, and I can't always "feel" her due to this.

As mentioned, she told me when she passed that she'd bring me the smell of coffee, which she has. I have more of a "knowing" when Mom is with me. I'll greet her and talk to her like she's there. The first year after she died, a white butterfly would come and greet me daily when I was in the backyard, and it was comforting knowing that she was letting her presence be known. Mom gave me a "singing clock"—which isn't really singing anymore when the hour strikes as that mechanism is failing—whose singing is significant because I know that it means Mom is reaching out to me. Even though it's only supposed to work during daylight hours, it's sung at night and at various times I've been distraught: Mom is trying to reassure me.

Mom is the one who always cared for me when I was sick growing up. When I am ill now, I always call upon her to take care of me.

Something interesting happened to me in 2022. I was walking around my bedroom, and I was suddenly taken to my knees with an inexplicable, debilitating pain in my gut. It felt like someone had stuck a shiv into my sternum. My phone and my watch were in the bathroom—a mere eight feet away—but the pain was so intense that I couldn't move. I lowered myself onto my knees, bent over, and rested my face on my hands while crying due to the pain. I felt like I was dying and thought about going to the hospital. However, due to Covid and the way the ER was being run, I'd stayed away from emergency trips. But I really was ready to go this time.

I knew that Farley Cat was coming over in a few minutes, but I had no clue how I'd get to my phone or watch, or how I would make it to answer the door. I called on Mom to please take care of me. Eventually, I was able to rise and walk downstairs when Farley Cat arrived.

I opened the door and sat down on the piano bench, with my elbows on my knees and my head hanging. Farley Cat started asking me questions so that she could figure out how to help me. I did raise my head once to look at her, but—when I did so—I felt "different." I attributed it to feeling so horrible.

When Farley Cat finally got me settled so that I was pain free (she stirred up some baking soda and it calmed down my tummy), she stayed for hours to make sure that I came out of my episode and was okay. She told me that she'd been horrified when I'd looked at her, even though she'd kept a calm disposition. It seemed that when I'd looked up at her, it had not been me. It had been my mom looking at her. Farley Cat said:

"You were as white as a ghost, and your face was your mom's."

She further said that my eyebrows "pointed up like [your mom's] and your mom was looking at me." I inquired how that could be, as

I was confused—we were both baffled. I ascertained that Mom had entered my body to help me out during my "imminent demise." Isn't that outlandish and cool all at the same time? Mom, once again, came to my rescue.

ADC is a real thing. CNN was documenting encounters that the living had had with their relatives who'd passed alone in the hospital due to COVID-19 (Blake 2021). It's nice to know that I'm not crazy, but I wouldn't care if people thought I was.

Out of curiosity, have any of you had communication from your deceased loved ones? I won't think that you're crazy. I do highly suggest that you keep track of these encounters, as—when time passes—you will forget most of the visits. They can be recorded in a journal, written in a log, or documented however works best for you. After Bono died, I stopped keeping track of all my encounters, but I later resumed. Now, when I read back in my documentation, I can re-experience the encounter and remember it vividly. Sometimes, when I have forgotten about it, the entry is a wonderful reminder that the Heavenly Realm is present in my life.

"PUT YOUR HEAD ON MY SHOULDER" AND PIERCE THE VEIL

ALL your loved ones want you to talk to them, even after they've passed. They are with you, watch over you, gently nudge you at times without taking away your free will, and want you to recognize them and to be remembered. They offer up guidance and help. They always want the best for us, and they hope that we'll find comfort in their presence for all time.

A vital component is that you must ask your loved ones for the help you need. In the last section, I asked Mom for help when I felt like

I was dying. I could not make the few steps to the bathroom; yet when I asked her for help, she assisted me by giving me the strength I needed.

I talk to my husband, mom, and dad in prayer twice a day: when I walk the doggies in the field, and just before I go to sleep at night. I also constantly babble to my deceased loved ones during the day. This small act will bring you closer to your loved ones and closer to piercing the Veil between Heaven and Earth, as it is fragile. They are not up in the sky looking down on us, but rather they are near us on a higher vibrational level.

I did not practice "piercing the Veil" until Bono died. Although Mom and Dad died first, they usually came to me in dreams, not while I carried on during my day. I remember Dad from two vivid dreams, and when Mom pierced the Veil just after she died. I will tell you about the two dreams from Dad now, and about Mom's final message to us at the end of this chapter.

DAD DREAM #1: "ALIVE AGAIN"

…I was walking, when—suddenly—there he was. I stopped dead in my tracks: I knew he "was alive." In my dream, I remarked that "you're supposed to be dead," and then crumpled against his chest and sobbed. I could feel his physical body as I lay against him in my dream. This was remarkable, as I didn't feel as though it were a dream.

It felt like I'd stumbled upon my dad, even though I knew in my rational mind he was dead. Yet, he came through to me for comfort in my dreams. When you can feel the physicalness of someone in a dream, it's phenomenal. If it's someone you love, then to feel their body and warmth against you is pure bliss…

DAD DREAM #2: POPS POPS IN

…Bono and I went to a restaurant, and I immediately noticed a Market America event going on. Bono and I had been business owners as part of that company. I was so embarrassed; I hadn't been to a business meeting in ages. We'd held a prominent position, and I was remiss for not remaining active. I tried to remain incognito: I didn't want anyone from the company to see me.

After we were seated, a man came up to our table—it was Pops. My mouth just dropped open, and I stared at him in amazement. He shook my husband's hand, and gave him a huge hug. When Dad and I were hugging, I wouldn't let go or stop crying. I was filled with complete happiness and love. He sat down with us and did not look at all as if he were ninety-five, but instead more like he did when I was a teenager. His hair was black, he had a black mustache, and he wore no glasses. We talked, and he told me that he was waiting for Mom.

I woke up, still amazed, and it was 5:55 a.m.—a good Angel number…

"THE END": PEOPLE DON'T WAKE UP UNTIL THEY'RE ABOUT TO DIE

I had no clue I'd be instrumental in helping people in my family transition to the other side. I didn't know this was part of my job description for this lifetime, as death was not a prevalent theme…yet. Helping someone transition out of their earthly body and into the Heavenly Realm was not an easy task. It was heart-wrenching, and layers upon layers of emotions encapsulated this decision. I found myself wrestling with a choice between honoring the wishes of the person who wanted to die, and satisfying relatives who strongly disagreed. "Stuck in the Middle" comes to mind; add scoops of guilt, loss, trauma, and suffering, and you could imagine my feelings.

I will discuss helping two beloved family members: Aunt Helen and Mom. I will also provide an example or two of ADCs where the flimsy veil was pierced.

HELPING AUNT HELEN END HER EARTHLY LIFE

My first experience with this was with my beloved Aunt Helen in 2009. She was a widow, and she'd fallen and was not discovered for five days. By the time she got to the hospital, her body was a wreck and she had pneumonia. Dad and I flew to California to help with her recovery.

Aunt Helen was a very petite lady, but she looked even smaller in the hospital bed. She was at Stanford Medical Center and was receiving the best care possible—I was impressed with the doctors and all attending to her. They put something down her throat to help her breathe, and she could only communicate with her eyes. They were doing all that they could for her. There was talk of moving her to a care facility once the hospital had exhausted their treatment options.

My father was distraught. Helen was his only sister, and his parents had passed. Their family unit had been extraordinarily close, and they'd called themselves "The Four Fieldbraves." Helen was living in California; she'd been considering moving to Oregon to be with her last remaining family members, and Pops had been ecstatic.

I was in constant contact with all of the family members in Oregon about her impending demise, and Dad had pretty much shut down and let me do everything. He couldn't make decisions or think properly—symptoms of grief that I'd later experience when my husband died. My son and niece were begging me not to let her die, as if I had any say in the matter. The stress was unbelievable, and that was the first time I became a parent to my father. As you know, later in life, I'd devote eight years to my parents' care, and we'd shift our roles: I'd become the parent and decision-maker, and they'd let me take care of them until their final breaths.

I called a nurse friend of mine, Jan, who explained to me what was happening to Helen's body: she was not improving. I told Jan that I'd promised my aunt years ago that I'd help her die if ever necessary. Jan intimated that Helen was not lying in bed thinking about what we'd discussed years ago; she suggested that I go talk to her to see how she felt about it now.

I made the trek to the hospital without Pops, as he'd disapprove of this conversation. I asked my aunt to open her eyes, as I needed to talk to her. I asked if she wanted me to help her die, and she nodded. I told her I would, and she went back to sleep. Upon leaving her room, I cried, came upon a nurse, fell into her arms sobbing, and told her Helen's wishes. She mentioned "comfort care"—the first time I'd heard this expression, and one I'd later hear often when my parents were dying.

I scheduled an appointment with the doctor, Dad, Aunt Helen, and myself for the next day. She was wide awake, and I explained to everyone what she wanted—these were her wishes. Pops and the doctor talked to her extensively about her decision and what would happen. The doctor wanted to make sure that she was "of sound mind." Dad didn't want this to happen, but we had to explain to him that it was not his choice but hers. She wanted to die: her body was dying, and she wanted to join her husband and family in Heaven.

Dad then wanted to set her up at a VA care facility, and only later facilitate her wish to die there. Perhaps he hoped she'd change her mind, and it'd give them some more time together. She frantically looked at me for support—I can still see the terror in her eyes—and I said:

"No, Dad, that is not what she wants."

He asked us to leave the room first so that he could speak with his sister. I waited outside, and—when the shell of my father walked out and passed me by without any acknowledgment—then the nurses and I went back into the room. They removed the tube from her throat and immediately began administering drugs to keep her comfortable. My aunt finally looked relaxed and at peace. She was now in charge of her own demise—free from pain and able to have relief.

A day or two later, Aunt Helen went to Heaven to join her husband, mother, and father.

ADC FROM AUNT HELEN AND UNCLE WALTER

The last night that I stayed at my aunt's house, something prevented me from sleeping—my aunt. I did not physically see my aunt, but I felt her. I could see colors swirling around the room, and I felt her presence. It was striking. The colors swirled and danced around the room as I sat stationary watching them. It was not scary, but rather lovely and comforting.

I was drawn to her bookcase and drawer, and she wanted me to look inside. She wouldn't stop. She was so insistent. I found some letters in the drawer that would've been hurtful if discovered by my family, so I removed them. She kept leading me to other items, but I couldn't figure out what I was supposed to find. I said that I had to sleep due to exhaustion, and she left.

Before my aunt's death, her husband had preceded her. She'd always told me about the times that he'd contacted her. Uncle Walter would open drawers and turn on and off lights—he'd never left her side while she was still living. In the hospital, I'd asked her if she'd seen him while lying in bed, and she'd nodded in the affirmative—he'd been waiting for her to come home.

While Dad and I were at my aunt's house, a fountain pen kept appearing. It'd appear out of nowhere, and I'd find it on a table or countertop. Dad always kept a pen in his shirt pocket, and it wasn't his. I asked Dad if he was playing tricks on me with the pen, and he confirmed he wasn't being a prankster. I looked at him, carried the pen, and put it in a pencil holder on top of a desk. Later, as Dad and I talked, I saw the pen on the floor. I called his attention to it, and we just stared at each other—neither of us spoke a word. My uncle was a mighty Spiritual form, and he used the pen to let his presence be known while we were there. He'd always been a mischievous person. I can see him gleefully smiling and laughing as he kept moving this pen about the house.

MOM PIERCES THE VEIL.

One day short of a year after my father died, my mother passed. It was about 11 a.m. as I sat by her side while she was "actively dying." Nurse Beth joined me while Mom transitioned and supported me during this very tender time. She knew the stages of dying and the proper meds, and she'd administer them as needed. She also noticed changes in the color of Mom's legs, feet, and other body parts; she told me what the body was doing in preparation for Mom's passing.

As strange as this sounds, nothing could've been more comforting than having her with me during Mom's final stages. Mom was so well attended to, and—for the last year—all she had wanted to do was to die and to be with Dad. As she neared the final days of her life, she knew that it was coming to an end—she welcomed it. When she'd wake up and still be on the Earth, her caregiver would apologize to her that she was still here. During the last two weeks before Mom passed, I'd noticed the changes in her. Toward the end, she could barely speak above a whisper, and I'd do most of the talking. She'd sweetly look at me and smile. Mom had the sweetest smile of anyone I know. It always expressed the love that we shared.

Nurse Beth stayed with me from 2:00 – 4:30 p.m., when Mom died. We talked and reminisced about Mom, I told stories about her life, and—sometimes—we didn't talk at all. I felt guilty about Nurse Beth staying with me, and I told her a few times she could leave if she had to.

She knew, from looking at me, that I was just saying that, and that it wasn't true. I thank my lucky stars that she stayed with me during that time.

Now, Mom lay there in her bed with both of us at her side: she had each of us attending to her and knowing of her desires. In retrospect, I know that her room was full of Spiritual forms from Heaven ready to take her Home—but I was not that in tune yet to receive their presence.

Nurse Beth noticed a radical change in Mom's breathing pattern—much longer pauses between each breath. At one point, she noted no breaths for forty-five seconds, and Mom's face color becoming ashen. Nurse Beth remarked that the time was coming near.

We were standing on either side of her bed, both of us with our hands on her shoulders and arms, while Nurse Beth was checking for a pulse in her wrist. After a few seconds, Mom took her last breath and was gone. As we were looking down on her, as she took her last breath, the overhead light flickered. She was saying goodbye. I didn't notice the light until Nurse Beth called my attention to it. While I raised my eyes to look at the light, it flashed. I was astonished.

Nurse Beth poked her head out the door to let the caregiver know what'd happened, and Kristin came into the room. Guess what happened next. Mom flickered the light one more time. Kristin looked amazed and said that light had never flickered in all the time she'd lived there. Mom had a special love for her, and that was evident when she said goodbye and "thank you."

"LIKE MOTHER LIKE DAUGHTER": KAREN PIERCES THE VEIL

I didn't actively practice "Piercing the Veil" and communicating with those who'd transitioned until after Bono passed. I'd sought help from psychic/mediums in connecting with people from the other side of the Veil. Now, I was the one experiencing this on my own. I gradually became aware of how Bono would interact with me, so I knew that it was him. He had a certain touch.

For years, I'd felt like someone was tracing their fingers across my shoulder blades and back, and I'd at once get body chills. I knew someone was trying to comfort me, but who? Recently, I asked my Guides while meditating, "Who has touched me on the back for so many years?" and I got an answer: Grandma Alice, Dad's mom who I loved dearly. Yet, for *years*, I didn't know how to connect with people behind the Veil. I do now. We all have this ability.

THE MEANING OF LIFE IS OFTEN REALIZED IN DEATH

In helping my aunt die, she was lucid and had an "awakening" about life. It was time to shed the shell of her body that housed her Spiritual form. She wanted to go Home. I found this also to be true with my parents as they aged. The "stuff" that they'd accumulated—what they'd thought was important—was trivial. Life was transitory, and what really was important was the love they'd experienced with family members and friends, the joy they'd brought to people, and the connections they'd made. Think of how simply the Beatles put it in their song, "The End."

What is truly important to me? What legacy do I wish to leave? What is my purpose? How can I be of service and help others? I'm not dying right now but having experienced several loved ones' deaths—and helping my own family to die—has "awakened me." I'm truly grateful for this lesson learned, and for not having to wait to learn it until I was on my deathbed.

FACEBOOK POST
FEBRUARY 20, 2021,

Senior year in high school, heading off to college—the world was at my feet. Now, all these years later, I would never have imagined all the adventures, twists, and turns that my life would take.

Oh, [look at all] the lessons I have learned, how I have grown as a person, and the ripples I have created—some good, some I would change. Life certainly is an interesting journey. I have found that what it boils down to is this: live a life filled with love, compassion, and empathy; let go of your ego; lend a hand; and honor the Golden Rule.

FACEBOOK POST
DECEMBER 24, 2021

[Bono] shocked someone last night. I set the Christmas table with the "good porcelain and silverware," and I knew that Mom and Dad were strongly present. These were items from my childhood and passed on to me. I whispered, "Merry Christmas to Mom, Dad, and Bono," and the rest of my night was spent in tears and grief. Yep, one thing can set you off for hours when it comes to grieving, and you just can't snap out of it.

During this time, [Bono's] colleague and mentor sent me a message. It stated, "Somehow, he told me to send you this song: [N]ights in White Satin." I am sure this person had never been contacted by my husband in Spiritual form and was completely taken aback. I imagine his colleague was quite shocked. However, my husband gave him a message that I needed to hear. I am so grateful that he passed along the message.

The song brought more tears, but the lyrics were very impactful, and they were tears of gratitude. So important because there are things I definitely want to achieve before my days are done.

I know that we are all experiencing challenges in our lives. I send everyone love and prayers for healing. —Namaste

FACEBOOK
DECEMBER 23, 2021

You may know that Bono reaches out to me to let his presence be known. My husband is an incredible and strong Spiritual form, and he comes to me in many ways—some are beyond what I could have ever imagined.

When I pour my morning coffee, I have a paper towel under the cup. Last year, upon lifting the cup on our wedding anniversary, I found his smiling face made by the coffee on the towel. My mouth dropped open, and I couldn't move. He knew how much I was struggling and wanted to show he was with me.

I didn't share this last year, as I was in shock and didn't want you all to think I was looney tunes. I am shedding caring about what others think and accepting all parts of myself. Bono comes to me in unimaginable ways—so unbelievable for even me to fathom. You will be surprised to see what happens on my journey in 2022. One of my favorite phrases is: "Buckle up, buttercup!" My ride has no bounds.

Forever in Touch:
Unbroken Connection and Loving Encounters with Bono

- After saying my prayers one night, and talking to my Guides, Angels, and Heavenly Helpers, I turned over to turn off the light. Bono pulled on the covers. I turned back in amazement to feel this happen and made a remark to him. I turned again to turn off the light, and he tugged on the covers again. He pulled on the covers three times.

- As I walked up the stairs, I was experiencing fatigue and sore muscles. I thought that it was getting harder for my body to move—stiff joints and stuff. Bono, with his humor, put the song "The Old Gray Mare" into my head.

- My daughter and I were talking about closing all of Carl's professional websites. This was just a few days after he'd died, and we were both still in shock and disbelief. While we were discussing it, I "saw him smile." I noticed the crinkles under his eyes, and the light from his soul shining from within. It was comforting, "seeing him smile." My daughter is also highly intuitive and in tune; when I mentioned I'd just seen Bono, she said she'd seen him too. We both received the same vision as we were sitting together.

chapter 17
"PRESERVE YOUR MEMORIES"

"Because" Whoever Dies First... Wins.

As I've previously discussed, in order to help me weather the trauma of losing my husband, I've relied heavily on growing my spirituality and my psychic abilities. That is one way I've been able to stay close to Bono, my parents, my doggies, and others who I love who have passed. Yet, there also exist more earthly means of retaining the love and good times you've had with people who are no longer physically present to share them with you. In this chapter, I present some of those ways of preserving your memories, along with advice on this topic from fellow grievers. In addition, I present you with a question that may make you think about just how you want to spend the time you have left on this Earth with your loved ones.

"PRESERVE YOUR MEMORIES":"HERE, THERE, AND EVERYWHERE"

If you are in a relationship with someone who you love deeply, cherish, and adore, I suggest that you do a few things. This way, if the love of your life passes before you, you will have something tangible to help during the painful periods that you will experience. In fact, do these for all your loved ones, so you'll have tactile memories to cherish them by when they pass.

MAKE AUDIO RECORDINGS OF YOUR LOVED ONES' VOICES

When they are gone, you'll miss hearing your loved one talk, and you'll find comfort in hearing their voice. Record a conversation, their singing—anything where you can hear their voice. Record a conversation of the two of you talking. Just enjoy bantering with your loved one. Make a recording that captures the true essence of your relationship: make sure to encapsulate the tone, the laughter, the playfulness, and the love that you experience with each other.

I have an audio recording of my husband's "greeting" for when people would call us. It's so comforting hearing his voice. I have a second recording of him calling me once when I was at work and singing "Happy Birthday" in one of his crazy voices. Bono could've done voice-overs, as he had such a diverse range of voices. I also used to have years of recordings of my parents calling to sing "Happy Birthday," but somehow, they all got deleted. This breaks my heart.

How I wish I'd recorded our conversations: to hear our banter, tone, and inflections, and to relive those memories, would be beyond precious. I miss Bono's laugh. His spontaneous laughter could fill a room and make everyone smile—it was infectious. I wish I'd captured a recording of him laughing. I truly didn't know how important this would be to me, still hearing all of my loved ones' actual voices once they passed. It's like having them here with me.

RECORD VIDEOS OF YOUR LOVED ONES

Do this no matter what they are doing. It doesn't have to be a grand video: it should just be something that makes you giggle or feel good. "Stupid stuff" is always good and will make you laugh. Aren't our lives full of "stupid stuff" that makes them fulfilling and fun? Not only do you get to view the videos, but also you get to relive the memories and the feelings that accompany watching them. This will surely—at some point in time—bring you peace, comfort, and smiles while experiencing your loss.

I have videos of Bono, but I regret not making more. I didn't expect him to leave so soon, but I treasure the few videos I do have. I watch them whenever I really miss him.

TAKE PICTURES OF YOUR LOVED ONES

This is a given: take pictures. Look at the stages of your relationship, and where you've come from and gone in your life. This will give you a greater appreciation for the time you had together and for how you've helped each other grow as people. Include yourself in those pictures, no matter how you look in the moment. When you look back on those pictures, you can recapture the feelings and memories, and not care about your looks at all.

I love looking back and seeing both the mundane daily life and the adventures that my husband and I shared. I love to look and see how we changed together as we aged, both as people and in our appearances. I framed pictures and put them up around the rooms of the house. Bono is in every room I enter, smiling at me, and he still sits with me on the table while I eat and entertain. I wonder if my friends ever wonder how long he will be there—or even care. Most people still sit down and say, "Hi, Carl," and I talk to that man every day and look into his kind eyes. Looking into his eyes was like looking into his beautiful soul.

While preparing a montage of photos to be put into a video for my husband's Celebration of Life (see Chapter 24), I noticed we were ALWAYS touching in every single picture. In each and every photo, we were intertwined in each other's arms, his arm was around me, we were leaning against each other, or I was latching onto him. I didn't notice this at the time the pictures were taken, but I've noticed it since Carl passed and I can see how palpable the greatness of our love was and still is. Seeing this closeness makes me feel wonderful, and it forever preserves the memories for me in a special way.

"WITH A LITTLE HELP FROM MY FRIENDS"

My friends, who've also faced the deaths of loved ones, use the strategies I've suggested along with a host of others to help with their losses and preserving their memories. I think you may find many of these accounts and strategies beneficial to your own grieving process.

PAM

"I have one picture of Ken and I in the bedroom, ha-ha. This year, it will [have been] twenty-nine years, and I have [another picture] of him beside his urn in the China cupboard. I also have one of Mike and I in the bedroom. And he [will have] been gone [for] twenty years this year. I also have one picture beside the ashes and hair [that] I kept, which—again—is in the China cupboard. Luckily, David understands [that] they were a part of [my life] and will never be forgotten.

"How much longer will they stay there? Probably until [either] we move, or I die. Most of my friends now never knew them, so I keep their pictures kind of private. Now [this] does not mean [that] I do not have other pictures. I gave Jodi and Scott many of them as Ken was their dad. I gave Michael and Daani pictures of Mike, as he was their dad. They both have children now, and they are [looking at] his pictures all the time to get to 'know' him. All my grandchildren have pictures of Ken. Even the twins now know who their grandpa is in Heaven."

CHERYL

"Karen—the passing of my parents, [my] birth mom, and some close friends…has left me with the strong sense, feeling, and belief that their Spirit[ual form]s are with me when I call, or—sometimes—even their presence is felt. It's a comforting way to still feel connected even without the ability to physically see them."

ROZ

"Grief is such a process, and [it is] different for everyone. It takes time, but for me I was blessed to [still] have been working in the media, which was a very demanding job requiring focus. So, most of my days were focused on my job, and it is when I went home at night [that] I missed him and would jump back into grief. However, I always felt his presence around me, and that was very comforting. I had my first granddaughter [also] living with us at that time, so that was a good distraction. Just take the time you need. Cherish the memories as they turn into smiles [at realizing] how blessed you were to have had a forever and always love of your life."

ELISA

"I have pictures scattered about the house, as well. Pictures are always comforting. Lately, memories—random memories—pop up in my mind. I used to sluff them [off] and continue with what I was doing. Now I embrace them, and [I] let them flow and fully emerge.

"I also have written letters to my loved ones. This is not only helpful, but I have learned it is recommended, [as well]. I talk to my loved ones. I used to 'call' them on their now-defunct phone number [a]nd just talk away. I know that they know, and I know that they hear."

JAMES

"What brought me comfort with the loss of my parents [was] that I did right by them. I did [for them] what they did for me when I was born. I fed them, cleaned them, [and] changed them. I would absolutely do it again in [a] heartbeat. My conscience is clear…"

HARRIET

"I have pics, some clothing, and just [the knowledge of] certain things [that] my folks love[d]. I wear a sweatshirt I got from my dad, because of its meaning—Green/Yellow U of O—and because he wore it—so it's like wearing a hug. I wear sweats [that] my mom had, but never got to wear because she passed—plus some jewelry which hadn't been stolen. I have my dad's marine blanket as well.

"I also occasionally have gone and done 'our things'…[I've gone] to certain places—restaurants, Portland haunts, Ashland, Carmel, Cannon Beach—[that I've] Google[d] to see if their friends are still here (most [are] not), [and] I make recipes they [used to like] or think of [what] their reaction[s] [would have been] when I make certain dishes. [T]he other day, I'm sure they assisted in furniture shopping as per the place. I think they are with me more than I realize, and maybe what I also miss is the opportunity to give back to them. Perhaps, there is a satisfaction in giving of their best parts expressed through me—wit, kindness, empathy, passion, courage, ways of seeing beauty and joy—for these are things of which I have a unique insight. [Y]ou, too, have a unique insight into Bono that no one else has run with it."

ALLEN

"My girls and I would light candles in the evening and listen to her and our favorite spiritual songs. This brought many tears yet gave us great comfort."

CHRIS

"On the first anniversary of John's death, I wrote [down] my thoughts about how I [had been] feeling since his death. I put [them] in an envelope [that I] kept on the fireplace mantel. I read the one [that] I [had written] a year earlier on the next anniversary and wrote a new one to add to the envelope this year. I will read them both on the next anniversary, and [I will] add a new one.

"Also, on the anniversary of his death, Taylor and I write a letter to John. Then, we burn it in the fire pit on the patio, and the smoke delivers the message to him.

"At Thanksgiving, we light tealights for John, and [we] keep them lit until the beginning of the new year—so he is remembered and with us during the holiday season.

"A long tradition in my family is that when someone is very sick and hospitalized, they get a bear who watches over them when family members are not there. John got his bear when he had a heart attack in March of 2006. The bear watched over him when he was in for his hip replacement in 2011, his lung surgery in 2019, and when he was in [the] ICU where he died. His bear is kept on our bed when it is made. I place it on his pillow every night when I go to bed, so he is with me. Its name is John Bear.

"I have a picture hanging in the hallway outside our bedroom. It is a [side-by-side] picture of John [from] when he graduated from high school [together with] a picture of John taken when he became a father in his mid-forties. I talk to that picture all the time."

BARB

"[Having lost] my dad and my son just a few months apart, certain music and symbols affected me]. When I would see [a] symbol or randomly hear [a] song that represented either one of them, I took it as a hello from [H]eaven. Also, pennies. Finding pennies. Always picking them up. My greatest gift from Danny was his amazing friends. They have been so great, including us in their lives. We are blessed. Now, it's been 18 years, and the sadness is [still] always there in my heart.

"But I get so much comfort [from] hearing stories—like [from] you—watching videos, looking at pictures, [and from] seeing [his] friends. Most of all, [I get comfort from] my family. I have an amazing mom [and] supportive siblings and extended family.

"When I lost Danny, you probably remember, I was in the right place[—at] Orenco. My Orenco family was over the top in helping me get through the loss. [The same was true of] several staff members where I had taught prior to Orenco. I cannot believe [all of the] amazing ways [in which] they supported us. I will never forget [that] incredible group of people. [Also,] I had to get back to school. It was my safe place. Everybody knew [what'd happened,] and—when I needed a break—Kerri or Tim would come in and cover so [that] I could pull myself together.

"Finally, a CD that was recorded by a dad that [had] lost his daughter [really affected me]. It had a series of songs [on it that he had written] and performed, some with his wife, as his way of getting through his loss. One song, 'A [L]ittle [F]arther [D]own the [R]oad,' especially helped me. [T]he lyrics reinforced the fact that—as life moves forward, and the further you are away from the tragedy—it somehow becomes a tiny bit easier. [Just listen to the song's lyrics and you'll see what I mean.] So, finally, Mrs. B., [it takes] time."

STACEY

"I was blessed to still have some voicemails on my phone from Tom. I had a friend take one of the voicemails and put it [in] a Q[R] code picture frame, so I can walk by it with my phone and scan it [in order to] hear his voice saying, 'I love you and I miss you.' It fills my heart with such love and joy, because I do know how much he really loved me—and I loved him back just the same. I also have pictures of us: [I have] a lot of [just] him and [of him] kissing me on the cheek. I miss that man more than anything, but I—like you—talk to him every day."

BECAUSE WHOEVER DIES FIRST...WINS...

(Trigger Warning: This section is raw and depressing. If you are entrenched in grief, you may want to skip it. Yet, it encompasses the meaning of this book. I strongly recommend you read on.)

Sorry if you find this offensive, but it is my truth. Whoever dies first in a relationship, wins.

You—the person left behind—may experience grief that is overwhelming, all-consuming, never-ending, and just plain brutal. Like me, your life will be ripped away, your brain may turn to mush, and you may be a former shell of yourself until you heal. Grief has no boundaries and no timeline. It rises up like a sneaker wave to consume one at any given moment. You can be merrily going about your day, and have an unexpected thought or memory, hear a song, or have some other seemingly innocent thing happen. At that moment, you may be suddenly transformed into a sobbing puddle of a human being with no end to the torment.

Grief will always be with you—for the rest of your life. Please know, the "deeper the love" the "deeper the grief," and grief is the price of love. How does that even seem fair? The person who departed gets off "easy," while life and its lessons continue on for the living. It can be torturous. Yes, it is said, "you grow around your grief", which you do, but it will never be gone. We can only hold on to our loved ones and the good memories in any ways we can.

When Bono died, I wanted to die too. I was once again enveloped by the raw emotions of grief and sorrow I'd experienced when I had planned on killing myself. There was no reason for me to carry on. The physical pain hit my body over, and over again, day…after day…after day. It was savage to get up daily and live through this time and loss. I saw the world through teary, bleary eyes, headaches from crying so much, and heartache. My heart was ripped from my body. I was just a little blip in this world; everyone would carry on without me. I could go. I could die. No one would miss me that much. No one had the love for me that my husband and parents had and now they were gone. My protectors. My family had always believed in me. Supported me. Taken care of me. Loved me. They had left without me. How could I endure life without them?

My grief was not just for my husband, but also for Mom and Dad. Compounded grief is a bitch. I felt the Universe was saying, "Let's see what she can take." I felt cheated when my husband died. I felt angry. I'd lost a life with him where we were going to live and flourish, and it had been ripped away from me. He got off easy. He got off scott-free. He was in Heaven, and was surrounded by his loved ones, my parents, and our pets—celebrating and having the time of his life. Bono had won. He'd died first and had won.

I was stuck in the muck of a life that had suddenly crumbled and was trampled upon. I was broken, devastated, angry, empty, and a complete mess. I tried my best, and just went through the motions of life while feeling lifeless inside. It was one of the hardest things I've ever experienced, and I thought it would never change.

Years before, a friend who had lost her husband had told me that she wanted to die. I could understand this on a certain level. She once remarked that it'd be so easy to turn the wheel into another car while driving and end her life. I was aghast. She not only would kill herself, but possibly also someone else. Yet, now, I understood. I felt her pain. Her loss of everything. Her loss of herself. I never did think about killing myself at this time, but I would have preferred to die than to live. My life was suddenly meaningless.

This is another important reason to preserve memories of your loved ones while you can. It's not only for the sake of keeping a part of them around or remembering good times; it's also for keeping *you* mentally healthy and reminding you that you'll be with them again one day and that good times in life are still possible. You need reasons to convince yourself to stick around. Because living the remainder of your life in honor of your loved one(s) who've passed and being the best person that you can be without them is the way to ensure you're all winners in the end.

DO YOU WANT TO BE RIGHT, OR DO YOU WANT TO BE HAPPY?

I have heard this phrase numerous times during my life, but I didn't truly understand the impact of these words until after losing my husband. If you were to die, right now, how would you feel? Would you feel regrets in your life? Have you said things that you wish could be "unsaid," or not said things and held back? Have you chased your dreams? Lived to your full potential? Have you left the world a better place?

I found, through the loss, to open myself up and to open my heart. To not live with anything unspoken—to speak my truth. To not live in regret. I know some of my family members have lived in regret of not having done certain things with my husband when he was alive. My husband would offer different adventures to these family members, only to be ignored; it hurt my husband. These family members have had to experience regret for things left undone and unsaid while Carl was still here, and that is a painful lesson to experience.

I look back on my own life, prior to Bono's passing, where I held myself back—in so many ways. I didn't always say what was on my mind, and I didn't take many of the adventures that I wanted to—the timing wasn't right, we didn't have enough money, or other seemingly important excuses. When Bono died, I lost my will to live. I truly didn't care if I got Covid and died; I found no pleasure in life.

"PRESERVE YOUR MEMORIES"

Once I made the decision to live, everything changed. I started living fully. I began pouring my innermost feelings out in a public forum, becoming vulnerable, and sharing the most intimate details of my life. I would never have done any of that before, because people can be so judgmental. Now, I don't care. If they don't accept me or my beliefs, then we part ways.

Do you know what happened when I started sharing my life and what I was experiencing? People started chiming in and sharing their own experiences. I had a deeper connection with the friends in my life. My heart opened, as did theirs. I made many new friends who'd had the same experience, and close bonds were formed. Our souls bonded together.

Bono and I had arguments and disagreements in our life together. I think every married couple must work together to find common ground—what is acceptable in a relationship and what is not. If we had an argument, we never went to bed angry. We never ignored each other for days, or until someone finally broke the ice. Carl had shared with me that his previous girlfriend would not talk to him for days if they'd had an argument. I couldn't even imagine that. This is probably because I always have something to say and could not remain silent. I couldn't imagine living with someone and ignoring them, getting huffy with them, or pretending they didn't exist.

If you are one of those people who goes to bed angry and ignores your loved ones, I implore you to *stop*. When your loved one is gone, regret is a horrible feeling to experience. Will you ever let go of that regret? It could take you until your own dying day to forgive yourself.

Do you want to be right, or do you want to be happy? What do you want to remember about your life as you take your last breath—the arguments you won, or the beautiful people and times you experienced?

Forever in Touch:
Unbroken Connection and Loving Encounters with Bono

- While sitting on the bed watching a video about my husband, I started crying. I was sobbing, and he gave me whole body shakes. I could feel him holding me. I could feel my body wrapped in his essence. I spoke aloud, and I told him that he couldn't wipe the tears from my face as he did so long ago. It was bittersweet.
- Bono brings me memories that are long forgotten. I was sitting in a hair salon. He brought me back to the memory of when we went to San Francisco; we inadvertently went to the Benefit Cosmetics corporate headquarters while I was looking for makeup. We met one of the Johnson Baby Shampoo Twins who own the company. She sent me to a clinic, and the stylist gave me three makeovers. During that time, Bono went around the neighborhood and waited patiently, which took hours. He was such a giving man. He was happy that I was having fun and being pampered. I am grateful for the happy memories he shares with me. For our entire life together, he loved and doted upon me—he always took such great care of me. I love when he puts our special memories in my mind.
- I inadvertently put up a post on Facebook with some personal information—as I walked downstairs, Bono told me to remove the post immediately. I had only taken a few steps when he urgently told me to take the post down. It's good I listened and didn't argue.

chapter 18
"DRAG"GED DOWN BY FAMILIAL "NET" LOSS

My Brain on Grief and Trauma

In an American Brain Foundation webinar on healing the brain after loss, Neurologist Dr. Lisa M. Shulman (2021)—Director of the University of Maryland Parkinson's Disease and Movement Disorders Center—said this about how grief rewires the brain.

> Traumatic loss is perceived as a threat to survival and defaults to protective survival and defense mechanisms. This response engages the fight or flight mechanism, which increases blood pressure and heart rate and releases specific hormones. Grief and loss affect the brain and body in many ways. They can cause changes in memory, behavior, sleep, and body function, affecting the immune system as well as the heart. [They] can also

lead to cognitive effects, such as brain fog. The brain's goal? Survival.

When Carl died, the *last* thing I wanted to do was to read a complex book on grief. I knew about the stages of grief, and they are not linear—one often meanders in and out of them. My brain chemistry changed *so much* when grief arrived. Here, I describe just a small digestible sampling of the biopsychosocial effects of grief on the body, mind, spirit, and behavior.

DEFINITION DOGGY BOX 9:
BIOPSYCHOSOCIAL ROSIE

"Bark! Bark! Rosie the Definition Doggy here again!"

"Mommy and I both know you didn't come here to read a difficult science book about grief. Hoomans are very complicated creatures, even more than us doggies. Mommy just wants to teach you a little about the psychological, biological, and social effects of grief on hoomans.

"I was asking some of her Spiritual Guides about it in the Heavenly Realm, and they told me that some hoomans created a model of health and wellness/illness that was later also used in psychology to show how these three different factors work together to explain a hooman's behavior. Grieving is one example of a hooman behavior (it's one of dogs' too.). They called the model the Biopsychosocial Approach, and it shows how hoomans' bodies (biology), minds (psychology), and environments (social) all interact to affect how they behave. It says none of those alone are enough to explain a hooman's mental health and actions (The Albert Team 2019).

> "Wow, poor Mommy. That pesky grief is hurting her in so many ways. I am so glad that she's had her children, her Heavenly Helpers, and us Spirits of her loved ones to help her get through it, and that she's so good at growth and tackling grief. Mommy is one tough hooman."

COGNITIVE AND CLINICAL PSYCHOLOGICAL EFFECTS: STAGES OF GRIEF, THE ILLUSION OF CLOSURE, AND SEEKING PSYCHOTHERAPEUTIC ASSISTANCE

It has been purported that there are five stages of grief; some instead suggest seven. As listed on healthline.com (Holland 2018), and with my commentary in italics, the seven stages of grief are:

- Shock and denial: (This is a state of disbelief and numbed feelings). *You may not believe your loved one is really gone. Perhaps that loved one is on a trip. Perhaps it is a mistake, and they are not really gone. How can he be gone? I just saw him this morning…a total state of disbelief.*

- Pain and guilt: You may feel the loss is unbearable, and that you're making others' lives harder because of your feelings and needs. *You may feel guilt or be angry at yourself (a form of pain) for what you didn't do or could've done. You may blame doctors for not preventing this death, or maybe you should've gone to different ones. You might be angry about and in pain from being left alone or feel guilty about being alive. Sometimes these feelings get misplaced: you may have rage at the person in front of you at the grocery store for taking so long, at the car driving too slowly, or at a brusque waiter—anything can trigger those emotions.*

- Anger and bargaining: You may lash out, telling God or a higher power that you'll do anything they ask if they'll only grant you relief from these feelings or this situation. *There can be anger at God: how could you let this happen, God? What, are you punishing me? I don't deserve this. Anger hides many emotions you are experiencing.*

- Depression: This may be a period of isolation and loneliness during which you process and reflect on the loss. *You have no direction and can't concentrate. Life has no meaning. You have no hope: a future looks bleak.*

- The upward turn: At this point, the stages of grief like anger and pain have died down, and you're left in a more calm and relaxed state.

- Reconstruction and working through: You can begin to put pieces of your life back together and move forward. *You can acknowledge your loss and start to live for the future. There is a finality to what has happened, but the memories of sadness, joy, and love will never leave you.*

- Acceptance and hope: This is a very gradual acceptance of the new way of life, and a feeling of possibility for the future. *The sadness may not fade. The grief will always make it to the forefront occasionally, yet you will no longer be immobilized by your sadness.*

After my parents and husband died, I was completely broken. I had no interest in doing anything except for lying in bed under the covers. Taking phone calls, or replying to texts or messages, was an insurmountable obstacle. My energy was non-existent, and I didn't care about anything other than my doggies.

However, I had to show up for life and liquidate the clinic and gym—which proved to be a whirlwind. I found that, while experiencing grief, the brain is in a total fog. You can't remember what you said or promised. You can't remember conversations. I lived in that stage for a long time. I knew my memory issues were frustrating to my family. I made many decisions I wouldn't have made if I were not grieving. I couldn't change that, and I had to let go and forgive myself. You brain can get so messed up during this traumatic process.

Before my losses, I'd made most of the decisions for the household. I'd run and steered the ship, and our life had always been full of activities we'd enjoyed. My grief made me pull inward. I couldn't be around friends that I'd known for years, nor could I be around groups of people, large or small. When going out in public, if I ran into a friend, I could only cry while stumbling through a conversation. You shut down as a person, and you wonder if your former self will ever return or if this is your new reality. I felt small—my life energy was held close to my heart and body for protection. I was in survival mode, going through the motions of life. I was a vacant person: full of pain, unbelievable sadness, and nonstop, uncontrollable crying.

I found myself experiencing all seven stages of grief. They're not linear; you can come and go from them many times as you slowly heal from trauma. It'd be nice to have a progression, and to know that once that stage was experienced it wouldn't return, but that doesn't happen.

SHOCK AND DENIAL

Oh, man, was I shocked. I felt like my husband was ripped away from me. He WAS. Here one day, and the next gone. How could this be? He was the epitome of healthy living. His career of twenty-four years was geared toward helping and improving the health of others, and becoming a kettlebell instructor only enhanced his healthy choices. Yet, he was gone. He'd left me alone. I kept expecting him to come home; he'd walk through the door, and we'd be together again.

We'd chatted numerous times before he died; he would live until he was ninety, and I planned on leaving by seventy-two. He wanted to live life to the fullest. I thought I'd still be pretty healthy by seventy-two, and it'd be a good time to check out before my body declined or illness set in. Yet, here at sixty-five, I was now a widow. I think what was so shocking was that—although there had been a few signs along the way that got pushed aside—there was nothing major wrong with my husband. There was nothing to warrant that he might be on death's doorstep, no infirmities, no diseases, or anything else out of the ordinary. He just died.

I've often thought about how I would've chosen for him to die. I would've liked to have been able to take care of him, make him comfortable, give him a peaceful end of life, and be with him when he drew his last breath. Sound like something else you've read earlier? This is exactly what happened with my parents. However, Bono would never have wanted me to nurse him until his last breath. He would not want to slowly die, to waste away, or to put any pressure on me. He went out like he would've wanted—quickly and peacefully. I would like to think, if given the choice, he might've stayed here longer in this lifetime. But we did not have the luxury of choice.

PAIN AND GUILT

It was so hard for me to accept others' help. I felt my pain and sadness would drag them down. I didn't want to be pitied. This was vital. I know that everyone could see the pain in my eyes; it's something you can't hide. I also could see the pain and sadness they had in their eyes for me; it can't be hidden. Who wants to be around someone who is constantly crying at the drop of a hat?

Yet, people kept offering me help, and slowly I started welcoming that. It was easy to accept food, as this is something I'd also offered grieving friends. My friends wanted to go above and beyond that. They wanted to do everything for me. I felt like a smooshed soul and realized that they truly loved and cared about me; they were helping me out of kindness, and not pity.

Worse than the pain, even worse than not wanting pity, was the guilt. I felt guilty. I felt that I was not in tune with my husband's needs. I should've called an ambulance (but he told me he was feeling better). Guilt was around every corner. Why didn't you do this? Why did you do that? You could have prevented this, Karen. Why did you go to sleep instead of being 100% sure he was okay? Logically, I know that it was not my fault. But grief throws logic out the window.

ANGER AND BARGAINING

Thankfully, I didn't stay too long in this stage. I experienced extreme anger toward God and my husband. I was angry at God for taking Bono first, and at Bono for leaving me. I was so pissed. When he told me that he died "for your growth," I became even angrier. How dare you? You don't get to make that decision for me. I was angrier at my husband than at Divinity during this time. I never tried to bargain my feelings away, but I did ask for strength to get through it all.

DEPRESSION

I have yet to meet a widow, or anyone who has experienced a great loss, who did not suffer from all-encompassing depression. My widow friends have handled it in different ways. One threw herself into activities and forced herself to travel and get out in life. Another started reading grief and spiritual books to help her understand what she was experiencing and what to expect.

As I've mentioned previously, I refused to take anti-depressants due to my history with them, and instead asked for anti-anxiety medication. I'm glad I did so, as it was very helpful in treating the anxiety and panic attacks I experienced when I started to re-enter life. At least initially, I needed these meds to soothe my broken self.

My doctor tried a couple of different ones, and I eventually found one I liked. He was apprehensive about possible side effects. This didn't faze me in the least—I was happy to die and go Home. However, I never abused the use of the medication, and it helped me to get through these tough times. His office also helped provide me with a counselor I could see to help counteract the depression and trauma.

THE UPWARD TURN

When a person is enveloped in such grief and trauma, they cannot see a way out. I thought I'd be in this swirling hurricane of anger, grief, depression, constant crying, and memory loss forever. However, little by little, small fragments of my old self returned to me. I think it took about twelve months for my laugh to return. I hadn't heard anything like it come from my lips—or felt any real joy—in such a long time, and it meant the world to me to experience it again.

I started to have more peaceful and calm days. I would like to say the crying stopped, but as I write this now—three years later—I am still crying. Yet, I have more good moments than bad. Life slowly does start to get better.

RECONSTRUCTION AND WORKING THROUGH

Carl died in November 2020. Yet, summer of 2022 is when I first truly started rebuilding and embracing my life. I'd slowly re-entered life before this, but that summer was a turning point. I wanted to feel alive and joyful again. This was the summer I decided to fly in a hot air balloon, went hang gliding, and hiked in the gorge. I'm scared of heights, but I wanted to try something I'd never done before. I never once felt fear in the hot air balloon. It was so quiet and peaceful flying over the countryside on a beautiful, sunny day. Landing was another story; it was bumpy, and I was thrown into my friend's lap. I'm sure she wasn't too thrilled having me land there.

I personally arranged the balloon ride and hang-gliding experiences for my friend and me. This was an enormous accomplishment. I could make decisions and orchestrate an outing again like before grief took over my life. I LOVED hang gliding. I was thrilled upon liftoff—being taken off the ground and into the sky by another pilot and plane. I found out the pilot in the other plane is involved with fighting wildfires, and that she dumps water on the fires. Pretty cool.

The pilot, a retired vet who now flew commercial planes, asked me if I wanted to fly, and I did. I was scared, and by the end of flying my hands were sweaty and hurt from grasping the wheel. YET, I FLEW. It was magical. There were no sounds; it was so quiet and serene. The pilot took control later, and he did things which caused me to cry out and scream. He took me for a wild ride…and I loved it.

I was now trying things I'd never wanted to do. I've told my friends many times that I no longer recognize myself. The inner struggle of grief and trauma changed me. It opened me up to want to try new experiences. It made me kinder, more loving, more trusting, and more "chill." I've changed, and there's no going back. I do like this "New Karen" quite a lot. Would you believe I'll likely go skydiving and paragliding this summer? Keep in mind I'm afraid of heights. But hey, I rode in a hot air balloon and a hang glider. Why not jump out of the plane and hurtle to the earth? Never in a million years would I have ever before considered this. Yet here I am.

I may seem like a daredevil now, but I'm also still constantly working hard to master the seventh stage of grief: acceptance and hope. Perhaps when I've finished writing this book for you and my lost loved ones—but also for myself and to honor my own grieving process—it may feel like a big step in that direction toward the fulfillment (but never "end") of my grief journey.

MAKING MEANING OUT OF LOSS

For me, I don't know if I could ever find an acceptable answer as to why my husband died so suddenly in his prime. I wasn't prepared for a "sudden loss," and I could've kept lamenting finding the meaning for years.

"It was his time. God has a plan. He left when he was meant to."

These all ring hollow to me. It wasn't until Bono gave me the reason, and my life unfolded as it has, that I truly understood why he died.

RELINQUISHING ONE'S DESIRE TO CONTROL AN UNCONTROLLABLE SITUATION

When my husband died, my entire world spiraled out of my control. I'd always said during my life that control is just an illusion. And now I was finding this statement to be quite true. I'd taught for thirty-one years in classrooms, where control is paramount, raised two children with two challenging ex-husbands, and taken care of my parents—everything was about juggling balls and control.

Now, poof! I had no control. I'd been overridden by a situation, not of my choosing, and I had to learn to adapt and find balance in life. I became the leaf on the stream, moving along the waters of life, trying not to get hung up on rocks (obstacles) or get stuck in stagnant water, and attempting to keep moving forward. Relinquishing my ability to control gave me a new attitude of peacefulness and the ability to "chill."

RECREATING IDENTITY AFTER LOSS

When I retired from teaching, I was no longer a teacher; I was a retired teacher. I was a substitute. While subbing, a child asked me, "Are you a real teacher?" That loss of identity was extremely hard: what defined me was gone. It was a difficult realization.

Now, suddenly, I was no longer "Carl and Karen" or "Dr. and Mrs. Bonofiglio." I was simply Karen. A widow. I had to stand alone. I didn't think I could do this; I didn't have the strength to be alone.

I'd had a protector for so much of my life, and now I had to fend for myself. Little by little, I was able to make this adjustment. I still remember crying on the way to gatherings because I was flying solo. I'd do things, and think, "Carl would be doing this for me." It was hard adapting, but—little by little—I succeeded.

BECOMING ACCUSTOMED TO AMBIVALENT FEELINGS

I became the queen of ambivalence. I experienced mixed and contradictory feelings for so many things. Things that used to upset me, or that I'd had to have certain ways, didn't affect me anymore. These feelings make it challenging to make decisions, and I relied on talking things over with my friends and family. The "Old Karen" had no problem being decisive, but the "New Karen" had to muddle through this challenge.

REDEFINING ONE'S RELATIONSHIP WITH WHOMEVER/WHATEVER THEY'VE LOST

This is a HUGE part of grief. With the loss, you redefine the person you were—or thought you were. I know that I've changed as a person through all my loss, and it has been pointed out to me lately. I do feel so strongly that Bono is still with me, and I talk to him like he is there; this connection has been so beneficial for my healing.

FINDING NEW HOPE

Hope barely raises its head when someone is encompassed by grief. I didn't have any hope for years. I didn't have the strength to be hopeful: I was focused on surviving. Only now, three years later, do I feel hopeful. Having a purpose has made me feel hopeful; writing this book has made me feel hopeful. I wanted to help as many people as I could who would experience this same situation. Focusing "outside" of myself has helped heal the" inside" of me.

SEEKING THERAPY

In addition to getting a prescription for anti-anxiety meds, as I mentioned above, I also reached out to my doctor about psychotherapeutic assistance. Early on, after Bono was called Home, I sought help from a therapist. I was hesitant, as I'd had questionable previous experiences with therapists from my darker period before Bono; when I'd seen one back then, all she'd do was nod her head. She wouldn't offer any clarification or advice—nothing to help me—and would just listen. I could do this with my friends, and they would also give me potentially useful advice.

However, counseling after Bono and my parents died was a godsend. At first, many practitioners wouldn't accept my insurance—a bitch of getting older, as the supplemental doesn't provide a lot of reimbursement to the counselors. Thankfully, my doctor's office did have a counselor that I was able to see before he moved away. His name was Paul. He was just a few inches taller than me, and his hair was below his shoulders. He had this laid back, wind-surfer dude, kind of attitude. I held nothing back from him—nothing.

Paul made no judgments on what I voiced, and he let me cry when I needed to. However, what he *did* do was actually help me. He offered me advice, gave me articles and other materials to read about grief, and was generally proactive in helping me navigate my path of grief and trauma. During this time, I was telling people that I see the dead, speak to the dead, and about many of my interactions with the Spiritual Realm: Paul was no exception. I told him my thoughts on Heaven, Hell, spirituality, reincarnation, and so forth. He never flinched. Instead, he listened.

I didn't know if he thought I was some woman who'd gone looney tunes, or anything at all about his beliefs. But he was a phenomenal therapist. Due to Covid, he decided to relocate back to his home in the gorge, which was too far for me to drive for sessions. I was sad to leave his care. His parting words surprised me; he explained that he felt the same way about life, death, Heaven, Hell, spirituality, and reincarnation. I was shocked. Yet, he remained a professional.

I also have a friend who is a counselor. Before Bono died, she'd helped me to process what I'd been experiencing with my parents. Every time we had a coffee date, I felt that I should pay her as I was getting a free counseling session. She continued to help me with Bono's passing, although Covid put a definite glitch in that. God truly sends those to you that you need, and—though Covid may taketh away—those people will often always remain with you in spirit. Thank God I had my therapists, doctor, and medication to help me get through the grief process.

BIOPSYCHOLOGICAL AND PHYSIOLOGICAL EFFECTS OF GRIEF: "ROCK(ING) YOU(R)" BODY "LIKE A HURRICANE"

Before experiencing the loss of my parents and husband, grief had been on the periphery of my life. I'd lost aunts, uncles, and my grandmothers—and had felt extreme sadness—but this was a mound next to the mountain of grief I've endured since my closest family members died. I've shown throughout this book how grief messes with your mind. However, I hadn't realized before the extent to which it has control over your whole body.

As Dr. Shulman touched on at the start of this chapter, grief can cause changes in the endocrine (hormone), nervous, and cardiovascular systems. It can also weaken the immune system, and this can make you more susceptible to illness. All these systems are controlled and influenced by the brain, and grief wreaks havoc on the brain. Finally, emotions associated with grief and the ways grief affects the body can create a vicious cycle in which they influence each other. This section illustrates a few ways in which the brain, the body, and grief can interact.

SAY WHAT? EXCUSE ME... YOU WANT ME TO DO WHAT?

A month after my husband died, I went to see my doctor to get on the anti-anxiety pills. There were times that I couldn't function—times when I was in a crying puddle on the floor—and I needed help. I needed to take medication, as trying to "tough it out" didn't work.

My doctor was concerned about my stress levels, and we had the following conversation. Let me preface this by saying that I like and admire my doctor: he always sits by me when he comes into the exam room, and we just chat. I don't have to sit on that silly table with the paper on it, and he talks to me. He's always looked at me while we've spoken, but this time he kept his eyes on the floor—we did not make eye contact. Our conversation went something like this:

Doctor: "Karen, are you having any sex?"
Me (*looking at him incredulously*): "Doc…my husband just died. Uh—no."
(*I wonder if he thought that I had men on the side.*)
Doctor: "Karen, do you masturbate?"
(*I am pretty sure no one has ever asked me this question in my life.*)
Me (*now in shock*): "…No."
Doctor: "Well, you should, as it is great for stress."
Me: "Carl will see me."
Doctor: "Carl will enjoy that."

After hearing his advice, and once the shock wore off, I did take him up on his suggestion. My naturopath was quite pleased that he'd addressed this with me. She was exuberant in her praise of him and his recommendation. Once again, I was shocked by this protocol and its acceptance by another doctor. You learn something new every day.

PAIN AND PANIC

My grief didn't stop there. This impressive, vital woman—who'd never had any difficulty making decisions—now had panic attacks. The panic attacks struck with no rhyme or reason. Nurse Beth, Farley Cat, and Michael helped me through these attacks. They could talk me down and help me decompress if my pill didn't work. Nurse Beth would talk me through upcoming situations in my life, and what might be in store that would trigger an attack—we would talk through different scenarios to manage the episode. She also encouraged me to have a "safety net" in place—someone who would be with me and help me if I was overcome with anxiety.

"TRY TO REMEMBER" A LULLABY FOR GRIEF AS "AUTUMN LEAVES" FALL: MEMORY/SLEEP EFFECTS

What struck me the most with how grief affected my body was the memory loss and brain fog. It was extremely hard for me to recall decisions and promises I'd made, which caused some unhappiness for my family. I started to take notes and write things down. I felt like I was getting dementia; not being able to remember important things was disconcerting. My executive function took a huge hit, and this affected my relationships and ability to function.

Even through all of the experiences I had with death, I was fortunately still always able to sleep. I've been able to sleep throughout my life without the aid of meds, gummies, relaxation tapes, or over-the-counter sleep aids. I am grateful that my sleep patterns didn't alter, as sleep offered peace and serenity during this dark, unforgiving time. Not everyone is so lucky.

GRIEF LIGHTNING—AN EMOTIONALLY WILD RIDE

Emotions label our experiences and act as signposts to guide our behavior. Steering clear of danger and seeking rewards is vital for maneuvering through our tricky environments and for survival (The Biology of Emotions 2012). Even though biopsychologists and neurobiologists aren't certain they completely understand the neurobiology of emotions, as I previously pointed out in the chapter about them, it is clear our emotions go haywire when it comes to grieving. This can affect numerous organs and body systems like those mentioned above, mess with our neurotransmitter levels, affect executive function, harm the sleep cycle, and can also trigger a whole host of psychological and related emotional issues—like depression, social and generalized anxiety, panic attacks, post-traumatic stress, anger issues, and even suicidal thoughts. Grief and its associated emotions can eventually be adaptive for us, as grief helps us steer clear of further danger and eventually allows us to be able to seek new rewards, but it can also be very harmful throughout the process due to the erratic nature of our emotions.

Like myself, some of my widow friends couldn't engage with others while grieving. It was too emotionally taxing. Life was so much easier living in a little bubble that didn't want to expand. I had a very close friend who lost her husband, and she kept me at arm's length for a long time. All she wanted to do was to eat a grilled cheese sandwich for breakfast and lunch and to be left alone. Her depression, social anxiety, and isolation went on for over seven years.

As she went through her process, she also developed panic attacks. If she were going to be late for an appointment, she'd freak out and go back to the safety of her house. She couldn't allow herself to ever just be late, and it took her years to get over this feeling of foreboding with the help of counseling. Seven years later, she still sees a counselor. It took her many, many years to make decisions, conquer her panic attacks, and re-enter life. She seemed shell-shocked to me. She's returned to her energetic, impressive self, but it took her a good seven years to get there.

Another friend had bouts of extreme anger at the unfairness of life. She couldn't understand why her husband had been taken away from her, and she was left trying to figure it all out. Like me, she felt weak. She started developing heart and digestive problems, and she still has them three years later. She also still doesn't sleep well; her sleep is disturbed, and she wakes up tired most mornings. She tends to catastrophize the future, but she's found strength in spirituality and finding feathers and signs from her husband.

Recently, I traveled to the Oregon coast. At the beach, I drew a heart in the sand, and inside the heart I wrote: Bono and Me. A widow friend saw it on Instagram and made a comment about it. I told her I still cry and can get swallowed up by my emotions. She mentioned it was now ten years since her husband had passed, and only around year eight had she stopped crying.

It truly amazes me when people carelessly spout platitudes. Carl would want you to be happy. You'll be happy again. Carl would want you to move on with your life. It's been long enough; you should be over most of this by now. I want to tell them, "Leave me the fuck alone and let me grieve how I need to and as much as I need." I may look okay on the outside, but no one knows the depth of swirling emotions from grief that lie below—or the lightning-strike physiological and psychological toll it can take on my body and soul.

As I went through the grieving process, and continue to do so, I feel a range of emotions which can change in a heartbeat. Most of my friends, are loving and caring and can commiserate with me. However, some have not experienced great loss, and these people sometimes don't know how to act or what to say (I'll discuss this further in the next chapter). Finding people who will help you and be there for you—whether they fully understand what you are experiencing or not—and having the strength to do so, is crucial to successfully navigating the grieving process. This leads us into the final realm of psychological effects of grief that I'll discuss in this chapter.

FAMILIAL AND SOCIAL PSYCHOLOGICAL EFFECTS OF GRIEF: GUIDED RE-ENTRY—FAMILY FOREVER

Telling my children about my panic attacks was one of the hardest parts—it felt like admitting that I was weak and needed help. My son, ever the therapist, expressed his concern and was "sorry that I was experiencing that." My daughter—well aware of panic attacks—was pleased that I'd informed her. They were my best safety nets in family situations. When people started asking me to join them, I admitted that I had anxiety and needed a safety net. The stigma and defeat I once felt

"DRAG"GED DOWN BY FAMILIAL "NET" LOSS

evaporated, and I established a team of friends who had my back and helped me out. Their support was crucial to my re-entering life and feeling strong and comfortable.

One of my first ventures out in a group was with my family, and we celebrated my daughter's birthday at Benihana hibachi for dinner. This type of restaurant has large islands throughout, where people gather around the chef as he cooks food for everyone at the table. The chef bangs his knife, makes a "show" out of everything he cooks, and banters with all of the people. The loudness and intensity in the restaurant are electrifying, and it's filled with the singing of "Happy Birthday" (it seems many people celebrate their birthdays there), loud voices, cooking noises, and so on. It frightened me to go to this place, whereas it used to be no big deal.

This was after I'd informed my children of my panic attacks, so I sat between them at the table. I more-or less watched the chef, but I didn't engage with him—I wonder if he could tell that being there was excruciatingly painful for me? I am ½ deaf, so conversations were difficult, and we had to speak loudly. I withdrew into myself, and I didn't interact too much with anyone—my in-laws tried to engage me, and I tried to be polite.

Toward the end of the evening, my nerves were frayed: I was exhausted, and I wanted to flee. My son could see it in my eyes. I took his arm after saying goodbye to our party of eight. He walked me to my car, and only then could I start releasing my emotions. I started crying and sobbed and sobbed. It was so overwhelming. I cried all the way home, and I was happy that my house was close by. Once I got home, I felt sheltered and protected. I embraced the solitude and quietness—that is, once the puppies settled down as they were also excited about my return.

My son is a licensed therapist. Both of my children were suffering the loss of the man who'd raised them like they were his own flesh and blood. He'd entered their lives when Victoria was three, and Nickolas eight. He was their father figure, and he'd called them his "son and daughter." The loss was hard on everyone in the family, and we were all grieving.

Nick tried to be the strong one for the family. He wanted to be there for me, his mom, and for his little sister. I believe he put his own grief on hold to try to hold us together; he was our glue. He stepped into the role of leader and helped with all of the family decisions. We had to liquidate the gym and office, find an attorney, and so much more, and he was there in the thick of things quietly and compassionately orchestrating it all.

When he'd come to visit and check on me, I knew that he was processing me as he would a client. It actually helped me, as it was like I was receiving therapy sessions. I knew I drove him crazy because I couldn't remember things I'd said, or promises I'd made, but now I know that that was a physical complication from the grief. I hope he understands that too. Nick is very level-headed and compassionate; however, Nick and I do not share the same spiritual beliefs. I'm sure it was hard to accept some of the things I told him. Seeing Bono, hearing Bono, messages from Bono—really Mom? Perhaps this is all in your head due to grieving.

He never embraced the Psychic/Spiritual Realm. He thought they were all shysters trying to take my money. He didn't want me to pay anyone, and he wanted me to "knock that shit off, Mom." Little did he know, I was now becoming "that shit" while growing my psychic abilities. I smile when I think how different our perspectives are on life. We love each other all the same

Bono's death hit my daughter hard. She's extremely sensitive and emotional. She's also very spiritual, like me. I love that we can share that part of my life. She has seen Bono flicker the lights in her bathroom, her baby monitor has picked up orbs, and she has received messages from Bono. He even turned on her downstairs TV one night, which frightened her husband.

Victoria is a quiet, yet outspoken, young lady. She patiently helped me with all of the bookkeeping chores, gathering info for taxes, and the paperwork aspect of dealing with death. I don't know what I would've done without her. I think I would've set fire to all of the paperwork, so I didn't have to deal with it. She's helped me out immensely, while quietly suffering with her own grief. Both of my children have been instrumental to my survival, and I love them dearly.

SECURING SOCIAL SUPPORTS: "YOU'VE GOT A FRIEND"

I've found that, for me, it is important to seek help when needed. Many people love and care about you, and they'll do *anything* to help. Having trusted people who can provide reliable advice and who you can count on is a godsend. If you stuff your feelings down, just know that they won't go away. They'll continue to rear their ugly heads until they're dealt with for good. Do you want to deal with these feelings of anguish and pain for the rest of your living days?

I did not desire this. I had many trusted people who I could rely on to help me through situations. I've introduced you to several of them in this book. I had a safety word in place: if I uttered it, someone—wherever I was—would come to help me. I reached out to my friends before an activity for good advice on how to handle myself and any potential issues. It was so endearing, because my friends would always pick up the phone and wouldn't let it go to voicemail. Sometimes, when I called, I was so anxious that I couldn't say anything at first. Some people would say, "take your time, but I want to know if you are okay." I would reply affirmatively, and that allowed the conversation to ensue. My friends treated me with love and caring, supporting me with open hearts. Asking for help was the best thing I could've done during this time. It helped me gain confidence, while giving me strategies on how to proceed.

"DRAG"GED DOWN BY FAMILIAL "NET" LOSS

FACEBOOK POST
DECEMBER 6, 2021

I feel like I am dying and constantly being reborn, on a daily basis. I can feel my magnificence and stand in my glory, or I can be beaten down and crushed. Tears still fall, but I know they are cleansing and must be experienced. Welcome to the world of loss, sorrow, and grief.

Forever in Touch:
Unbroken Connection and Loving Encounters with Bono

- I experienced a bizarre dream. In this dream, an animated man told me a story about his friend's strange name, which was supposed to be funny because his friend was bald. (Dreams can be so weird). I felt Bono behind me, slightly pushing me toward this man. He wanted me to put my head on this man's chest for comfort. I told Bono when I awoke that I wasn't ready, it was too soon, and that I wanted to fall onto his chest in my dreams.

chapter 19
"HELP!"

How To Comfort Those Who Have Lost Their Loves

When Bono passed, my world was torn apart by searingly painful grief. Just putting one foot in front of the other was exhausting, and the tears didn't stop—the grief was all-consuming. During that time, it was difficult to find the strength to reach out to others for help. Mastering that ability came later. Initially, I relied on others' caring natures to step in and take charge, lend assistance, or even simply offer kind, meaningful words. Happily, many people were up for these tasks.

However, as a bystander to grief, or even as a griever to a lesser degree (i.e., not the spouse; child; parent; etc. of the person who has passed), it's important to know when you're being helpful and when you may be unintentionally making the bereaved just plain feel worse. It's especially difficult to know what to say to someone who has lost a relatively young spouse or child, as such tragedies are not the norm. In this chapter, I describe reactions to my husband's death I got from strangers and acquaintances, as well as proper etiquette for comforting widows.

"WITH OR WITHOUT YOU": UNBELIEVABLE KINDNESS FROM STRANGERS

When Bono left to party with his family in Heaven, I was left with quite a lot of work to do to keep me busy. In addition to handling the usual items when a loved one passes, I had to organize my husband's paperwork at the clinic and gym, liquidate my husband's assets there, get an X-ray machine removed; the list goes on and on. My husband and I split the bills in our marriage. I made the house payment, and paid the cleaning ladies, homeowners and auto insurances, and my health insurance. Bono took care of the cable, internet, power, rent where he had his office and gym, his health insurance, City of Beaverton, gas, waste management, and the security system. We also had other small accounts that we handled. My name was on some of the bills; on others, it was not. The latter posed a problem.

Each company was different when I called them to explain why the bill should now be in my name, but every company expressed words of kindness and empathy toward me and my situation with each call. I was pretty broken while making the calls, and cried through the conversations, yet I was met with patience. Some companies wanted a death certificate; others didn't. It would've been easier if all of the bills were in both of our names. If you are in this predicament, you may want to rectify this and include both names on household expenses.

I would call these companies, and the representatives would stay on the phone and walk me through the process of changing the accounts over. The compassion and empathy in their voices came through over the phone, as did their genuine caring about my loss. All of them. Every single one. Even talking to Social Security—it wasn't like dealing with a government agency. I was working with someone who cared. The gal had solace in her voice, took her time with me, was kind in her explanation, and we had a genuine and heartfelt conversation.

When I contacted the rental agency for Bono's business, I could hardly get the words out. After reviewing the contract, an associate spoke to me and called me back. My husband had put a termination clause in the contract, as he'd had heart problems five years prior to his death. He would've been released from rent if he'd closed due to health problems, but ninety days' written notice would've been needed for him to be removed from the contract. I replied to the associate:

"It would be hard to give ninety days' notice if you were dead."

This item was never again addressed between us.

This same agency was trying to find a renter as my family and friends were going through my husband's items and liquidating. If they wanted to show the space, even though I wasn't required to, I'd make sure to be there while the agent and renters walked through. The agent and I had a very nice relationship, although he was seeing me at the worst time in my life.

In addition, my husband had received authorization to build a room for taking x-rays of his patients. Everything had to be inspected and up to code for this room, and he was to tear it down when he left the premises. The company decided to let the room stand, and not require me to have the space torn down. Those were tears of relief.

The agency that held his lease had hundreds of rental properties. Bono had been the only one who'd come into the office to pay his rent—everyone knew him. Whenever Bono had wanted to make physical changes, he'd constantly checked with the agency before doing so. He'd been well-liked in the office—especially by the construction and maintenance crew. Everyone who'd known him lamented his departure. The staff always treated me compassionately; an office who'd known and missed my husband extended to me so much grace.

They went through the building after it was vacated and found some things that needed to be restored and fixed; it was about a $5,000 bill for his estate. Since he had a history—and a friendship—with the agency, it was written off. There was no money owed. I had constant tears flowing down my face for the generosity and sympathy shown to me.

Bono had an X-ray machine that had to be dismantled, drained, and properly disposed of due to the chemicals. The only fellow who would do this work was in Seattle, Washington, and we lived outside of Portland, Oregon. This was a good three-hour drive for the man. He offered to do the service for $900. Before coming to Portland, he explained my husband's death to his wife. It seems that her first husband had died from an unexpected heart attack, probably just like mine. She told her husband not to charge me anything. Nothing. Nada. The pain, loss, and anguish negated any charges. I was on my knees in gratitude, and I penned a letter of thanks to them both.

I'd called the storage unit, identified myself, and remarked that I'd be responsible for the bill since my husband had died. There was silence on the phone. The lady receiving the call was sucker punched and could only utter, "Carl died?" I had a hard time keeping my composure with these calls, and this one was the most painful for me. My husband had had a relationship with these people—they were friends. She streamlined and made everything easy for me.

As I worked through contacting all of the businesses, I was amazed at the relationships that my husband had made with people. It wasn't that I was surprised that he would've done so, as he had a very affable nature. I'd never thought about it. I never knew of the connections and relationships he'd created outside of our marriage. This was a lesson for me, as I'd been too wrapped up in what I was doing in my life. I wished I'd asked more about the intricacies of his.

THANK YOU: INFINITE GRATITUDE AND POSITIVE ATTITUDE

I have infinite gratitude for everyone who helped me with the process. I truly could not have done it alone—my brain had gone to mush, decisions were hard to make, and my memory had taken a vacation. I felt like a shadow of my former self. I found—during my darkest days—that people met my pain and grief with compassion, empathy, and support. It was comforting to hear a change in people when you explained why you were calling, and to see how their humanity came out in dealing with me. People "took my hand," and helped me with the required processes when I was down to the lowest of lows. I was treated like a person—not simply like a client.

Looking back, I see how much these interactions have impacted me. Three years later, I now come completely from a state of gratitude in my life. I express gratitude to everyone all the time. I thank people for the smallest of things. Kindness and an attitude of gratitude are how you live your life. It is you—your essence. You aren't just kind and giving gratitude; you live it daily in everything you do—in every interaction, every email you write, phone conversation you make, text you send…in every freaking thing.

There is a secret in this. It is about the flow of energy. Some call it "The Law of Attraction"; what you give out comes back to you (Atkinson, 2023). What you send out in your wake to the universe will come back to you. And like energy attracts like energy.

Life will always have its ups and downs—that's life. Life is full of lessons, blessings, challenges, and gratification. That is why we are here on this earth—to grow our souls. We come here for our soul's evolution. I believe I chose these lessons to experience before I came into this body for my soul's evolution and growth. Guess what. If I don't get the lessons and the growth, I get to come back another time and do it all over again.

Believe me, I DON'T want to live through this misery one more second than I have to.

Think about yourself—what comes back to you in your life? If you like what is happening, continue down that path. If you don't, change your attitude and your mind and you will change your inner being. Have you ever noticed how some people constantly complain about their lives and what "happens" to them (AKA "victimhood")? Also, do you notice the people that still have stuff "happen" to them, but their outlook is different? What people do you prefer to be near? Who raises your vibration and lifts you up? Do you ever feel tired and sapped when you spend time with the wrong person—as if they've sucked the life out of you. They *have*, and you have to replenish your soul. Do you have other friends with whom you experience great happiness, love, and laughter and from whom you leave feeling energized? Sure, you do. These are friends that you should keep close to your heart, so you can feed each other's souls.

I could've easily become a victim and changed my entire thought patterns. Why did God take the three most prominent people in my life away in thirteen months? Why me? What did I do? I could've traveled this road to my dying day. People would've listened, commiserated with me, and totally understood my viewpoint. In doing so, in feeling sorry for my circumstances, I would've lowered my own vibrations as well as those of the people around me. I would've also still endured my loss, grief, and trauma. My life would be full of misery, pain, and victimhood.

There are times in your life, whether you're grieving or not, that you can get in a funk. You may feel defeated, down, depressed, hopeless, or worse. I've experienced this not only with loss, but also with other things that have happened to me in my life. When this occurs, when you may feel hopelessness and lost in loss, perhaps there are avenues to help. Relief can be found with a good, competent therapist, or through a religious institution that resonates with you. There are also "help hotlines" to guide you toward finding the help you seek. Health care professionals have lists of avenues to help with your feelings. There will be light at the end of the tunnel, and it may take some striving to get to that light, but don't give up hope. Many times, the road to travel seems insurmountable; finding your way to the top can be empowering and gratifying.

AT A LOSS FOR WORDS? "MEET ME HALFWAY"

It seems that when someone loses a parent, words flow freely to help with the grieving. Losing parents is a sad, but common, part of life for most people. This is not so for a woman who has lost her husband. Many people do not know how to convey their feelings effectively, and they are usually shocked by the news—this is especially true for friends who know you and your partner primarily as a couple and not individually.

If you're struggling with the best way to show support for someone who has lost a spouse, it's important to keep in mind what not to say and what to say to convey support.

WHAT NOT TO SAY TO A RECENT WIDOW

- *How are you?* Well, I feel like dying, I'm suffocating in grief and shock, and I feel freakin' awful. No one's doing well if they've lost their beloved—don't ask.
- *Call me if you need help.* The grieving person does need help, but they will not call. It is tough to talk on the phone, or even to text, when experiencing a devastating loss. Know that the grieving spouse does need help and is overwhelmed. Take it upon yourself to think "how" you can help.
- *You're still young enough/beautiful enough/have many years left to meet someone else.* What? My husband just died, and now

you are telling me to replace that beloved, exceptional person? What is wrong with you?

- *[Husband] would want you to be happy.* Then he shouldn't have fucking died. If he wanted me to be happy, then he shouldn't have left. There were so many times I wanted to say this to people, but with most I held my tongue as they were well-meaning and trying to make me feel better. It made me feel the complete opposite.

- *You have such beautiful memories to sustain you.* I don't want memories to sustain me. I want my husband. I want him here in the flesh. Don't offer platitudes. The grief is still too raw and fresh. When you lose someone, you don't revel in the memories. You suffer from the loss and trauma and experience angst.

Above all, widows do not want pity. They want to feel loved and supported. Instead, focus your energy on conveying that support.

WHAT TO SAY TO A RECENT WIDOW

- *I'm here for you.* Anytime of the day or night, I am here for you. If you need a shoulder to cry on, someone to listen, or someone to share a cup of tea with—I am always here for you. I will drop whatever I am doing and take care of you. You are not alone; others share your pain and want to help you in any way they can.

- *You are in my thoughts.* Knowing that I was not forgotten, once the initial shock had worn off, was very heartwarming. Just a simple text saying, "I am holding you close to my heart," or a caring text with an added "there is no need to respond," is wonderful. The latter was texted to me many times by different friends, and it took a lot of the pressure off of me. Eliciting a text conversation is overwhelming for the grieving. It takes so much energy to think and reply. Sending thoughtful texts without expecting, or wanting, a reply was wonderful.

- *I have been keeping you and your family uplifted in prayer.* Prayer is so strong—it is a connection to the Heavenly Realm and to the Divine. Knowing that a multitude of people were praying for me and lifting me up was phenomenal. Prayers can serve as a telephone line to the divine world. And always give gratitude once you have prayed. Show your thankfulness and appreciation.

- *Tell the grieving, "I love you."* Love is the answer. Love heals. Love crosses all boundaries. These three simple words can help mend the deep wounds someone has. Just hearing those three words would make me cry in gratitude. Someone loved and cared about me while I was facing this turbulent sea and being tossed around in a swirl of pain, grief, and suffocation under the sneaker waves of loss.

- *My heart is breaking for you.* My heart is too. Thank you for coming from a place of caring and compassion in dealing with me, and for understanding this unrelenting pain. I could feel others' pain and compassion for me—and it came across as sympathy or empathy...not simply pity.

- *Be honest about your feelings.* I know it is hard to know what to say—it used to be for me too. Let them know. "I am at a loss for words, but please know that I love and care about you and that I am holding you close."

If you want to provide help and support beyond kind words, then initiate action*:*

- *Offer to help, or just do it.* Cut their lawn, drop off food, and write thank-you notes for them. Let them know you'll phone, text, or both for an assignment. The widow's brain has shut down, but yours still works. How can you help? What can you do for someone who is immobilized and paralyzed by grief on a daily basis?

  One of my friends prepaid $100 to one of my favorite restaurants, and I ordered the food because cooking was not essential. Another gave me a $250 gift card to an eatery, spoke to the manager, and was told that he would "personally deliver the food." When my husband died, I lived on coffee, tequila, and chocolate. Eating was not a priority. In addition to your spirit shutting down, so does your body. You truly don't care about food, but—when you decide you need nourishment—cooking is overwhelming to think about. Having money at a restaurant, food, or a gift card—as well as having food delivered—was glorious.

- *Widows want their loss acknowledged—not glossed over.* Speak the name of the dead spouse; don't avoid it. All of a sudden, the person who died loses a name. ("I am so sorry for your loss." How about "I am so sorry for the loss of *Carl*—he was a magnificent man who touched my life in so many ways.")

Death is difficult to discuss; I truly understand. I didn't know what to say, or how to say it, until I experienced my own loss and spoke with other widows. I feel it is especially very difficult when you knew the two as a couple, and now one is gone. You can be at a loss for words, your brain might freeze, and you may say whatever pops into your head while trying to make the griever feel better. I hope these tips will help to ease you into a conversation with one who has lost their spouse and assist you in grasping how to express yourself meaningfully.

FACEBOOK POST
NOVEMBER 22, 2021

Kindness matters—no matter how small the act.

About a week ago, I had an extremely rough day—since I have experienced many of these in the past, I knew that it had to run its course no matter how much agony was involved. I canceled an appointment and didn't even try to get out of the house; I had tried that in the past, and it only made matters worse. I had to go through the process as it was intended. I was pretty much a sobbing mess of my former self, going from room to room and experiencing loss, pain, and grief. You can't think happy thoughts to raise your vibrations or count your blessings—you just have to experience. I am glad those days have subsided, and I will endure the ones that still insist on coming.

Shortly after that day, an order showed up on my doorstep. In addition, a friend swung by and brought me a tasty bag of chocolates with a lovely note from his wife—she had reached out via text, knowing of the painful day that I had just recently experienced.

The friend who shipped me the order would not let me pay, even though I asked her three times for the amount. She said:

"We have been blessed, and we want to bless others."

Since my husband died, my heart and emotions have expanded beyond my comprehension, and I live in a very raw state. Normally, I would have thought, "that is so kind." Yet, this time, I cried when she wouldn't charge me, and again on the day the package arrived. It wasn't about the money; it was about her soft, kind, and gracious heart. Those tears were in appreciation. That someone just cared about me. See's Candies are one of my favorites, but my tears were due to the beautiful note on the bag—which I still have. This was a small act of kindness from someone who wanted to share her love and brighten my day when she knew that I had suffered. She also calls me "Doll" sometimes, which always makes me snicker—I like it.

Everyone, *everyone*, everyone is fighting some sort of battle—even you who are reading this post. We don't get out of this life unscathed—I don't care who you are. Kindness costs nothing, but it is priceless. On my walks, I ask:

"How can I be of service today? Present me with a way to make a difference in someone's life."

This morning, I already know my act of kindness, and it brings me a smile knowing that someone will smile back at me for the small act that I'll perform. The feelings received are invaluable for the both of us.
—Namaste

FACEBOOK POST
DECEMBER 14, 2021

I went running errands, and I was in such a funk and felt very disheveled looking. The gas station attendant was a young man, and when he greeted me, he asked how I was doing. I told him, "Not too well," but I didn't go into details. He stopped and stood in my window, started a conversation, and was sorry I was having a bad day. He talked about Christmas, my festive nails, and he kept calling me "Hun." I don't find it offensive when people speak in that manner, as I do as well. It was a nice, soft word for me to hear.

Everything started to change when he got me to laugh, and my spirits were lifted. He kept checking on me as my tank filled, and I could see his eyes crinkle when he was smiling. I was well attended to. After we finished up, I slipped him a Christmas bonus. He refused it, and he said that I didn't have to do that.

I remarked, "That's what makes it so fun."

My spirits definitely turned around as I drove away. A sweet soul was put on my path today.

FACEBOOK POST
JANUARY 1, 2021

I am glad that the year has passed—with all of the milestones of the last two months and the office liquidation. I had a morning when I awoke happy the other day, which was such a blessing. I made a shift yesterday, and I have been able to become once again appreciative of everything in my life. Little bits of my former self are re-emerging.

Replying to your posts is like climbing a mountain—I don't have the tenacity just yet. It will come, and I will get stronger. How can I not? I have the love and support from my family and friends.

Happy 2021. May God's blessings shower upon you and bestow upon each of you a bright, healthy, and peaceful new year.

"HELP!"

Forever in Touch:
Unbroken Connection and Loving Encounters with Bono

I could feel Carl's arms around me on the patio bench. He hugged me from behind, and we rocked back and forth. I stroked his legs. He was so comforting.

chapter 20
"I NEED YOU"

The Stronger the Love, the Deeper the Grief

It has been said that "the stronger the love, the deeper the grief," and it's hard to argue with this statement. You've read about my experiences with Bono's passing and my state of being. A friend reached out to me ten months later to see if I was doing anything fun. I had to stop and think. Fun? Not really. I'm just going through the motions of life, healing, and trying to regain my strength and stamina, so as to keep putting one foot in front of the other. I have fun moments with friends—such as going out to lunch and playing Mahjong—but no new or exciting trips. I still hit a "wall" from 4 to 5 p.m., and I lose my energy. Grief sucks. Yet, I know all this grief is not a punishment, but a lesson, and life's primary purpose is what you do with your lessons.

I had never planned on writing a book. In the '80s, a psychic medium told me I'd write a book someday, and I scoffed at those words. I was a schoolteacher with two young children, had gone through a divorce, and was headed for another. I could hardly keep my head above water, although I could've written books about crazy men you should never marry. It would've been so much easier if I'd taken my parents' advice and not married my first or second husband: Bono was my third. My parents only gave me their blessings when I married Bono. Yet, I would not have been blessed with my two phenomenal children if my life had not led me down those roads. Everything, no matter how small or insignificant, is intended in your life. Life is full of lessons, and expansion of our souls and our spiritual growth, while we take up space in this world.

During these times, I certainly tested my Angels. I felt my first husband was so obsessed when we separated that he'd kill me. I had these feelings so many times, and at that time I was not so spiritual. Had I been in tune, I'd have taken precautions against him as I was receiving warning signs and not paying attention. My Birth Angels made sure I didn't leave prematurely.

This man *still* holds animosity toward me. We haven't talked since Nick graduated with his master's a decade ago. He used to call me "that bitch," and he once spit in my face when I handed my son to him during a visitation. It's unfathomable to me how one can hold on to anger and treat another in this way. He'll go to his grave without an apology ever uttered from his lips to me. Yet, I believe that when he passes, he will have many regrets about how he lived and how he could've learned his lessons in a way toward growth, enlightenment, love, and acceptance.

I hold no animosity toward him, and I've forgiven him. I had to work through a lot of anger in my forgiveness, but I was able to do so with help from my counselor and my coach. On my morning walks with the pups, I'd talk to this man. I'd speak everything I wanted to say to his face: You fucked me up. You fucked up your son. You treated me like shit and cheated on me. I didn't matter to you; you only cared about yourself. Yet, it was through being honest with my emotions that I could forgive him. We're all doing the best we can, and he thinks that's his best.

When I went through my second divorce, I thought I was defective because I couldn't make two marriages work—and I became suicidal. When contemplating suicide, the pain is so intense that killing yourself seems like the only way to get relief. Anyway, what does it matter? You're merely a burden to others and your life doesn't make a difference. I was really going to do it. Thank God divine intervention ensued in the form of Bink's eyes and soul. My Angels intervened, and I never pondered suicide again. I regained my life and started living once more.

When I look back, I would've destroyed so many lives if I'd taken my own. My parents would've been devastated, and my children would've gone to live with their fathers—with horrible consequences. I was the apple of Pops' eye, and it would've broken him. Mom would've been ruined and tried to hold the family together. My parents' lives would've been destroyed; their "little girl"—who they'd showered with love, and helped to become a powerful, responsible young woman—had taken her life. I shudder to think what my loss would've done to them.

Both of my ex-husbands were unfit to be fathers. Both battled their own demons and wouldn't have given the necessary care to the children. The kids would've been separated, with one living in Nevada and the other in Oregon. I think my ex-husbands would've been ill-prepared to help my kids process my death. Everyone in my family would've been changed forever, and not in a beneficial way. I would've been responsible for causing them so much pain.

I was a teacher during this time: how would my students have understood? I was their role model. The ripple effect of my death would've been huge in the school; I'd taught there for many years, and many students had come through my door. The impact my suicide would've had—not only on my students, but also on every student and their families who knew of me—would've been astronomical. Elementary school kids wouldn't have had the skills to process what had happened. My coworkers would have also been stunned; I'd never complained, nor had I taken any of my angst to the workplace, so they only knew a bit about my situation. School had always been a safe haven for me. The school counselor would've been very busy working with the children impacted by my death, and I would've tarnished my very nice legacy.

At the time, a lot of these suicidal feelings came from my second husband poisoning my mind. For those who know me now, it's unfathomable that I'd turn my back on my parents—but I did. He twisted them and my life with them, and I became brainwashed. This man would malign my parents and friends. We'd go to family events or spend time with my friends, and—immediately after we left—he'd point out all their frailties and find fault with them. Never were there kind words: only criticism. He isolated me from my parents and friends: I believed the thoughts he put in my head. He tried to control me, and it worked for a while. It was when I was at my breaking point—when I'd decided to live and to stand up to him—that I was set free.

My parents were my everything in life—my cheerleaders. They wouldn't accept my getting a "C" in a high school class; that grade was "average," and I wasn't average in their minds. They'd always been there for me: to lose me would've been like losing a huge part of themselves. My parents and I were close, and we shared a great deal of love. I'd seen how my father had reacted when he'd lost his sister—to lose his daughter would've been unendurable. My mother—the woman who'd given birth to me—wouldn't have understood, and she would've blamed herself and questioned her abilities as a mom. My death could've broken up my family.

I know that both of my ex-husbands loved our kids. Yet, each became estranged from his kid during the teenage and young adulthood years. Can you imagine that as a parent—not seeing your children for years, blaming them for the loss of contact, and not loving or nurturing them? Both men walked away from their kids. They didn't talk to them for years—their conversations, or texts, were periodic. Neither was meant for fatherhood at that point in their lives.

Looking back, and seeing where their lives took them, I know my children wouldn't have received the love and care that they needed—even as adults. Those children would've turned out completely differently, and I shudder to think of how. Perhaps they would've become stronger and more resilient than I could imagine: the process would've been painful, but it also could've reaped many rewards regarding their inner strength and fortitude. Thankfully, we'll never know.

Thank you, my loving and wise Birth Angels, for your divine intervention. I know you had realized the ramifications: without your assistance, I would never have learned to grow into the soul that I have to this day. Even when my husband passed—and I had no will left to live and wanted to die—I never contemplated suicide. I was in the deepest grief, but—due to my past experiences—I knew the horrible ripples it would've put out to my children, family, and friends. I'm so grateful that I learned that lesson and was better prepared to tackle grief this time around.

FACEBOOK POST
DECEMBER 16, 2021

I took an arrow through my heart today.

Remember my friend, Chris? The person who I had connected with, and the one who gets all the goodies that I bake and make? A man who wanted the truth, and he got every harrowing experience of my life over the last year?

I hadn't seen him at the school for days, which is highly unusual as we'd usually talked three to four times a week. While walking the dogs, he came from the back of the field and not the parking lot, as he was on leave and didn't want his colleagues to see him. He came to share with me why I hadn't seen him lately. His younger brother had died unexpectedly from a heart attack. The news sucker-punched me, but the most challenging part was seeing the pain in his eyes. I knew what he was experiencing, and what his future would hold. My heart was so heavy for him.

We walked and talked, and I gave him space. I offered a few suggestions and told him what he may experience moving forward. I felt honored and humbled that he came to share with me.

We are so interconnected.

I was just some broad walking her dogs. I said "hi," and we struck up a conversation—and then a friendship. The young kid at the gas station talked to me and lifted my spirits when I was in a funk. We can help each other out in every small deed that we do.

I am so sorry if I come across as "preachy," but experiencing three deaths in a short amount of time has opened my heart, and I appreciate every little thing.

We hugged goodbye, and we had never hugged before. Just two lost souls connected, trying to find our way.

SECTION IV

"ELEVATION"

GROWING THROUGH GRIEF

chapter 21
MY EPIPHANIES

> How lucky I am to have something that
> makes saying goodbye so hard.
> -WINNIE THE POOH, A.A. MILNE

"I LIVED"!

While traveling on the road of grief, many epiphanies came to me. I don't want to minimize any of my experiences during this time, but I had several noticeable shifts that helped both in my growth and my grieving process.

I CLAIMED MY POWER BACK

I was married for twenty-six years to a man who could repair and build anything. He had terrific talents, whether it be replacing the brakes on my car, creating a workbench, or figuring out how I messed up my phone or computer—along with many more. He called himself my

"Fireman," because he was constantly rescuing me. He'd make sounds like a firetruck when he came to help. He actually enjoyed "saving me," and never questioned me when I asked or balked at his chores. I think I was the first woman who created a "Honey-Do List" for him.

While growing up, my father was never taught how to repair or build. His father had been a minister in an upper caste in India, and he'd had all the chores completed by staff. Thus, Pops was never taught how to mend or restore. I worked by his side out in the yard, and I knew how to correctly trim trees from working in our orchard, how to run a mower and tiller, and the proper way to edge a lawn. However, Pops had to hire people when something needed to be done in the house, and I was the same way. I was my father's daughter; I'd never been taught these skills.

When Bono died—in addition to having feelings of anger, sadness, numbness, yearning, and shock—I felt weak and disempowered. My husband had treated me like a queen. We'd both taken care of each other in different ways. After his death, I reached out to people and asked for help, but I always felt pitiful and helpless.

On May 26, 2021, I had the epiphany that I would no longer be a weak woman—I reclaimed my power. I still had to ask for help and learn in the process, but it came from a different stance. I could stand in my power and ask for help, and it wasn't from a powerless, pitiful perspective. I have learned to be resourceful and how to do things along the way. Before I met Bono, I'd lost my power. When we met, I regained my strength, but it dimmed once again when he passed. It felt incredible to start getting my power back. Learning to ask for help is a strength in itself—and one can learn in the process of being assisted.

I DECIDED TO LIVE

Having lost my parents and husband in quick succession, I hadn't cared if I lived or died. I'd actually wanted to die and to join them in Heaven.

I'd felt that my kids had the strength and good character necessary to survive my death, but that I had to stay here for my doggies. They'd already lost their daddy, were grieving, and had special needs. I had to stay here for them. I'd soldiered on through my grief, trying to make it one more day—just doing the best that I could. It had been the most challenging time of my life—and I'd lived through some difficult moments.

I just decided to live. I decided that I wouldn't focus on dying or wanting to join everyone in Heaven; instead, I'd start living my life again. This thought didn't give me any more energy, but it did cause a change in my awareness. This shift was instrumental in my grief process. Many widows have experienced this defining moment in their lives; it seems you make an inward shift and decide you will live and create a new life. One of my widow friends had the same epiphany, and she said to herself, "Naw, Imma gonna live." For myself, this was not a decision that I spent a lot of time thinking about; I just woke up one day and decided "to live."

When you lose your beloved, your identity is wiped clean. You are no longer "Mr. and Mrs." or "Dr. and Mrs." Bonofiglio: you are just yourself. You can't define yourself as a couple. No more, "my husband and I." You are a widow. Your husband (or wife) has died. You enter a new, foreign, and unforgiving world. When I wrote cards after Bono died, I would add his name. Christmas and birthday gifts were given by both of us, even though he was deceased.

In learning to embrace being "just Karen," I started to stand in my own light. I became a self-empowered woman again—not defined by anyone but herself. This is a slow and gradual process in which you change. I remember when I retired from teaching, I was no longer "a teacher" but rather a "former teacher" or a "retired teacher". We have these labels attached to us, and then *poof* they are gone. I am now "Karen Bonofiglio" but I know that label will change as I continue experiencing life. I have many more adventures to embark on and much more growing to do until the day I leave this world. If you are reading this book, I am now, "Karen Bonofiglio, Author." Who would have thought? Certainly not me.

I RESOLVED TO GO BEYOND MYSELF AND REACH OUT TO OTHERS

When writing on Facebook, my rule was never to complain or to put up anything negative. Everyone experiences crap in their own lives, and they didn't need to know my problems. I was always a quiet, private person, and I didn't share any vulnerabilities from my life. That changed when Bono died. I poured my heart out into my searing, gut-wrenching posts, and I exposed my vulnerability and virtually all the pain my soul was suffering. I'd cry while writing these posts. I would never have thought I could expose myself in this manner.

I put up posts about seeing a psychic medium, and never in a million years would I have written about that—I was divinely inspired to do so. People can be so judgmental, but my tribe grew and supported me. I made many new widow friends—people interested in spirituality, who appreciated the rawness of my posts, and who liked what I'd written—as my contributions helped them deal with their own significant losses. Yet, this relationship I had on Facebook was twofold. I was lifted up and supported by my friends. Reading their replies always made me cry; there was so much love and support coming to me through this social media. Tears are cleansing. Tears must fall. Stifling the emotions will never heal the soul. I'll never lose the grief inside me, but I'll grow around it. Even after a year, I still shed tears daily; this is very common.

I found that being my true, authentic self, and showing my vulnerability, made me "human." Other people had experienced the same tragedies, but they did not articulate their feelings or write about them. My posts of that nature became a safe place for others who related to them to share their innermost feelings and express them without judgments. When I wrote a post about the time in my life that I'd contemplated suicide, it generated a multitude of replies; so many friends were at that point once in their lives, and they shared this on my thread. Sharing openly can be very cathartic and cleansing for the deep, hidden secrets we keep tucked away.

I LEARNED TO APPRECIATE LIFE

Through my grief, I learned to appreciate EVERYTHING. No matter how minuscule it may seem, it can be life-changing: seeing the Big Dipper in the morning sky, or the sunrise over a frosty field of grass; laughter upon seeing my doggies' crazy antics; everything. Start now: think of five things you are grateful for. Do this daily and see how "having gratitude" will transform your life. Think of five things you are thankful for about yourself—you'll find, at first, that it's much harder to praise yourself than it is to praise others. Do this daily as well—be changed.

Back when Pops, Mom, and Bono died, I quit appreciating. I was not grateful. When I had this epiphany, I FORCED myself to seek gratitude and appreciation. On most of the doors of my house, I wrote in large words on paper, "GIVE GRATITUDE." Every time, *every time* I saw a paper, I would stop in my tracks and speak words aloud about my blessings in life:

I am so grateful for all the love I experience from my family and friends. I am grateful that I get to see my puppies when I open my eyes every morning. I am grateful for fresh air and morning walks with my doggies. I am grateful to all of my Heavenly Helpers. I am grateful for another breath of air in my lungs. I am grateful for being upright (Me).

Once you begin doing this, you will start living a life of gratitude and kindness. It is not simply something you do—it becomes who you are.

A friend of mine, Carlos, shared the idea of a gratitude jar on Facebook, which I started using on the first of every year. It need not run for a year; you could make it a monthly jar and start out with something more manageable. He'd deposit slips of paper in the jar daily with all the things for which he was grateful written on them. It wasn't just one drop of gratitude—he'd mentioned any and all things. I started doing this, and the slips of paper could contain one statement or many statements to add to the jar. Doing it daily was easiest for me as my day was still fresh in my mind, and I could remember all the blessings—no matter how minute.

At the end of the year, Carlos would have a celebration. He'd take the slips of paper and read each one from the previous year. When you read the paper, not only do you remember that event, you get to experience it again along with all the "good feels" it gave you. It becomes very celebratory. I told two of my girlfriends about that jar, and they thought about doing the same. This upcoming New Year's Eve, we will gather together and each read our slips of paper, and we will undoubtedly discuss some of the events of the year that have slipped our minds. I know food and beverages will be involved, and that we will create a new tradition—making our connection, bond, and friendship even stronger.

This tool differs from a gratitude journal. I wrote in a gratitude journal for years, listing five things for which I was grateful in every entry. When the journal was done, I did not revisit the blessings, fun, and gratitude I'd had during the year. The gratitude jar solidifies your experiences and is more festive. I love it.

FACEBOOK POST
DECEMBER 28, 2021

I have mentioned how hard it is to live in my body—that I am not bipolar, but my life is.

Since Carl died, I have experienced extreme highs and lows. I get feelings where I can't contain my soul, and it wants to explode out of this shell. I am just overcome, and it is freaking amazing.

While talking to Tracy last night, I finally figured out why and what state I am in while experiencing these explosions. It is due to living in love and gratitude. That simple. Feeling and expressing love and appreciation [ignites] my explosive soul. One must live in a state of gratitude, which in turn encompasses love.

When Bono died, I posted huge signs around the house that said, "Give Thanks": because I was not in a thankful mood. I would stop and say at least five reasons I was thankful daily. I also would say five reasons why I was thankful about myself, such as "I am thankful for my ingenuity" and "I am thankful that I love and care about people."

Stop and try it for yourself and see how you feel. Trying to make it about yourself is challenging.

Enjoy your day and keep on shining your light.

Forever in Touch:
Unbroken Connection and Loving Encounters with Bono

- I saw a snake on my front doorstep. I love snakes, and I hadn't seen one since I was a little girl. I was in awe and transfixed. I looked up the symbology of a snake, and it meant transformation and rebirth. I shared the story with Binks, Vivi, and Tracy.

Chapter 22

"ALL YOU NEED IS LOVE"

My "Widows' Club" The Janda Sisters

The Indonesian word Janda has many meanings, and one of them is "widow." Many of my friends had also lost their husbands, and we came together monthly to meet for lunch and mutual support. This was invaluable to all of us—we'd lost our husbands under different circumstances and at different times. We shared our experiences and grief, gave suggestions, shared books, and were heartfully there for each other. Close friendships became closer, and I learned how precious life was and to never take anything for granted—it could change in a heartbeat.

A NAME FOR OUR GROUP AND TAKING BACK OUR LIVES

When I had this divinely inspired idea for the widows to meet, I posted about it on Facebook. I told my friends I was starting a club. It was not just for "cool kids," but for women who'd lost their spouses. I asked if they had suggestions for names, and boy did they. They ranged from:

- Until Death Do Us Partners
- WOW- Walking Onward Women
- Widows with New Beginnings
- Black Widows (just no)
- Making Times with Friends
- The Empty Hearts Club
- Widows' Journeys
- LBT Club- Lonely but Together

I eventually chose the suggested name "Janda" Sisters because it sounded upbeat, and not a downer like "widows" (even though it means "previously married" and now widowed or divorced). It also has a very relevant meaning, in that Indonesian janda are often stigmatized in that culture due to people not knowing what to make of them (the men see them as sexually available, even promiscuous, and wives often then see them as a threat to their marriages; Parker et al. 2016). Others' uncertainty of what to make of widows—and how to interact with us at all as we are suddenly mysterious, "single" or "uncoupled" women—is also often more subtly a major part of our continued social experience in my own culture, as I've shared in this book.

Using this name for our group is, in a way, a form of reclaiming the name for all women, and of asserting the idea that we can make of our widowhood whatever we want to (just as Indonesian janda hopefully will be able to), and that our own personal lives—as well as our roles as mothers, daughters, friends, and as part of a social network of people like ourselves—don't have to end forever due to losing our partners. We may feel like we want them to, but our group is a way to fight that feeling as well as any stigma that comes with having lost a husband.

MEMBERS AND MEETINGS: CONSTANT CAMARADERIE

I explained to my friends on Facebook that I didn't *want* them to join the club, but that they were welcome to do so when the time came. One gal asked if her father could join as he was a widower. Since this was so new to us, we were only comfortable with women joining then, but at this point I feel that we could introduce men to this club.

Having my widows' club has been highly beneficial. I've been living in a time where most meetings are managed with Zoom due to COVID-19. Sitting together in a room with people who share my pain is more advantageous for me than any Zoom conference. We gather monthly, if not more often, to talk about what we're experiencing as part of our grief. We've blossomed through these friendships. Not only do we meet monthly, but we've also gone to the movies together, visited food carts, and one sister and I even bought season tickets to Thorns matches.

Some of us also text each other each morning to make sure we're upright and breathing. We joke and say things like, "I'm on this side of the grass," "I am upright," or "I am alive." In addition, we share what's happening in our lives that day, and have a small conversation. We know that we can call or text each other at any time for support. We instituted a rule: you have to check in by 11 a.m. (quite a long grace period, I think). If you don't, we'll reach out to your emergency contacts, which we've previously shared. We had to use this emergency procedure once, but the sister was okay: she just had bad reception on the mountain where she lives.

We agreed to meet on the first Thursday of each month. I've found that changing the date complicates things, so we have tried to keep the meeting set the same. Consistency is very helpful when you are grieving. Sometimes not everyone is there, but most times they are.

Our meetings are sounding boards for what's occurring in our lives. We share and discuss the best options for how to handle situations and the best possible outcomes; it's a nice support group of like-minded ladies who've bonded over loss and grief. No discussion topic is off-limits.

JANDA SISTERS READING RECOMMENDATIONS

We also share book suggestions with each other. Some deal with grief, while others concern different aspects of the afterlife. We don't discuss and analyze the book in the same way that a book club would, but rather we share how this book has helped us and provided insights.

Here are some books we've shared (Appendix IV has a longer list of suggested readings):

- *Dying to be Me* by Anita Moorjani
- *It's Okay That You're Not Okay* by Megan Devine
- *Signs from the Afterlife* by Lyn Ragan
- *Signs: The Secret Language of the Universe* by Laura Lynne Jackson
- *I'm Still With You* by Sherrie Dillard
- *Finding Meaning: The Sixth Stage of Grief* by David Kessler
- *When Breath Becomes Air* by Paul Kalanithi
- *Reaching to Heaven* by James Van Praagh
- *Messages from the Masters* by Brian Weiss MD.
- *Journey of Souls* and *Destiny of Souls* by Dr. Michael Newton

THE JANDA PROMISE

My friend Betsy is a psychologist. When I told her about my support group of widows, she suggested we write up rules to serve as guidelines. We did, and we call this The Janda Promise. It's served us well, and this group overall has been one of the best tools I've had to tackle grief.

THE JANDA PROMISE

1. What happens in Janda Sisters, stays in Janda Sisters: We are to respect the confidentiality of each group member.
2. Each gathering would have a facilitator for the meeting: This could be one constant person, or we can switch between group members.
3. No interrupting each other: Let the sister speak freely.
4. Check out at the beginning of each meeting who needs "airtime" and what they would like to talk about: The facilitator would make a list of people and their subjects.
5. Keep talk to about five minutes per person, but you can possibly go a bit over the allotted time: I brought a darling toy monkey, Bob, to Janda. Now, he joins us regularly; when someone speaks, they hold Bob or have him sitting nearby. Bob is always very respectful and follows the rules.
6. NO discussion of politics or religions

FACEBOOK POST
JULY 2, 2021

I had this brainiac idea when I was in the shower today. I am going to form a club. It is not a "cool kids" club, but a "widows' club" where we will meet monthly for a luncheon.

It could be a wonderful support group between friends, as many of my friends have lost their husbands. If you can't join this club, you are blessed, and hold on tightly to your loved ones. Should there come a time that you could join this club, you would be welcomed with open arms.

My quandary: what to call the club? Widows' club is so "meh." One friend suggested "black widows"—that was a resounding "no." Perhaps you are more creative than me and can help me come up with a name—something upbeat. It is not an easy task.

Forever in Touch:
Unbroken Connection and Loving Encounters with Bono

- My husband has communicated to me numerous times how proud he is of me. He has applauded me in undertaking the writing of this book, and in gathering friends in a support group—just to mention two. Since our Janda Sisters have bonded together, I am sure our husbands have also connected in the Heavenly Realm. Even though they are behind the Veil, they still learn and grow with us; it is a symbiotic association.

chapter 23
"A CELEBRATION" TIME?

The Dreaded Holidays, Anniversaries, and the "Birthday" Song

Holidays. They used to bring me such joy. Thanksgiving was my favorite. Gathering around a table with loved ones and sharing food brought so much love to my heart. Now, it also brings stress, high anxiety, tears, fears, and other unpleasant feelings. I am now actually one of those people who dreads the holidays—from October 1 – December 31. Anniversaries can be even more difficult to cope with, or to figure out how to appropriately honor. In this chapter, I will teach you some tools I have learned for navigating this difficult time of the year for all grievers.

SPIRIT BOX #21: HOME REMEMBERING THE HOLIDAYS

"Bono again. It's Christmas. A lovely time of year. Our ways of celebrating it changed over the years. When they were growing up, we'd let the kids open one gift on Christmas Eve, and then the rest on Christmas. The first one we celebrated together, I slowly opened a gift and folded up the paper to use next year. I saw the glances Nick and Victoria exchanged with Karen. They were used to ripping all the wrapping paper off the box, and I eventually joined in their fracas.

"Later, as the kids grew up, got married, and had partners, we shared them with the other side of the family. Ever since I met Karen, we always went out on Christmas Eve for dinner at a Chinese restaurant. We called it 'Chinese Christmas Eve,' and the restaurant was always packed with others who had the same idea. We started opening our gifts on Christmas Eve, and the kids would open their gifts with the other side of the family on Christmas Day. However, that day, we'd all gather together for a meal with Grammy and Bapu (you know them as Mom and Pops) with the other side of Karen's family. Isn't that right, Mom and Pops?"

"That's right, Carl, isn't it, Ruthie?"

"Yes, Ted. Thanksgiving dinner was always a feast when the girls were growing up. I'd make my special shrimp aspic salad, made only on the holidays, and we'd have the traditional fixings. Oh, how we loved those moments; I'm so happy we experienced them as a family."

"Me too, Ruthie."

"Me three."

"SEE YOU IN SEPTEMBER": RACING AGAINST TIME AND BEING PREPARED FOR ALL OCCASIONS

Depending on your traditions, people celebrate holidays at all different times of the year, though for many people the most important and frequent holidays cluster around the fall and wintertime. For me, Mom and Dad died in October, and Bono died in November. Right off the bat, there are three death dates. I do not call these the "anniversaries" of their passing, as this sounds too celebratory. In November, Thanksgiving involves the gathering of family. In December, I honor Bono on his birthday: December 8. Then comes Christmas Eve, Christmas, and New Year's Eve—our wedding anniversary. I chose December 31 for our wedding date as it was usually celebratory and festive. People were partying and welcoming in the New Year. What a perfect day to celebrate our marriage and union.

Thanksgiving was a recent topic for the widows' club. All of us had different situations. I was dealing with getting together with a combined family that I did not know well, and I was experiencing panic attacks. One group member was alone; if I'd known this, then she would've been invited to my celebration. The other ladies had various ways of celebrating.

We found there were several ways in which we could make the holidays more bearable.

PLAN AHEAD

Do this so that you are not blindsided. With whom will you be celebrating? Where? What's your part in the celebration, and how does it pan out? It's better not to have unforeseen circumstances. Knowing the details and predicting the outcomes will allow you to set yourself up for success.

One Janda Sister has two celebrations with her family. She doesn't try to orchestrate a celebration as she had done for so many years. She lets her children make their plans, and she then figures out how she can integrate herself into them. She's always welcome, and her celebrations may be with one part of the family, two separate celebrations, or combined. She, like all of us, has learned to give up control of the situation and decide for herself how to fit in.

My first Thanksgiving as a widow, I suffered from panic attacks. I let my kids know, and they were receptive to my news. Do you know how hard that was to admit to my kids? It was excruciatingly painful, yet they were both caring and compassionate. Telling them was painful but freeing. As our celebration that year was winding down, my son and I locked eyes, and he knew that it was time for me to leave. He put his arm around me, and I started crying. Everyone helped me get packed up and ready to go home. I was never ashamed or embarrassed, and—frankly—I was proud of myself that I was able to stay so long at the gathering.

Other Janda Sisters were able to make plans with their children and didn't wait to be asked to a celebration. They were able to celebrate at their own houses and invite their families over. Hosting in your own house can be overwhelming, but it also controls the environment. If you have to step away due to grief, it's not so obvious. However, even if family members bring dishes, holidays and parties involve a lot of planning. Ask yourself, are you up for that?

Then there is the set-up, cooking, and baking, both beforehand and on the day of the celebration. To top it off, cleanup heads the top of the list after a tasty meal has been eaten, and exhaustion may set in. Remember how much energy it requires to host a gathering? The Janda Sisters who hosted had their family members bring food, as well as help with the cleanup. I found it easier to attend the holiday at a different house, and to leave when necessary.

SET A TIMEFRAME

Plan to give yourself periodic self-checks and potential time limits for your presence at the celebration. It's okay if you are the first one to leave. Honor yourself and be in tune with your needs. The others at the gathering will understand. You don't have to stay until the last person leaves the home. Many widows are highly stressed, and they don't have enough energy for that. They know how long they will last, and they tell the hostess of their personal need to honor their time frame. Families are incredibly understanding and want to help however they can. I knew my MAX time was three hours, and if I had to leave earlier I would.

KNOW YOUR LIMITATIONS

What can you handle? Is the party too large? Too many unexpected guests? People you don't know? Too far to travel? If you are uncomfortable, it's okay to decline. Put your mental health above all else—do not show up due to obligation.

Looking back at my first Thanksgiving as a widow, I wish I would have had the strength to decline the invitation. I definitely wanted to be with my kids and celebrate. However, the blending of the families was extremely hard on me. I was trying to rise above, even though a year later I was not quite ready. I learned to honor my limitations, because when I didn't, I took a step backward. In time, I grew back my strength and power—but it took quite a while.

I think blending the holiday was hard for me, as I wasn't ready to be in a celebratory mood. My family and extended family gathered in the tradition of celebration: laughter, good food, spirits, and sharing stories. And I wasn't ready. I was forcing myself to be happy, forcing myself to interact, and forcing myself to be there. I thought I was strong enough, but I wasn't.

Looking back, I pushed myself too much. I was torn between wanting to be with my kids and wanting to stay home. I love my kids so much, so that decision won out—but it wasn't the best choice for me. I wasn't happy. I wish I would've taken a step back, and not gone to the celebrations. It has taken me a good three years to truly feel happiness: a good three years to want to gather with a group of people, even though these were my family members. I didn't want to be the sad, empty person in the crowd—but I was. I have learned how to set boundaries and take care of myself. I have learned to say "no" and to decline invitations.

I wish I would've sat quietly and thought about what I was getting into. I wish I would've meditated and asked my Guides for guidance. What would be best for me? I wish I would've taken the time to recognize and honor my feelings and insecurities instead of just doing "what I should do." I know my family would not have questioned me if I didn't come to the holiday celebrations, but I felt obligated. I have learned, from that year, to honor my truth and what is best for me. I have learned to say no; I found out I didn't have to always say yes.

START NEW TRADITIONS: "NEW YEAR'S DAY"

This can be done for yourself, personally. One Janda Sister lights a candle at Thanksgiving, and it burns until January 1. She is making

"A CELEBRATION" TIME?

and creating new memories and honoring the passing of her husband. She speaks freely to her husband whenever she lights and blows out the candle, and she keeps the connection up with him. Another Janda Sister writes a message and then burns it. She sends it to her loved one in Heaven. As I mentioned previously, I adopted the tradition of creating a Gratitude Jar to read my entries from and give thanks every New Year's Day for all of the great things in my life—large and small—and for living a life of gratitude. By starting new traditions, you can honor the people who are no longer present in your life, and it is a beautiful way to connect with them.

Tracy and I have come up with new ideas on how to release "what doesn't serve us." We gather pinecones and have a fire ritual of releasing. We have done this on New Year's Eve, when we are at the beach, or when we just feel stuck in our lives. We take slips of paper and write down all the things we want to release from our lives and stuff them into the pinecone. We then start a fire, and Tracy usually says a spiritual cleansing prayer before we put our pinecones in the burning fire. It is very satisfying to see these worries burn and drift away with the smoke.

I've also started a new tradition with the pups since Carl died. I am usually very careful about the food they consume. However, now whenever there is a holiday celebration, I use the food to give them a special meal of what I have dined on. I must tell you: they embrace and love this new tradition. I don't give them any sweets from the regular dinner, but I do pick up some healthy frosted treats at the holistic pet store in my area. They definitely love to party.

Tracy and I now take two annual trips to the Oregon Coast—we make our own holiday. We stay in a gorgeous beach house that one of my friends owns. We unplug from reality, take time for ourselves, and do what brings us joy. Whether it be walking up and down the shoreline, building a fire and making s'mores, or shopping in the coastal town, it's our own thing. The puppies also benefit from these trips, and joyfully partake in herding seagulls and crows as they gallivant through the sand. My doggies are not water dogs: they never run in the water or surf.

Tracy and I also get together every other week. We're such good friends, and we use this time to help us heal, grow, celebrate our accomplishments, and just to enjoy our friendship. Sometimes celebrations are warranted more often than annually. Our biweekly outings usually involve an adult beverage in the form of a martini, reading our tarot cards, and a tasty dinner. We've started taking fun "fieldtrips" when we get together. We discuss local events and make a day of it with our new adventures. Many people tell me that "everybody needs a Tracy."

"MOST WONDERFUL TIME OF THE YEAR"? JANDA SISTERS' SUGGESTIONS FOR WIDOWS' FAMILY AND FRIENDS

The group also had suggestions for family and friends. Check in with them during the holidays. Be in tune with their grief; there are no timelines for grieving, and it will never be done. It helps to remember that grief is on the inside, and mourning is on the outside.

Grief always involves internal thoughts and feelings that we have when our loved one dies. Think of grief as a receptacle that holds all of your experiences, thoughts, and feelings about your loved one. It keeps swirling and percolating around in your body, and it never stops letting its presence be known.

Mourning is what others see you do. Crying. Expressing your thoughts and feelings. Praying. Writing letters to your loved ones. Chatting with them as if they were there. Celebrating and remembering anniversary dates, holidays, and other important milestones. And honoring your deceased loved ones at the same time.

"A DAY WITHOUT" YOU: COPING ON CHEERLESS ANNIVERSARIES AND BIRTHDAYS

Any anniversary after your loved one passes comes loaded with extra emotion. Wedding anniversaries, birthdays, the anniversary of their passing: each of these hits like a ton of bricks and reminds you of what you've lost.

SPIRIT BOX #22: BIRTHDAY BLUES, BUT ALWAYS AROUND

"Kare Kare, you used to enjoy celebrating birthdays. But now, not so much. Why?"

"Dad, since you died, it breaks my heart not to be celebrating with you. It brings me feelings of longing for and loss of what will never be again."

"We haven't left you, Sweetheart. You can feel us, but not see us. We speak to you, and you hear. We leave you signs, and you notice them. We are the wind that blows the hair from your face, and the music on the radio that soothes your soul; we are with you forever. We're but a thought away. Mom and I must leave you and your readers now, but remember: call to us, or think of us; we'll be by your side. You are so beautiful. Thank you for all you've done for us."

On the anniversary date of her husband's passing, a fellow widow put pen to paper and wrote about what she'd experienced during the first year after his death and how it had affected her. I plan on doing the same. She sealed this in an envelope to read the following year. I've gained so much wisdom from others walking the same road. They each have a special way of honoring their loved ones, and they always choose the one perfect for themselves.

As I write this book, three wedding anniversaries have passed since my husband left, and I have handled them all differently.

ANNIVERSARY #1 SINCE MY BONO DIED: 12/31/20

During our first wedding anniversary apart, I was steeped in grief. My pain was raw, fresh, and suffocating—as the occasion was occurring seven weeks after he died. I was not in a celebratory mood, and I couldn't fathom being around anyone. I actually wanted to crawl into a fetal position and die. At this point in time, I found such comfort and security in my bed, and I welcomed sleep and naps. That was one place where I could be free from the unrelenting pain—at least until I awoke and remembered my situation.

Covid had hit hard, and restaurants were open for takeout or outside dining. There is a wonderful restaurant in our area, Di Carli, that serves delicious takeout food from a set menu. My hubby and I would dine at this exquisite restaurant for special occasions.

I ordered two dinners to go, as I could eat one the next night. I remember something with homemade pasta was an option, as well as a crisp Caesar salad and dessert. It was a decadent dinner, and it would be perfect for me to eat while looking at the framed photo of Bono on my table and chatting with him.

As I sat at the table, a multitude of emotions engulfed me. I did cry through a lot of the meal, but I was also overcome with the love that we shared. This was at a time when I could feel his presence strongly, which was comforting while I celebrated our marriage. I was always amazed at the abundance of tears that I could cry daily, only to start over again the next day. I'd thought, "Surely, I will run out."—but that never happened.

I know that if I had asked friends over, I would've been a sobbing mess and wouldn't have been in a celebratory mood. I learned self-preservation early on, and I knew how to take care of myself. I knew that if I'd reached out to others, I would've been invited in and taken care of. However, I didn't desire such hospitality. I was in the early stages of grief—before I began to understand it—and I needed to be alone. The way I celebrated our anniversary was perfect.

ANNIVERSARY #2 SINCE MY BONO DIED: 12/31/21

On our second anniversary since his passing, I invited my Janda Sisters, Nurse Beth, and Vivi to celebrate Carl at a luncheon. It was a small gathering of supportive friends who were experiencing their own trying times during this season of festivities. We talked about Bono, our lives without our loved ones, and welcomed the new year.

It was festive, but it was very low key and done during the afternoon. Restaurants had now reopened, but I still couldn't comfortably go out at night. Yet, this way of celebrating—with a small number of friends—was my choice, and it was ideal. It had taken me a year before I could celebrate with others, and even then, I kept the number of invites to a minimum.

ANNIVERSARY #3 SINCE MY BONO DIED: 12/31/22

When the third anniversary date rolled around, I was starting to get my power back and there were more glimpses of my old self. I didn't want to go anywhere. I wanted to stay home, have a couple of friends over, have a buffet style dinner, and drink martinis.

That is exactly what I did. We shared stories about Bono, and our favorite memories. This anniversary had the most celebratory "feel" to it, and I attribute this to "time." Grief is not ever going away, but I was getting better at managing it.

As I look back from the first year (when I could hardly make decisions and wanted to be alone), to the second year (tentatively going out with some friends), and to now (experiencing fun, laughter, and joy when we celebrated), this third celebration definitely felt the best.

SPIRIT BOX #23: BONO'S BIRTHDAY BALLOONS

"Honey! Do you remember when we celebrated your sixtieth birthday? I brought sixty balloons for you and filled the living room with them. I remember the surprise on your face. I also picked up your favorite cake, German Chocolate, from the Beaverton Bakery. We had so many of our friends over, delightful food, and it was a party full of love and celebration of YOU, my wonderful, crazy woman. I was so overjoyed to honor and celebrate you."

FACEBOOK POST

DECEMBER 12, 2021

I try to put up light and fun posts, but I think this one, once again, will tear my heart out. Dag nabbit.

I tried to ignore something, [but I] have been told to share this with you numerous times. Previously, I was an extroverted, though private, person. I loved parties, gathering in large groups, outings, and being surrounded by friends. Once Bono died, my brain turned to mush—I turned inward for my survival. It was hard for me to see people because I could see my pain in their eyes. I couldn't remember promises I made, conversations I had, [or] decisions I made. One of my most challenging aspects was [that] I started having panic attacks. Are you kidding me? I could handle anything and take on the world. I survived two failed marriages [and] a brush with suicide, and now death and grief were going to take me down?

On Thanksgiving, I did pretty well for a few hours. We were combining families, and I was adjusting. As things were winding down, my son looked at me and could see in my eyes that I was not doing well. He put his arm around me, and I just cried. He knew I had to leave, and everyone was very kind and understanding.

I believe I am supposed to share this with you, as you may need safety nets. You may not have panic attacks, but [you might still] need something in place with your friends and family to help you out. At a gathering for my hubby's day of death, Nurse Beth wanted me to have a word to say so that she would know I needed help. People are always willing to help, love, and protect each other. We just have to reach out and be honest and vulnerable so [that] they can help. Heaven knows, I have.

I returned to Beaverton Florist after a year-plus absence. I could barely walk through those doors, even though I know and love many of the ladies. Sure, I cried when I went in, but they understood. However, I cleared that hurdle and can walk in there now. Grief presents mountains that we have to conquer. They knew I was going to my widows' club luncheon and provided beautiful roses for us. I have a friend who gave me a new mantra— "I am doing the best I can." I know you are too.

Forever in Touch:
Unbroken Connection and Loving Encounters with Bono

- I was nervous about celebrating Thanksgiving. It was the first time mixing the two families together, and I had anxiety. I knew Bono stayed with me all day, and at the end of the day, I saw his fleeting shadow during the celebration.

- I was fearful of getting the COVID-19 shot—I hate needles, and I didn't want to experience any potential side effects. I was telling my husband how much I needed to hold and feel him. He put the song "Hold Me Now" into my head.

chapter 24
"YOU ARE SO BEAUTIFUL"

A "Celebration" Of Life

I don't like funerals. They are too full of death. It's not the passing that's important; it's the impact that the person had while they were still alive. With this in mind, I began planning Bono's Celebration of Life.

SPIRIT BOX #24: "IT'S MY PARTY"

"I know I was so excited to attend."

Although my husband passed in November 2020, I was unable to hold a memorial for him until the summer of 2022. I kept waiting for

Covid restrictions to lift so that we could gather without masks, partake in good food, and have a celebratory celebration.

Becky was my eyes and ears during the planning stages. I told her what I'd envisioned, and she helped me to create that vision. Unbelievable. It was *still* hard for me to make decisions and to retain info in my brain. At the first meeting with the minister at my church, we talked through everything and then went out to my car. Becky told me "What she'd heard" to make sure that it was accurate. I jotted down more notes in my notepad to help me.

Many people helped to create this Celebration of life. I was in constant contact with my minister, David, and he had to deal with a fragile, stressed, and grieving widow. I asked my friends for help. I learned to ask for help. This had been so hard for me to do initially when Bono had died, as I'd seen it as a sign of weakness. I later found out that people WANT to dive in and help. They truly want to help with the process.

I asked Vivi to create a video that captured Bono's life. The final product was beautiful, and it still brings me to tears when I watch his magnificent life unfold. I revel in the pictures of the life we created with the kids and our love and adventures. I'd go back and forth with her—change this picture here, different song there please, and so on—and it came out perfectly. My husband has sent me many songs to let me know that he's always with me. Many of those songs were playing while friends filed into the church, just as they've been throughout this book.

Jan, Ruth, and Becky created a standing "Memorial Board" and displayed key items on the table around it. Bono had had a rich, full life. People saw him variously as Musician, Doctor, Husband, and Dragon Boat Champ Rower: they were all getting the true picture of this man.

My husband had a myriad of designer, Disney, and spectacular ties. Linda displayed them on a table, and she gave ties to people who wanted them. It was so heartwarming to see people come up to me after the service with his ties on. One friend took a picture of one of the ties displayed at her home in an altar with the picture of Bono from the service. This man had an impact on so many people in his life.

My husband was a foodie. A buffet of Indian food was served—with some of his favorite dishes ready for the taking. Mom, Dad, and I had become long-time friends with another family who ran an Indian restaurant. They saw me through the deaths of the three most important people in my life, and they kindly catered this event for my husband.

At the service, I spoke for over an hour. I wanted to honor my husband, and to let people know all that he'd done with his life. People were able to hear our stories, and to see my hubby in a new light. I'd framed a picture of Bono when he'd attended PCC at the same time as I did—but we'd never met then. This was displayed in the front of the church.

At the same time, I didn't want a guest book for people to sign, or for me to look at their names in years later. Becky and her husband, John, distributed papers and pens when people entered the church, on which they were to write their favorite memory, story, or anything they wanted to about Doc. Afterward, they could put those in the basket under the photo of Carl.

My longest friend, Todd, whom I've known since I was five, and another friend whom I've known since middle school, Debbie, passed out the programs as people entered the hall. Todd and I had met at the church where the service was being held way back in kindergarten.

It took a HUGE TRIBE of friends to help me with this memorial, not to mention all of the people who helped set up beforehand and take down and clean up afterward. No one wanted me to worry or fret—they just wanted me to be in the moment while honoring my husband.

A large portion of my eulogy below consists of stories about and attributes of Bono and our relationship, as well as his life with my family, friends, and all our loves. If you've heard enough about the man, the myth, the legend that was my husband, and if you want to skip past it, I won't fault you for that. However, reading it may remind you that, while you can hear many different parts of stories and pieces of information about a human being at various times, hearing them all together better illustrates that the person's whole is greater than the sum of their parts.

MY EULOGY FOR MY HUSBAND: "YOU ARE THE SUNSHINE OF MY LIFE"

First of all, I want to thank you all for being here to honor my beloved husband and show your love and support for our family. Just having you in the room shows how much Bono touched parts of your lives, whether you knew him or learned from him from me. We are all grateful.

Where is Terri? Terri, stand up. I want to thank you for releasing me from the confines of brevity. I have waited so long to honor my husband. I have a lot to say.

Did you enjoy the music upon entering the sanctuary? These are some of the songs that my husband has brought me since he passed. Since Carl died, he has contacted me in a variety of ways. I have seen him as an apparition many times, and he looks like he did when we met—vigorous and handsome as hell. He speaks to me, sends me music, and gives me full body chills. He still has his sense of humor. A couple of times, I was extremely exhausted, and he put the song "The Old Gray Mare" into my head, which made me smile through my fatigue.

Secondly, it seems that, since my husband died, my language has gotten a little saltier. If something slips out, I apologize in advance. I might call upon Jesus today or drop the F-bomb. It's like a burp; it just comes out. Give me grace. Lastly, this is audience participation. As a retired schoolteacher, I'm not used to a quiet audience. You may call out or participate. I'm half-deaf, though, so make sure your voice is heard.

"YOU ARE SO BEAUTIFUL"

This is my church where I grew up, was baptized, and in which I have a friend, Todd, whom I met at around five years of age and who is here today celebrating my husband's legacy. It's the church where I married my first husband, and where I'll honor my last husband.

I've always hated the award shows where people would thank all of those who helped them on their travels. Now I see why they did that. Their hearts were full of gratitude, and it had to be expressed. Bear with me, as I want to thank my team that has helped. They helped me create my vision, as I still have trouble making decisions, and we talked through things to make this the most beautiful service for Bono. Do me a favor, I know that you can't count some of these people as there are many from online, but would you keep track of everyone I mention?

Moral support—my children and family members. All of you here, you are lifting me up and holding me in love and light. My Facebook friends who always lent encouragement when I had nothing left to give. No one ever gave up on me. All of you listed in the other categories also fall into Moral Support. My friends who listened to me and let me cry: Nurse Beth, Victoria and Nick, Todd, Jill from high school, Marilyn, Terri, Jan, my Janda Sisters, Becky, Cindy Sue, Tracy, Toni, Vivi, Michael, Dylan, and Pookie.

The worker bees—the people who helped with set-up on Friday and some added helpers for take down on Saturday. Farley Cat, Becky and John, Deanna and Wayne, Elis, Jody and Scott, Mike and Nadine, Linda, Tracy, Debbie, and my Indian family—who are all there in a heartbeat to support me. There are about ten of them here today. Also, of course, I want to thank Victoria, Nick, and the love of his life, Leah.

Wait, there's more.

Then there was the minister, Poor David. He had to deal with an anxious, grieving widow, and I am not an easy person at times. I thank the AV Crew who are creating a video for me, and Chad with his mad skills on the piano.

Jyoti, my sissy, who has catered this event and who has tried to make the arrangements as easy as possible for me in order to take away the stress of having everything work. Please enjoy the food that was created with love after the service. If I missed anyone, my deepest apologies. Did you count and figure out how many helped with this event? Lots.

Now, we may begin.

This man. This man. He died too soon. He did everything right. He lived a healthy lifestyle, exercised almost daily swinging bells, and this major meat eater became a vegetarian for his health. He'd had fun with his friends playing poker and playing in the band. Yet, he was taken away too soon, and is missed incredibly.

You all know my husband is here, taking this in, with that big ole grin on his face—holding me up as I talk and always supporting me. His love and support have never wavered. The Veil is very thin, and he reaches out to me all the time. I understand he has also visited some of you, and I am glad that you have shared your stories with me. He continues to be incredible in death. Although we know his Spiritual form, he is not dead, but rather fully alive and vibrant.

My husband never had a chance once we met. I was his type, and he loved my eyes and my ability to cook. We had a love that not many will experience, which is baffling to me. We had total and complete love for each other. We both cherished and took care of each other. I know my family felt he spoiled me, and he did. No argument there—but I reciprocated in kind. I took care of him as much as he took care of me. I can honestly say that I changed a lightbulb once in the twenty-six years that we were together. I only did that because he was out of town, and I couldn't see in the closet.

Bono was my type: tall, dark, and handsome. Those eyes. Look at those eyes. How could I *not* fall head over heels for this man? And think of his grin, zest for life, and laughter—I was putty in his hands.

"YOU ARE SO BEAUTIFUL"

My mom was the one who introduced us. If you knew my mom, she was relentless, and would never give up. She was like a dog with a bone. She had seen my chiro adjust my neck, and was aghast. She kept telling me to go see her chiro. Doc was having a toy drive for a free evaluation. I was poor at the time, and I brought a very cheap toy into his clinic for my appointment. I was embarrassed with my toy, but it was the best I could do.

I'll never forget the moment I walked into his office. I turned to look at him, and he at me. We both froze. I just uttered "hi," and he said the same. I could feel the energy between us. I've NEVER felt this before—it was electrifying and sensational. We just stared at each other and didn't move. I finally broke the spell and threw the toy quickly under his tree. I did not know that my future husband was a "kid at heart" and loved toys. He sat down next to me, took the toy from under the tree, and admired it. I truly was embarrassed, but that dissipated.

He became my doctor, and I his patient. He had a girlfriend, and I had a boyfriend. We were both respectful of those relationships, but—whenever I was in his office—we could not negate our mutual attraction. I remember asking him why he didn't marry his girlfriend, and he replied, "Why ruin a good thing?" I was shocked by his answer. I couldn't have known he'd been married before, and it must have left a bad taste in his mouth.

Our relationship began as a friendship. Although we were dating other people, he came over to hang out at the house. My two children, Nick and Victoria—who were three and eight at the time—were in the house, as well as my girlfriend, Vivi. We'd all cook together, and Bono and I would go play racquetball. He never won a match—ever. He was too tall. He was a good foot taller than me, and I could get the ball down really close to the ground. We were both highly competitive, and I enjoyed beating this big, tall, handsome doctor.

Eventually, I broke up with my boyfriend. When I was at Bono's office, I lay down on the adjusting table, eyes closed. He asked me about "Rob," and I told him that we'd broken up. A single tear ran down my face, and he gently wiped it away. It was such a tender moment that it is etched in my memory. Once he wiped that tear from my face, we never stopped touching. I was not privy to how he broke up with his girlfriend.

I wonder if my husband knew what he was getting into. We started dating, and the kids came along with the territory—my kids can be quite outspoken and have no filters. Both of my children had strong personalities, and there were two ex-husbands in the background. I'm surprised he didn't run for the hills. I explained to my husband early on that blood is thicker than water, and that my kids always come first. He accepted this. What a wild ride our family had.

He took on the role of "father" in the family. Not only was he there for me, but he was always present for my children. Nick was a Boy Scout, who became an Eagle Scout, and Bono became part of the troop. He was gladly accepted among Nick's friends and the other parents. They used to go on campouts. Bono returned from one campout and let me know that Nick would scream in his sleep while camping. He was still asleep but screaming. Bono was only startled once and came running, and later on he just let it run its course and let Nick scream.

All my family eats off each other's plates—even my parents and sister. If we were in a restaurant, we would sample the other person's dish and it was no big deal. We still do this to this day. This was new for Bono, and he started sampling with gusto. I remember when he took a bite of my hamburger and only about a quarter of it was left. I just sat there stunned. We had etiquette; it was a small sample, and he had to learn.

Once, when we were eating at home, Bono had prepared a shrimp and pasta dish for the kids and me. I was saving some shrimp, and—out of the corner of my eye—I could see my son's fork coming for my plate. Since we were eating the same food, I was not giving up my coveted shrimp. The dining room chairs were on wheels, and Nick and I struggled over my food. We were pushing each other around the kitchen, struggling with each other, and Carl just stared at us. Yet, he stayed. I think we left him speechless many times.

Victoria was another story. She may have seemed quiet growing up, but she had her definite opinions and let them be known. She'd ride him around like a horsey, but, thankfully, she didn't kick him. One time, he was driving with her, and she matter-of-factly told him:

"You're not the boss of me."

My husband was not a curser, but he told her to "knock that shit off."

I think that was the last of that.

Once, when Carl came out to leave, Victoria looked at him aghast, and said (with quite the attitude):

"You're not wearing that outfit, are you?"

Poor Bono never had a chance against the three of us. I don't remember if he wore that outfit or if he changed.

He would drive Victoria to school, and they would stop at Starbucks occasionally and get her a crumbly coffee cake. He always remarked that a great deal was left on the table and less in Binky's mouth. Binks loved her coffee cake. I was not the only one in this package deal—he had an instant family. Yet, he loved them like they were his own. There was no second guessing that, and he called them his son and his daughter. He loved and was proud of his family. Even though he called me "Crazy Woman," I knew he loved me with every breath.

We grew together as a family, and we faced obstacles but always overcame them. I think that one of the reasons that Bono and I had such a loving relationship is that we were friends first. We both truly loved, cherished, honored, and appreciated each other. Our love could be felt by others. We took care of each other, and we were always attentive to each other's needs.

Bono was the first of my husbands to accept me for who I was. He didn't try to control me or stifle my voice, and he accepted all my frailties and quirkiness—he let me be me. He was the only man who I received both my mother's and father's blessings to marry. I felt so honored to be his wife. We were so devoted to each other. I could tell you story upon story of what he'd do for me, but then you would know how much I was spoiled. He rarely told me no.

Would you say that my husband was adventurous? I sure would. He introduced me to body shots. We would belly-up to the bar at the Gypsy and take body shots off each other. It was really fun, and you may want to try it.

He introduced me to Dragon Boats and to the phrase "paddle till you puke." Those were such fun days on the river, paddling against different teams in different divisions. Bono sat in the back of the boat, and his reach was so long that he could reach two benches in front of him to stroke the water. I swear, he was the one driving from the back of the boat. He was a freaking beast. In all the time we were together, he was constantly surprising me. He studied and learned Italian for when we were to travel to Italy—it was beautiful hearing him say those words.

He decided that he was going to get his motorcycle license, and he ended up buying a Harley. He would ride his Harley out to school, and stride upstairs in his leathers, holding his helmet out in front of him. The kids were always happy to see him, and I wanted to jump on the back of the motorcycle and leave with him.

We cooked side by side in the kitchen, and those were some of my favorite times together. He became quite the grill master, and we ate many racks of ribs until he perfected his recipe. Remember, Binks, all those ribs we ate? He loved when I cooked Indian food, and I liked when he cooked Thai. He could never understand why Victoria and

"YOU ARE SO BEAUTIFUL"

I would make 300 Christmas cookies and give them away. He always got more than his fair share, and then he started joining us in making cookies. "Fruitcake cookies" were his specialty—which was odd, as I was the only one in the family who liked fruitcake—and most people loved his cookies.

He was always striving to become a better person. He kept talking to me about the need for a scoliosis doctor in the area. He became a Clear Certified Doctor for non-surgical treatment for scoliosis—the only one on the west coast—and he had patients fly in from Hawaii and come up from Palm Springs to seek his services.

I used to get migraines and had an S-curve in my neck—you are supposed to have a C-curve. My migraines were so painful that I would go to St. V's and get shots of Demerol for the pain. He put the correct curve in my neck, and I became migraine free.

Did he stop there? No. He turned part of his office into a kettlebell gym and became a StrongFirst® Kettlebell Instructor. He taught daily classes, and he incorporated the bells into his patients' therapy.

Wait. There's more. He joined a band. Tracy and I became his groupies, and we'd follow him from bar to bar. Later, he started his own band, and he enjoyed his Friday nights with his bandmates.

My husband was FREAKING AMAZING. He was always a fun spirit, full of adventures, and constantly growing and learning. Yet, he was the most tender and humble man I knew. He was always so patient and kind to the kids and me, and never raised his voice; he only lifted us up and showered us with love and caring.

You have a part now. Can you say, "you bet"?

Was I spoiled? You bet. Did I find unconditional love and acceptance? You bet. Did he accept me as a flawed human and continue to love me? You bet. We were a perfect match.

I was honored to be called "Crazy Woman" and "The Wife." His death crushed me—my soul died with him. I didn't care if I lived or died, and—quite frankly—I preferred to die. However, once again, he reached out from behind the Veil to contact me and spur me on to live. I was surviving on coffee, tequila, and chocolate. Not quite the breakfast of champions.

His spirit was strong on this Earth, and [his Spiritual form] remained so after he died. I know he is proud of me and the kids. I know he is proud that—through my grief—I have embarked on a journey of self-discovery and constantly learning new things, just as he had done. I know he is proud that I have written a book about grief and trauma, and that I have helped other people along the way. I know he is especially proud that I made the decision to live.

I know that our love will never die, and that he waits for me to come Home. When my days are done, I will gladly take his hand and go Home with him. Until then, he will live in my memories and in all the ways that he continues to contact and comfort me. He has never left my side. I love you, husband, more than you could ever imagine.

MY HUSBAND'S OBITUARY:
Dr. Carl Louis Bonofiglio Jr.

(Similar words were written in the pamphlet handed out at his Celebration of Life)

Dr. Carl passed quietly at home in Beaverton, Oregon, of a heart condition on November 8, 2020.

Carl was born Dec. 8, 1952, in Portland, and was the youngest of three children. He was surrounded by a large extended family of aunts, uncles, cousins, and later nieces and nephews.

Born with a zest for life and laughter, Carl always greeted people with a big smile and generosity. He had a knack for teasing laughter out of anyone and was often a mentor to clients in need. Towering over most, this gentle giant left an impression on everyone he'd meet.

Music was Carl's soul song. Playing in music groups in Portland and San Francisco, he became proficient as a bass guitarist, drummer, saxophonist, and pianist. Living in the Pacific Northwest, Carl was fond of the outdoors, enjoying fly fishing, skiing, cycling and Dragon Boat Racing through the seasons.

After graduating from Cleveland Chiropractic College in Los Angeles, California, in 1987 with a B.S. in Human Biology and a Doctor of Chiropractic degree, he returned to Portland to open a clinic in Beaverton.

One day, a client came into the clinic seeking treatment and the sparks flew. That day, he met the love of his life, Karen, who soon became his wife. He also became a loving father and mentor to a son, Nickolas, and daughter, Victoria, whom he loved as his own.

Carl is loved by his wife, Karen Bonofiglio, children, son, Nickolas, and daughter, Victoria Koopman; brother Ralph Bonofiglio, and sister, Esther Brown, as well as many other family members and friends.

He is deeply missed and cherished in all our hearts. A good man, gone too soon.

FACEBOOK POST
JULY 6, 2021

"Those Were the Days" plays in the background

Bono and I, when we first connected—be still my heart.

I have been thinking about Doc's "Celebration of Life." I talked with my minister yesterday, as the church just reopened with masks and safety precautions. I am going to wait for his celebration so that people don't have to wear masks and are able to mingle.

We loved to entertain and throw parties. I want to honor him with a huge party/celebration, as that is what he would want—everyone happy and having a good time. We will have a wonderful service; then fun, friends, music, food, and beverages. It seems as though his celebration will be more toward Fall.

It always bothered him when I cried. I don't think I can have this celebration without shedding some tears. However, he may be used to them by now. I will keep you posted when I know the date to honor my hubby.

Forever in Touch:
Unbroken Connection and Loving Encounters with Bono

- I saw a flash of Bono getting out of his car, and he was wearing his red coat. He had a big grin on his face as he walked toward the house. I love seeing him in apparition form.

- While lying in bed, I told Bono I missed feeling him. He gave me body chills later, and he was looking down on me while I lay there. I wondered what it would be like to kiss him. I urgently and suddenly had a vision/memory of Bono and I kissing when we first dated. We were at a Thai restaurant, and we were standing around waiting for another couple. Bono and I turned to each other and had a very long and tender kiss. When we stopped, one of the customers applauded our kiss. I'm not sure that my husband wants me to kiss him, but rather he wanted me to remember that that kiss was always memorable.

chapter 25
GRIEF IS THE PRICE OF LOVE

A Heart That Is Broken Is a Heart That Has Been "Faithfully" In Love

"HEART AND SOUL": WHOEVER DIES LAST... HAS A LOT OF GROWING TO DO

If I could tell you anything, it would be that no matter how you envision or plan, your life can change in an instant—beautifully or horrifically. In the grand scheme of things, it's not what happened at that moment that is important, but your journey afterward. You are probably thinking, "I know, Karen, I know. You are not telling me anything new." Until you have this experience, however, you will not know what it does to your heart and soul. I am not the only one who will experience significant loss, and it grieves me to know that others will also walk this road. If you are in a loving relationship, one of you will probably leave first—and the person left behind will experience extreme trauma and suffering.

Thus, the title of my book: *Whoever Dies First…Wins*. The person who left/died got off easy; the person left behind has lessons to be learned regarding loss, grief, and trauma. These are not exactly wonderful experiences, but they're lessons, nonetheless. How will you handle those lessons? I moved beyond "coffee, tequila, and chocolate" to create a beautiful life.

Was it easy? HELL NO. I wanted to die so many times and have the pain end, but I rose up continually. I didn't really think about it at the time, but I just kept moving forward and rejoining life. I found love. I found beauty. I found a depth for spirituality that I thought I would never experience. People have told me that I am an "abnormally happy person," and it has served me well the sixty-seven years I've been on this planet. Other people have told me that I "need to be more cynical." No, I am good. I will live looking through the lenses of my Pollyanna Glasses until my last breath. I will always look for the lesson in the situation and embrace LOVE.

BONO'S BLESSING

My husband and I experienced a love that is not found too often. We adored, cherished, and supported each other. He was my everything, and I was his. Early on, after his death, I was lying on his jammies and sobbing. I was so angry with him. Why did you leave me? Why did you go? This was "our time" now. He told me, "for your growth," which made me even angrier. I could still grow with him here—little did I know how prophetic his words were.

Had he not passed, I would not have experienced all that I have these past few years. I have grown incredibly: spiritually, psychically, empathetically, in tune with others, deeper love and friendships, more appreciation for everything, and in tune with my emotions. Would I trade it all to have him back? In a heartbeat. Yet, my pain and vulnerability have brought me new friends and more revelations—some painful and some not. People have loved and supported me—I was lifted up in my darkest days. And I survived and decided to live.

With great love comes great loss. Many of you will take this walk. Grieve in your own way. Listen to your heart; go where it leads. I never in a million years would have expressed my spirituality or vulnerability before my loss. However, in doing so, it has been one of my greatest healers. Regardless of how you choose to grieve, just remember it's the journey—mine could've been quite different had I not had support, and I love and appreciate all who've supported me.

Early on, when my husband died, I would've traded all of my spiritual and personal growth to have him back. To touch him again. To hear his voice and laugh. To be held and cherished. To take care of him and be taken care of. To live out our lives into our golden years together. To have the life that we put on hold as I took care of my aging parents.

If you were to ask me that now, I don't think I would give the same answer. Even though Bono is on the other side of the Veil, I feel his presence all the time and know that he is near me daily. He is trying to nudge and support me from the Heavenly Realm as I experience my new life. He was correct when he said that he died "for your growth." As angry as that made me, he was absolutely right. I would've never grown as a person like I have had he stayed on this Earth.

FILLING UP THAT GRATITUDE JAR

I have a DEEP APPRECIATION for everything in life: the wind on my face, seeing the Big Dipper in the early morning sky, ice crystals frozen on the grass, the puppies' loving eyes staring into my face—my heart is wide-open and vulnerable. All I want in life is to make a difference and to live the best life I can. I want to eventually go "Home" and hear, "well done." I desire to look back and be proud of my life and the difference I made.

When I taught school, I found it extremely fulfilling. I loved seeing the excitement in children's eyes as they unearthed new discoveries and hearing their innocent comments. I truly loved my calling as an educator, and I wanted to be the best teacher possible. But this new path was rooted in helping humanity, and ultimately in helping them deal with the inevitable: Death.

I could've quickly headed down the road of tequila, coffee, and chocolate and shut down as a person. I promised my husband early on that I wouldn't become an alcoholic or abuse drugs. I have kept my promise, and I've flourished as a soul. Many new people entered my life that I would never have met if he hadn't died. The expression of my soul has grown exponentially.

Do I still have my deep grief? Yes. I still cry daily, but I get up after I fall. I'm crying right now as I write these words. If you're experiencing grief right now, you know how incapacitating it can be. I don't know exactly how you feel; only you know that. Yet, I can relate to the pain, sorrow, and other feelings that accompany profound loss.

LESSONS LEARNED THROUGH GROWTH FROM GRIEF: "DON'T STOP BELIEVING"

You will take your own walk. Take what resonates within your soul from me, and then add your own wisdom. These are some of the most important things that facilitated my healing:

- *I decided to live.* If, and when you make that decision, true healing will begin. I have talked to other widows who also made the decision to live. I woke up one morning and made that choice. That was a turning point in this journey.

- *Although I was taken to my knees, I kept getting up.* Sometimes, I may have spent all day in bed, but little daily steps would propel me on. I learned to be easy on myself and not to push. I listened to my body. If I wanted to rest and be in my jammies all day, I honored that. I learned to say "no." I was stretched too thin in my daily activities, so I learned how to cut back. At first, it was because I didn't have the energy, but later on I did it to preserve my love and appreciation for my life. I slowed down and enjoyed it.

- *I sought help from my friends.* It was SO HARD to ask people to do things for me, as it made me feel weak. My husband had been my "knight in shining armor," and we both had taken care of each other. He could do and fix anything. I decided not to be a weak woman, and I used strength in asking for help. I remember one friend helping me asked me to get a ratchet out of the garage for her. I said, "Sure. What's a ratchet?" I have learned and grown so much in just the few years since my profound loss.

  When I started doing things for myself, I felt extremely proud. I'd raise my arms in the air and yell "Score." I accomplished things I never had before, and it felt good. This was empowering and made me feel more proficient.

- *I surrounded myself with my tribe.* It was painful to join in activities that once brought me joy. I would have a panic attack before entering events, but I eventually made myself go in— very slowly. Everyone always showed up to me in love, didn't care if I was a slobbering mess, and the pain in their eyes turned to kindness and understanding. When Bono and my parents died, I hated seeing the pain in someone's eyes, as it was like looking back into a reflection of myself. Above all, I didn't want to be pitied.

Moving past these fears was essential to my healing process. I slowly allowed myself back to seeing my friends. If I had to cancel at the last minute, people understood. Little by little, I felt more comfortable in acclimating myself back into my social circles, and now I don't give it a second thought. I don't have to have a safe word, plan my escape, or any other strategies of avoidance. I can just enjoy the time with people I care about.

- *When there was a milestone event—like my husband's birthday, death day, my birthday, or our anniversary—I'd invite friends to be with me.* If I stayed home, I would be a slobbering mess. If I went out with friends to honor and celebrate, I was uplifted. Please know that this is what worked for me—you need to find the solution and balance for yourself. I also found that when the second year of his death came, I didn't necessarily want to be out and celebrating. I was happy to stay home with just a couple of friends and honor him. I found out there's no certain way to honor our dead; just the most comfortable way for you.

- *I have a stronger relationship with God, the Archangels, my Birth Angels, my Guides, and all my Heavenly Helpers. I write in my journal daily to my Guides and my husband.* I write questions, and I'm provided with answers. As I moved on into the next year of my husband's death, I started taking classes with Renee Terrill to develop that trait in me. I took classes on "Healing with the Angels" and "Channeling/Mediumship."

People think that I'm lucky to have this connection with the Heavenly Realm. Yet, I'm not special, as we all have this ability. I have embraced it all my life, but it was ignited when Bono died. I sought comfort with God/Divinity and my Heavenly Helpers, and I frequently stop and talk to them during the day.

- *While just trying to make sense of it all, I sought the help of psychic mediums.* My husband and my parents would come forward and give me messages and affirmation of themselves. To hear that they loved me, missed me, and were proud of all I have done and endured made me feel accomplished. I'd done quite a bit with all these losses. For me, talking to a psychic is like a tune up and improves my mental health. There are some charlatans out there, as in any profession, and one must be discerning.
- *I sought counseling.* Talking to someone helped me immensely. Being validated and offered advice was reassuring.
- *My soul was on fire.* While living in complete gratitude, I found it hard to live in my body. I knew that there was so much more to myself than this body, which housed a spectacular being. We are all lights of God, yet we are dimmed once we enter our bodies. I have discussed how our life is full of lessons, and it is how we handle these lessons and what we do with them that is important. I was thrown some major hardballs: the losses of my father, my mother, and my husband in just thirteen months. It truly took me to my knees.

Yet, it taught me to appreciate everything in life. (If I can be candid, I still don't appreciate bugs.) Once I started mindfully connecting to Source and my Heavenly Helpers, I found it difficult to live in my body. It was electrified. I love that feeling. Sometimes, I wondered how my body could hold this fiery spirit which resided in it.

Would I trade all of this to have my husband back? It truly is a tricky question. It was my deepest desire to live out our golden years together. We were going to travel, buy a new house, and live in pure happiness, love, and bliss. We had a special love that not many people have. I was a lucky chick to have him, and he was me. Yes, I would love to have that back and live out my life with him until my days are done.

However, the advancement of my soul wouldn't have happened. I know that he is still with me on my walk Home. His love for me is overwhelming, and he is so proud of what I've accomplished. I am too. I went to Hell, and I came back. On some days, I want him back, and on others, I'm proud of what I've accomplished. My answer will change on any given day.

I don't know where life will lead me, but I have clues. I will make a difference to many people. It fills my heart to overflowing knowing that I've helped someone. Know that I love you as you read my words. I genuinely love all of you reading this book. Know that you are loved.

Namaste,
Karen

SPIRIT BOX #25: BONO REMEMBERS "THE BEST OF TIMES"

"Oh, the day we wed. Such a happy day for us both. Together with all the family and the kids before we joined as husband and wife. We pledged our love to each other, which grew stronger as the days and years flew by. Our undying love.

"Our honeymoon was in Leavenworth, Washington, and we were transported into a snowy, picturesque, winter wonderland. We discovered a magical place to call our own: the sleigh ride in the snow. This sounded so romantic, but snow was thrown over us during the entire ride. Bbbbrrrr. Hot chocolate in the barn took off the chill. I learned to not trust you in the snow after you pushed me down the snowbank. I tried to grab you to have you join me in the tumble, but I wasn't quick enough. Walking hand in hand—arms around each other's waists—we shopped in stores and enjoyed German food and each other. Such a remarkable way to begin our lives together. May it last forever."

PARTING FACEBOOK POSTS: "LET IT BE"

FACEBOOK POST
SEPTEMBER 11, 2021

Ashes to ashes, dust to dust.

Today is the second of my birthday celebrations. The birthday person gets to choose the activity—hiking, archery, or whatever they want—and then break bread in celebration. Today I chose to scatter the ashes of Pops, Mom, and Bono, and we are having more of a commemoration.

The kids, their partners, one of my nieces, and I will be heading west for the scattering, and although Pops, Mom, and Bono are already together in Heaven, they will also rest together here. I imagine my children will scatter my ashes in the same place when my walk on Earth is done.

Not sure if I will be able to respond to your posts…it's going to be an emotional day.

FACEBOOK POST
MAY 28, 2023

In October and November, it will have been four years since Pops passed, and three years since Mom and Bono joined him. These last few years are the hardest I've ever endured, yet my evolution at a soul level has also grown exponentially.

The last few days have been full of pain, suffering, and angst, but I know everything I/we experience is meant to happen. It's for "our growth." We have free choice in how we handle it, but the lessons and trials will still be presented.

Losing my family members changed me. Grief changed me. Grief changes anyone it touches. I'm not the same person I was three years ago. Having an intense and loving relationship with my parents and husband created shared characteristics with those people; now that they're gone, I'm finding out who I am now. I've embraced many new adventures I would've never thought I'd go on, and I've made many new friends in my life and on social media; I treasure all these friendships. I have so much love for everything and everyone in my life, and a deep sense of compassion and gratitude.

I've told my friends countless times that I don't recognize the person I have become. I know they don't understand as I can see it on their faces. My kids have noticed a huge change. They have remarked, "Mom, you are so chill." I have come to appreciate every lesson and blessing in my life. I can find beauty in everything, and in most situations. It doesn't necessarily mean that life is easier, but my perspective is different.

Yet, I yearn to die. I can hardly wait to die—however, we never die, we just leave this existence. Don't say, "Karen, you should not think like that. Embrace life. Start anew. Carl wants you to be happy." Don't "should" on me, and I won't "should" on you. Deal?

If we are still here on this planet, we have not completed our purpose. Will my purpose be complete when I finish my first book, and can I then be released from the confines of my body? I don't think so; I know I have more to do. Will my purpose be done with my second book about grief written for children? I still don't think so. Will my purpose be achieved when I find a new love with someone as I had with Bono? I still think I will remain here.

I always thought I'd die young: at sixty-five – seventy-two-years. Your body's still doing well, and your mind is intact. Nope. I foresee a long life. So, we'll walk this journey together, and laugh, love, feel heartache and pain, live, and learn from each other as our souls grow and expand. Cheers to expansion.

You can accept or reject anything and everything I say.

Isn't that cool about free choice?

Mom just reached out to me, so I know that I have her support and was supposed to write this post. Funny how the universe works.

Complete love for you all—yes, all.

Namaste, Karen

Forever in Touch: Unbroken Connection and Loving Encounters with Bono

- It was hard integrating myself back into my former life. I went to play Mahjong with friends that I've known for years, and it was brutal walking through the front door. I took a deep breath and walked in, and I immediately felt welcomed when my friends embraced me. During the game, I told Bono I was having fun, and he put "Never Ending Song of Love" in my head. He is always by my side.
- While sitting on the concrete bench outside, Bono held me from behind and rocked me as I cried. He now rocks me every morning while I stare at the stars in the dark sky—it is very comforting.

Tears are part of the mending of rips in the psyche where energy has leaked away. The matter is serious, but the worst does not occur—our light is not stolen—for tears make us conscious.

Sometimes a woman says, "I am tired of crying, I want it to stop." But it is her soul that is making tears, and they are her protection. So, she must keep on till the time of need is over.

CLARISSA P. ESTES
(2022: Midwives of the Soul on Facebook.com)

SECTION V

"SHADOWS OF THE NIGHT"

COMMUNICATIONS AND ENCOUNTERS

> *Always remember you are braver than you believe, stronger than you seem, smarter than you think, and loved more than you know.*
>
> —Christopher Robin, A.A. Milne
>
> *The Complete Tales of Winnie-the-Pooh*

SPIRIT BOX #26: "I WILL REMEMBER YOU"

"We, as Spiritual forms, try to make ourselves known to the people we've left behind. We can do things that'll make you think of us, such as putting a special song or memory in your head, leaving signs for you to find, coming to you in dreams, and more. If you decide to visit a medium or a psychic/medium, we can come forward and offer you words of comfort or answer questions.

"Me and the Boys in the Band have also prepared some great songs just for your delight, and I'll be sending those along to you shortly. I'm sure you'll be familiar with many of them.

I bid adieu, for now, to my beautiful bride, and to you readers—for now…but not forever."

DEFINITION DOGGY BOX 10:
WE SEE MORE DOGGIES IN YOUR FUTURE, BUT WE'RE STILL HERE!

All Three Doggies: "For years, Mommy has taken classes on how to access and increase her ability to be a psychic. She even took one from a world-renowned psychic who admonished her for not using her gifts. A psychic uses the abilities of the Clairs. A psychic will be open and honest about the good and bad that may come up in a reading. A true and pure psychic never asks for more money, or tells you a curse, or bad luck will be removed, or a love spell needs to be cast. Such a psychic doesn't want to know your history, why you are there, or anything about you. As they give the reading, listen to them. Ask questions, and you'll usually receive answers. Validate the info that makes sense. A psychic provides clarity and insight to the living.

"A medium acts as a conduit to bridge the gap between the living and dead. A medium communicates with their own Spiritual Guides, or perhaps with an Archangel of their choice, to receive messages from someone who has transitioned in order to bring forth a message. For example, a medium may give you info from you Uncle David or friend Jess who've passed.

"The key difference between psychics and mediums is that a psychic can speak with an individual's deceased loved ones and also channel that person's Spirit Guides, as well as offer guidance on questions that person may have. They "see" different avenues that person may take. (Remember how Mommy was told in the ' Os she'd write a book? That psychic saw this info and shared it with her). A medium speaks with the deceased and acts as a conduit between the person having the reading and those coming through to visit; but they don't access a person's Guides or see future possibilities the way a psychic does. Sometimes, lines blur between types of spiritualists (e.g., a psychic/medium) and their methods, but these are basic descriptions."

Rosie: "Bark! Bark! Bark! Now it is time for us to say so long for now to you readers. Remember, I am the noisy one, and I will continue to be so until Mommy comes home to Heaven. Then, I will run to her furiously, while barking at the top of my lungs. I bid you all a barky adieu. Perhaps we may meet another time."

Mr. Vin: "I'm so glad he's gone, Isabel. Between your howlin' and his barkin', I could hardly get a word in. Maybe it's good I went deaf—I didn't have to hear you. But I do wuv you."

Isabel: "Oh, Vinni, you were just jealous of my fast, long legs, because you had short stubby ones and couldn't keep up with me. I wuv you too, but it is time for us to join Roosevelt and leave. Woof! Woof! We are so glad we had this time with you all."

Appendix I
"OOGUM BOOGUM":

PSYCHIC AND MEDIUM READING EXCERPTS

As you should be aware by now, spirituality, connecting with people who have passed away, and making connections with my Spirit Guides, Birth Angels, and family members, have all been a source of comfort and enlightenment for me throughout my grieving process.

I have included parts of some readings that I've had since my husband transitioned and decided to leave for Heaven. These readings were, and still are, eye-opening for me. My commentary can be found in italics throughout and in the paragraphs after each session.

BEAVERTON PSYCHIC #1: THEA STROM

December 10, 2020 *(a month after my husband had passed)*

Psychic: "There are two males there. His energy is amazing, and he has said 'I am home with everyone else.' Many parties were given, and he was well taken care of.

"His passing was quick and unexpected. It was nothing out of the ordinary—his time to go. There was nothing in his system that hurt him—that was not the cause. He loves Binks and Boy like they were his children.

"He is apologizing to you. Sorry you had to be busy."

Zero to ten with how much I had to do. It's overwhelming. (Bono is slinking behind me.)

"He feels your levels of frustration and anger. He is sorry things were not set up for an easy transition.

"He likes the ideas that are being thrown around financially. He is proud he has a life insurance policy for you."

Bono is optimistic, but I am stuck in my thoughts. What am I going to do now?

"Give it some time. You are going on a rollercoaster ride and will have a lot to deal with. You will figure out your path.

"He acknowledges the milestones and sees that being very gut-wrenching. One of your most challenging to process. Your future will be different, and he is excited. Traveling is in the cards for you. He will make sure you feel his presence. His connection to you is very personal."

We have a sacred connection, and he will not leave me.

"Carl wants you to know that life will be beautiful again. He wants you to be happy. You will find love again. Your soul will grow exponentially, and you will do things you never imagined. It was his time to leave for your expansion."

I've taken bits and pieces of my reading to share with you, the reader. This psychic and I have a lot of history, and she normally wouldn't have talked to someone who had experienced such death and trauma the month before. Yet, she knew that I'd be receptive.

The two males who stepped forward were definitely my husband and father: the two most beloved and prominent people in my life. The closeness and the relationship I'd had with both of these men was incredible.

With regard to Bono apologizing about my anger and frustration, I had a lot to be exasperated about. I had to close his clinic and gym down, sell items, and deal with property management, vendors, creditors, and so on. The list was endless. I had to be on point and show up to work my arse off and get things done with my family's assistance. I made many poor decisions at that time. It's recommended that a grieving person wait a year before making any monumental decisions, and I was doing this as soon as my husband died. It was agonizing, and I let people make decisions for me. Many decisions I would've made differently. I just wanted to crawl into a fetal [position] and lay under all of my blankets and comforters and cry.

I was mad at him for dying. For leaving me with all of this. For leaving me with things I didn't understand and know how to deal with. Mad because he said he would live until he was ninety, and now he was not here. Mad because our life was just beginning all over again and didn't have a chance to take seed and blossom. Promises were not kept. A life we desired was now ripped away from me, and I was the one suffering. He was having a grand time in Heaven.

I am not surprised about there being many celebrations for my husband as most of his family members were already in Heaven.

I am glad that he had a life insurance policy as well, and if you do not have one for your loved ones—get one. They don't need to worry about money at this point in time. I was grateful for his foresight.

As for hearing that life through the holidays would be gut wrenching and a rollercoaster—I was already aware. He passed at one of the worst times of the year to die. Holidays, birthdays, and anniversary dates all rolled into the upcoming two months. Thinking about traveling was foreign to me. We always travel together, so I shoved it out of my mind.

When she told me that he wanted me to be happy, I replied, "then he shouldn't have fucking died." And regarding finding me a new man, I remarked, "Well good luck with that. How can you improve on perfection?" The last thing I wanted in my life was another man.

Even so, these words my husband spoke through the psychic proved to be prophetic.

"CALIFORNIA" PSYCHIC

May 2, 2021

Psychic: "We have predetermined exit points. He left, but you still have a life path left. Their job [*Dad, Mom, and Carl*] is to pass it off to you. Carl is peeking in and wants to come through. He struggled a lot. At the end of his life, things were getting rough for him. He felt the stress. He had cardiac issues. He felt blessed to be with you. She really goes out of her way to help people- (*meaning me*). Did you have a miscarriage? *(I did.)* Your daughter is with him.

"It was very celebratory when he died. I see him clinking glasses with your parents.

"You will have a different relationship, and your husband will find you a partner. *(Why?)* He learned his lessons. The loved ones that remain still have needs to fulfill and should find pleasurable company.

"Have you written any books? You are supposed to write two or three books. Nonfiction. Write a trauma guide—this is part of your life's purpose. Dealing with trauma. It is the magic equation in your life lessons—trauma and grief. It will help others deal with and experience grief. You have duality, Karen—a teacher and a healer. Soulmate in your blueprint.

"You have two Birth Angels and six Spiritual Helpers. Ask a question and get an answer in real time. Meditation is excellent for balancing. Guides are here for help, while family plays another role. Guides help you manifest. You must be clear, consistent, and concise with your choices. Repetitiveness—have clarity with your Guides. Your Guides are for health, healing, trauma, business/financial, and two Native American: pathfinder and ritualistic healer/shaman.

"In three years, you will have another mate. Now Carl does not feel sorry for you. This is part of your life path.

He helps me fulfill my destiny.

"You will help people with their grief. Since this resonates, you know it is true—you know that on a deeper level. You will be of service helping people with grief across all age brackets—three different books with the same theme. They are a launching pad for other things.

"You will have your house in two years.

"Talk in REAL TIME with your Guides. Work on manifestation. Quit wasting time. The clearer the question, the more precise the answer. For example, 'Is Bob Jones the right partner?'

Three years for a guy. The universe does not distinguish between marriages of companionship and marriages of the heart. This is already in your blueprint."

Please keep in mind these excerpts have been edited. This California psychic was one of the absolute best I've had in my life. He gave me direction in my life, and I was so thankful for clarification about my Birth Angels and the types of Guides that were with me. Many years prior, I'd been told I had a huge team of Angels helping me, and how they stepped in when it was their time. This psychic was able to home in on my Guides.

He reiterated what I'd been told by other psychics: [he said] I'd write a few books. I didn't like the time frame he'd given me for finding a house, but it actually happened just when he'd said it would. I was given that info in 2021: in 2023, I purchased my house. As for finding a new soul mate, the jury's still out on that. I have a wonderful, loving relationship with a man, but he can't give me a commitment, so he is obviously not perfect for me. Other men have entered my life, but nothing has rocked my world like Bono. We'll see when this comes to fruition.

He's not the only psychic who suggested I chat with my Heavenly Helpers "in real time." Stopping and finding time to connect with them is very advantageous. Feeling overwhelmed? Ground yourself and talk to them. I've learned to "ask more" as they want to help us.

BEAVERTON PSYCHIC #1: THEA STROM VISIT #2

September 22, 2021

> Psychic: "Your parents are coming in to acknowledge your birthday. 'Happy Birthday.'
>
> "Bono is working as your assistant and scheduler. He is trying to lighten your load, as you have booked yourself too much. He has learned skills on the other side. Don't overthink how you write about him as far as the book is concerned. You have complete creative freedom and full support; let your creative juices flow.
>
> "As for Chris (*my friend who lost his brother*), you are stepping more into a very natural role for you; things are coming full circle."

Through my experiences of loss, I can understand what others are going through. This is one of my incredible blessings—mirroring for others.

> "Why your extreme grief? Guides are answering. There is a clear distinction—this did not happen because of you. Your family had their purpose and plans. It is about how you navigate and adapt to your own experience. You were feeling extreme grief, but now you can experience more joy. The purpose—you've expanded into the whole experience of life. Before, life was pleasant, but your gifts were limited. You have developed in all directions. Now you are helping others. This is the gift.

> (*Husband is talking in the background*) — "You are soulmates. You have added a different aspect and are now closer. He knows you on a deeper level and loves the closeness.
>
> "Someone is falling apart. You are supporting and holding her up emotionally. Gentle support and gratitude. Small things have a ripple effect."

I knew who this psychic was referring to, and she was experiencing a deep depression.

> "Your soul desires more relationships with new souls—Husband wants you to be open to the fact. You don't see the positive of being in a relationship. It would not be giving him up. Be open to the idea there is someone out there who will be a fantastic benefit."

Bono stated that he really loved the scattering of the ashes.

> "Your father—he loves you so much. He knows it is a little overwhelming. He's proud of how you put one foot in front of the other. Truly amazed. None of them (*Dad, Mom, or Bono*) would have wanted all this happening to you—all this loss. Loss after loss after loss. Dad has been watching you and is so proud of you."

I'm surviving.

> "There are a lot of bright moments coming. Ups and down, too, but life will be making sense again. A significant shift in the spring mentally. This will get better.

"I see a bunny. This means new beginnings… Hard to welcome in if you keep the past. Husband—you will have a lot of jobs. Keep working on projects and mentoring. Mentoring will grow.

"I see nothing terrible going forward—slow, gradual growth of building things."

BEAVERTON PSYCHIC #2: RENEE TERRILL

December 7, 2022

Beaverton Psychic #2: "Bono steps in. He will be sending more helpers for your journey. Male companionship. Not all at the same time—it is not going to rain men. The departure of his energy from you has changed things. He realizes male energy is essential for you. Very important to have male energy around. This is a different form of male energy, for companionship. If you choose to have someone in your life, Bono will make his opinions known if he doesn't like someone; people will be more like friends, spiritual, and will keep entering your life. You need masculine energy. He did not realize how much you needed that."

Bono: "I need to tell you that you're doing great. I love you so much. I am so proud of you. When I left, I was sure of the plan, but I've since seen these ups and downs. I will know what the plan is, and it is a good plan, yet I couldn't help but wonder when I left. Then I see you making such spiritual growth. My wife's growth is a marvel; it's amazing, like a star from the other side in the sky. Keep it up. You are doing great."

Psychic: "Your husband is so happy with you. He has absolute joy. So in love with you. He has a fun Spirit. Your Dad just pulled up in a very old car, 1950 Impala? Wearing a hat and suit. Waving out the window at you. Beaming smile, I'm great. The house he is in front of has significance. There is a holiday gathering in the house, and everyone is inside. He is beaming ear to ear. He is putting his arms around you—I miss you. Mom is in the rocking chair—very content. Dad is showing me a flowered trellis that he made. I did this. They both miss being with you. They are around you a lot, enjoying the family. Bono is around his sister and your family, not really around his brother or his family."

Bono: "You've done great. Hang in there. I know it's hard. I'm completely with you all the time. I am so committed to finding happiness for you, I will see you again."

Psychic: "He has an overwhelming love for you. He says: I love this person so much. You are his project. He will see you again. He is quite a character."

Guides: "All that you've been through, you will not lack support. People are coming to you in different ways, different forms. People will enter your life; you will never be alone. You could have been alone. Because when you lose someone, some people isolate. You could have shut-off, you could have said 'that's enough for me.' You will receive support in physical and spiritual connections—you will always have support. We are so proud of you, and you will look back and be really proud of your life."

When I had my reading with this [last] psychic, it was like my husband, the psychic, and I were having an intimate conversation. She could connect with him so easily. Her style resonated with me, and she also spoke about me writing at least two books. She felt the second book would be for children and its theme would be death and recovery. It's funny, I had asked this psychic if I would get my house in this upcoming year. She'd said, "Yes, in winter. Wait, I also heard June." I found my house in winter and closed on it in February 2023; I had to be out of the house I was living in by the month of June. She was correct on both counts. Our family also had a white impala when I was very young.

When my parents and my husband were still living, I started to feel bored with my life. I felt like I wasn't really accomplishing anything. I took care of my parents, made lunch dates with my friends, and had a blissful married life which included having our wonderful puppies. I felt like something was missing. I was missing the mark. I was unfulfilled, but I couldn't put my finger on what was causing these feelings. My parents needed me—that wasn't going to change. Life with my hubby was on hold while I took care of them. This longing was bubbling up in me—the desire for something more fulfilling.

I could never have guessed that through all of their deaths, I would find myself and my purpose. I actually found my purpose in life. I had worn many hats: daughter, mother, wife, schoolteacher, mentor, and Jazzercise Instructor, among others. Now, my life was morphing for my growth as a soul. I was in the "college of life," which was preparing me for what came after all my loss. The prep work was done, and now came my chance to live up to and experience my soul's full potential.

I actually didn't realize this until just now. What an epiphany. I prepped for my life's purpose up until my mid-sixties, and now an entirely new chapter—a new book—was unfolding for me.

Namaste, Karen

Forever in Touch:
Unbroken Connection and Loving Encounters with Bono

- I saw something flash across the landing upstairs, like when you have a visit by a ghost. This was the first time he appeared to me this way.

- Bono rang the doorbell, and both dogs went crazy. I looked out the window upstairs, and there were no vehicles in or around the driveway. No one was at the door. I went downstairs and opened the door—no one was there. There was no person on the doorbell camera. My husband was being a prankster.

In Loving Memory of
Carl Louis Bonofiglio
Husband, father, friend, brother—the Love of my life
My everything
The man who captured my heart and soul
You will never be forgotten because you are a part of me
I am grateful and blessed to have been you wife
I love you, Bono
With every part of my being.

Appendix II: "SILLY LOVE SONGS": BONO'S PLAYLIST

1. "Never Ending Song of Love" - Delaney & Bonnie
2. "Here, There and Everywhere" - The Beatles
3. "Always on My Mind" - Willie Nelson
4. "1960s Batman Theme" - Jason Legget
5. "Oogum Boogum Song" - Brenton Wood
6. "See You in September" - The Happenings
7. "Baby Elephant Walk" - Henry Mancini
8. "You're the Inspiration" - Chicago
9. "Dragnet Theme" - Ray Anthony and his Orchestra
10. "The Rain, the Park and Other Things" - The Cowsills
11. "Good Morning Starshine" - Oliver
12. "Sunshine" - Gabrielle
13. "Don't Worry Baby" - The Beach Boys
14. "Highway Star" - Deep Purple
15. "All You Need Is Love" - The Beatles
16. "Morning Girl" - Neon Philharmonic
17. "Downtown" - Petula Clark
18. "I Will" - The Beatles
19. "Along the Navajo Trail" - Bing Crosby

20. "Across the Universe" - The Beatles
21. "I Need You" - The Beatles
22. "Tip Toe Through the Tulips" – Tiny Tim
23. "Put Your Head on my Shoulder" - Paul Anka
24. "Sunshine of Your Love" - Cream
25. "A Song for You" - Leon Russell
26. "My Love" - Paul McCartney and Wings
27. "Till There Was You" - The Beatles
28. "You are the Reason" - Callum Scott
29. "The Beatles Birthday Song" - The Beatles
30. "Silly Love Songs" – Paul McCartney & Wings
31. "Good Morning" - The Beatles
32. "Bleeding Love" - Leona Lewis
33. "Last Kiss" - J. Frank Wilson and The Cavaliers
34. "You Are So Beautiful" - Joe Cocker
35. "Hold me Now" - Thompson Twins

Appendix III: "SUNSHINE OF YOUR LOVE": SOME MORE LOVING ENCOUNTERS FROM BEYOND THE VEIL

- When Victoria, Mitch, and I were at the table in the clinic, we heard a loud noise coming from the exam room—no one was in that room. It sounded like something had fallen. We all stopped and looked at each other, eyes wide open, as no one else was in the clinic. We all went to the exam room, and nothing had fallen or was out of place.

- Bono has brought a multitude of songs to me: through the radio, in my mind, and through friends. They come morning, noon, and night. Usually, the song's message has something to do with what I am experiencing at the time. He tries to lift me up through music, and it is very embracing. Bono's Playlist can be found in Appendix II, and also as part of the chapter titles throughout this book. Many of these songs I'd been familiar with, and many others I had not known before Bono brought them to me.

- I was very stressed having to liquidate Bono's clinic, workspace, and gym. Since his therapies were specialized, his items were used by specific chiropractors. Covid was at its peak, and I didn't know if they would sell; you had to be trained to work with them. Bono left me two pennies and told me, "Be patient and don't worry." It was very comforting having him acknowledge my unfortunate circumstances and trying to offer me solace.

- Bono constantly gives me chills and full body shakes to let me know he's still with me. I've learned to stop whatever I'm doing and chat with him when this happens. His chills and shakes feel different than others. He has a special way of touching me so that I know it is him. The love is overwhelming and incredible.

- I was having a very rough day and wanted my old life back. I wanted to wake up from this nightmare and return to normal. Bono gave me a subtle body shake—just softly to let me know he was there. Since I was in bed, I soon fell asleep. I dreamed of him holding me and stroking me as he used to in a very private way. I snuggled my face deeply into his chest and could feel his muscular body and touch. It was so honest and comforting.

- I want to lose weight. I have a horrible sugar addiction. I beseeched my husband and Guides to help me lose weight and to take away my sweet tooth. Three days later, I noticed that I hadn't wanted anything sweet; I had no cravings. The same a week later. I thanked them all gratefully. I got a huge body chill in confirmation that they'd heard me.

- I met my friend for lunch who I haven't seen in about five years. We cried about Bono and reminisced. She isn't doing well. She has PTSD from being raped; now, she also has anxiety attacks, difficulty leaving her home, and has taken a leave of absence from work. We talked about her seeing a therapist, and Bono came to me fiercely. She saw my entire body shake, and her eyes widened. I told her Bono was adamant that she should see one.

- I was standing in Bono's music room, when I became overcome with grief and started sobbing. I turned toward the center of the room and asked Bono to help me. I cried out in anguish and pain—please take this away from me. Help me. I *immediately* calmed down, and although I couldn't "feel" him, I knew that he was there helping me.

- While sitting with one of my doggies in the swing, I looked up at the door and felt Bono's strong presence. He was "standing" in the doorway—holding the door jamb with both hands—looking at me and smiling at us.

- I was sitting on the swing, missing Bono. Suddenly, I looked up, and I saw him looking down at me from the upstairs window. He looked young and boyish—early twenties. Can you imagine? You're living alone, and you look up to see your dead husband looking down at you with a big smile on his face? It was startling, but it made me feel good.

- While I was sitting on the bed, Bono came and sat next to me and gave me body chills. I started crying, and I asked him if he ever got tired of "hanging around with the sorry-ass woman who cries so much?" He put the song "Never Ending Song of Love" in my head.

- I awoke to use the bathroom around midnight, and I heard the TV downstairs. I'd gone to sleep at 9:00 pm, and the TV hadn't been on then—nor had there been any noise coming from downstairs. I had to walk downstairs to turn off the TV, and it was quite disconcerting. I asked Bono not to do that again, as it gave me the creeps.

- I was pretty bummed about how Nick treated me after he visited. Nick had been so patient and kind when Bono passed, but today not so much and he was irritated. I was despondent, and Bono gave me a body chill to let me know he was by my side. It was very comforting, and I felt his arms around me.

- I was doing my usual morning routine, and I felt overwhelmed. I wasn't thinking about Bono or my parents, so there were no memories that would have denoted grief. I just felt overwhelmed. I couldn't pinpoint anything. I started sobbing, and not knowing why. It was so odd. Maddy stood by me, looking in my eyes, wagging her tail, and barking—as if to say, "It's okay, Mom." I then realized why I felt this way. I knew the room was filled—JUST FILLED—with Spiritual forms, and I was feeling their love and energy.

- On January 15, 2022, I read about the death of a beloved teacher of mine, Dr. Hew Len. I took his Ho'oponopono (traditional Hawaiian practice of forgiveness and reconciliation) courses, and I also met him personally. One time, when he came back from lunch, I happened to be in the hall when he entered the building. I threw myself into his arms—full body hug—and shouted: "Dr. Hew Len!"

  - He held on tight and didn't let go. He said I was the only person who called him by the correct name.
  - Upon reading of his death, I cried. I knew that a great spirit had transcended. Upon looking up, I saw his Spiritual form standing to my left; he was leaning on the back of the chair, wearing his ever-present baseball

cap. I was shocked. I thought: "Why me? Why is he visiting me? I am a nobody."

- He left, and I decided that I would never minimize myself again. My light shines brightly: we had a wonderful connection in life, and he came to show me he was just fine. I am forever grateful for his visit.

- I was having lunch with Nurse Beth, and we discussed the usual topics. I also asked what she thought about rebirth/reincarnation. She really didn't know. She said we are made of energy, but she doesn't know where that energy goes when the body departs.

  - She discussed a family dog she used to have named Poncho. She extolled her love of him and his antics. Yet, she wasn't told about his death until a year later. As an adult, she also had a great connection with a puppy she adopted named Alex. They adored each other and engaged in the same antics as she had with Poncho. I said that "it sounds like Poncho came back as Alex." As she pondered this, I felt Poncho's Spiritual form give me full body chills. I'd never been contacted by an animal like this: it was incredible.

- While writing a post on Facebook about grief, and using Nurse Beth's graphic, I was enveloped in a sweet smell; I knew that Mom was by my side.

- I have a "singing clock" that works during daylight hours. As I was petting the puppies at night and talking to my Heavenly Helpers, the clock started singing at 9 p.m., when it was pitch dark. Mom was letting me know she was around.

- As I was sitting at the table, I spoke aloud and told my mom, "Happy Mother's Day." I could feel her presence with me. About thirty minutes later, two clocks sang their songs; the Christmas Clock and the Singing Clock. Those clocks have not worked or sung their song over the last couple of months. Mom was letting her presence be known.

- Mom made her presence known today with both clocks singing at the same time. They haven't sung since she visited me on Mother's Day. Gosh, I love my mom.

- Last night, I was super tired and crawled into bed. I noticed I was rubbing my comforter with my thumb, and this was something Mom had taught me to do when I needed to relax to fall asleep. I cried out, "Mom! You're here!" I felt her presence and her hand on the side of my face. Tears of love and gratitude flowed.

- I was posting about grief on Facebook. It was emotionally difficult to compose the post. I was writing about how I knew that Bono was proud of me; my parents were also proud that I'd weathered this storm of all of them passing. I kept smelling something sweet, and I knew it was Mom. She always brings me sweet smells.

- I went to bed, but I'd forgotten something in the other room. I walked from my bedroom into the Great room, and I felt so much energy. I knew that room was filled with Spiritual forms. I looked, but couldn't see anyone; yet, I asked if any were here, and I was told yes.

- I've been asking Bono to come to me in a dream that I would remember afterward. Last night, I dreamt of us standing in the kitchen of our old house. He was to the right of me, and we were in front of the kitchen window. As I stood next to him, I felt his "presence" and comfort. When I was around him, I felt safe, protected, and taken care of.

- I looked up at him, and I noticed he was wearing a baseball cap, a white t-shirt with a logo, and blue jeans. I'd given him some anchovies, or some sort of fish, in a clear plastic bag. He saw the price, which was high, and he was so grateful for what I'd presented him with. In my dream, what stood out to me was his presence and the feelings I received with having him near me. It was very comforting. He is still taking care of me.

- I had an unusual dream. I was on the tennis courts at the school, and I knew the pups were behind me. Another pup came onto the courts, and I got pissed off because the owner was not there. I then saw the owner; we locked eyes, and he saw I was not pleased. Later, I was at a school as a teacher, and he was also there.

  - We started noticing each other, and there was an attraction. Later, I was tucked under his arm with my hand on his stomach the way Carl and I used to hold each other. I COULD FEEL HIM PHYSICALLY in my dream, just like when I'd felt Bono and my father at previous times. He was tall, and had black and gray hair. Is this a premonition?

- I went to Bethany's Table with Becky, Nadine, and Cheryl. Cheryl asked about my husband, and she found out that he'd died in the house. She wanted to know more, so I told her the circumstances. I cried. Bono then came to me and gave me a body chill and shake to let me know that he was with me.

- Bono wrapped his arms around me from behind when I was reaching into the cupboard at night, and he gave me the usual body chills. I'd screwed up, and I talked to my husband and thanked him for "saving my ass." He gave me body chills in confirmation.
- I have felt my husband's Spiritual form twice in the house recently:
    - I was leaning against the counter, gazing at his picture, and crying tears of joy and gratitude. I could feel him behind me with his arms around me.
    - I was alone in the house. I walked into the Great room, and I just knew he was there. I stopped to chat with him about my new house.
- What happened here is freaky crazy. Even for me, it is crazy.
    - I was tuned in to Renee's mediumship class, and I heard some LOUD voices coming from the kitchen. They were so loud that Maddy started barking. I left class to investigate. It turned out that my Sonos speakers were on, and two people were talking.
    - I picked up my phone to turn off the Bluetooth so the speakers wouldn't play, but it wasn't on. THE SPEAKERS WILL NOT PLAY WITHOUT BLUETOOTH. I stood there flabbergasted. I unplugged the speakers, and when I plugged them back in the voices continued. I turned off my phone, but the voices reappeared. WTF.
    - I realized that the two people talking were Bono and me. I was asking him if he "was going to go back to work." Now I was shocked. I have no audios of

conversations that I know of on my phone. I found the voice recording app and it was playing, so I stopped the conversation and the speaking stopped. I was beside myself—I couldn't understand what was happening. I left to rejoin the class.
- The next morning, I went to listen to the conversation between my husband and me, but there was none. There was no audio of us talking in the list. My head almost exploded. Bono has never quite reached out to me like this. I was freaked out when the speakers were not connected but were still playing; now, however, it turns out that I'd heard our voices talking and there was no audio. WTF?
- Bono had taken over my Sonos.

- I was editing the first chapter of my book—where I find Bono on the floor when he died. I experienced that night over and over again, like it was a movie playing in my head. I spiraled down and was crying, stumbling all over the house, and full of pain and angst. I even had to take a pill for help.
  - The next morning, when I came out into the Great room, the TV was on. Bono had turned this on in affirmation that he was here with me, comforting me, and letting me know he will always be with me.

- While editing my book, I reread Chapter 1 about Bono's death and finding him on the floor. It was like watching myself in a movie going through that entire night; yet, simultaneously, experiencing everything I saw and felt while watching. It felt like shards of glass were ripping me apart, and my tears fell in a constant stream from my face.

- I actually got mad.
- "Seriously, God. I have to keep doing this again and again? Why is this pain so raw and fresh?"
- I had to take three chill pills over a couple of days, due to the pain and angst, whereas I usually only take three per month max. It wasn't good. I almost called Nurse Beth and Terri crying. I have many friends to call, but these two ladies can get me through the pain and will take my call anytime, day or night.
- I had a brainiac idea last night. I wanted to see orbs. I wanted to see the celestial bodies which are around all of us all of the time. My daughter has captured them on her baby monitor. It is so cool to see them fly around the room and hover over the baby.
  - In my house, I have a couple of indoor cameras. I waited until dark, and started filming in my bedroom. Oh my God. My room had orbs flying all around it. The orbs were of different sizes and intensities, with some zooming by and others moving up and down. My mouth dropped open in amazement. I called out to Bono to see him, and a very bright orb zoomed by. I tell ya, knowing and seeing my Heavenly Team in my room lifted me from my funk, and I was so happy and, on a body, high. I wanted to call my friends and tell them. However, due to the time, I only called Tracy.
- Today I am broken. My heart is shattered. Suffocating grief is taking over and resistant

- to leaving. Coach Jeff told me to pay attention to what triggers my grief. That was easy. I was making banana bread. Some of my most loving and memorable times with Bono were in the kitchen. We'd work side-by-side, whether baking or cooking. We'd often "accidentally" run into each other, sharing a hug or a kiss. These were my favorite times. I loved to come up behind him, throw my hands around his waist, and latch onto him.
  - I remember once coming up to him while he was doing food prep. I lifted his arm, and climbed under it. He looked down at me, and inquired what I wanted. I started to sing, in my off-key voice, "I Want You to Want Me" by Cheap Trick, which elicited a huge grin. I loved to make him smile. He'd have those crinkly lines around his eyes, and his light shone brightly.
  - Today, as I was chopping pecans, he told me I wasn't doing it correctly (which I knew, but I didn't care). I asked him to come up behind me and put his arms around me to help me chop. He obliged; I could feel him behind me and holding my arms and hands.
  - He spoke into my ear and told me, "You know, I haven't left you baby." As tears streamed down my face, this comfort was able to break through to me.
  - I have been told that you have to grow around the grief. I've been told that it will diminish. I find that to be true, until it's not.

- I just closed on my house two days ago, and I received the keys yesterday. I've experienced mixed emotions: great jubilation, but also sadness as I like where I live and my neighbors. I reminded myself that I make friends wherever I go, and I'd do so there.
  - I came downstairs this morning, and the TV was on. It wasn't on when I went to bed, as the dogs and I had been down there for our nighttime ritual. The sound was down so that I wouldn't hear it during the night. Bono came to me to provide comfort and to let me know "you've got this." When he'd previously turned on that same TV, I'd told him that it scared me to hear voices talking. This time, he turned the sound off. What a man.
  - Bono came to me via the light in the morning. Messages were:
    - Don't rush things
    - Everything has its own timing
    - Enjoy your life—the journey is the most powerful part

When my parents and husband passed, my spirituality, psychic abilities, open heart, and raw feelings grew exponentially. These are not the only times my husband has reached out to me, but many of the most memorable. I know that he is continually with me, watching over me, nudging me in decisions made, and always loving and supporting me. Just wait until I return Home to be with him, Mom, and Pops. What rejoicing there will be.

Appendix IV: LIST OF RECOMMENDED READINGS

BOOKS ABOUT SPIRITUALITY

Dillard, Sherrie. 2020. *I'm Still with You.* Woodbury, Minn.: Llewellyn Worldwide, Ltd.

Dooley, Mike. 2016. *Top Ten Things Dead People Want to Tell You.* Carlsbad, Calif.: Hay House.

Dyer, Wayne W. 2003. *There's a Spiritual Solution to Every Problem.* New York: Quill.

Dyer, Wayne W. 2012. *Change Your Thoughts, Change Your Life: Living the Wisdom of the Tao.* Carlsbad, Calif.: Hay House.

Frederick, Sue. 2013. *Bridges to Heaven.* New York: St. Martin's Press.

Martin, Joel, and Patricia Romanowski. 1998. *Love Beyond Life: The Healing Power of After-Death Communications.* New York.: Dell.

Newton, Michael. 1994. *Journey of Souls: Case Studies of Life Between Lives, Fifth Revised Edition.* St. Paul, Minn.: Llewellyn Publications.

Newton, Michael. 2012. *Destiny of Souls: New Case Studies of Life between Lives*. St. Paul, Minn.: Llewellyn Publications.

Van Praagh, James. 2000. *Reaching to Heaven*. New York: Signet.

Weiss, Brian L. 2001. *Messages from the Masters: Tapping into the Power of Love*. New York: Warner Books.

BOOKS ABOUT DEATH AND GRIEF

Devine, Megan. 2018. *It's Ok That You're Not Ok: Meeting Grief and Loss in a Culture That Doesn't Understand*. Boulder, CO: Sounds True.

Gore, Ariel. 2014. *The End of Eve*. Portland, Oregon: Hawthorne Books.

Kalanithi, Paul. 2016. *When Breath Becomes Air*. New York: Random House USA.

Kessler, David. 2020. *Finding Meaning: The Sixth Stage of Grief*. New York: Simon and Schuster.

Kübler-Ross, Elisabeth. 1969. *On Death and Dying*. London: Routledge.

Burns, Lucy. 2020. "Elisabeth Kübler-Ross: The Rise and Fall of the Five Stages of Grief." *BBC News*, July 2, 2020, sec. Stories. https://www.bbc.com/news/stories-53267505.

Levine, Stephen, and Ondrea Levine. 2001. *Who Dies?: An Investigation of Conscious Living and Conscious Dying*. Park West, Dublin: Gateway.

Moorjani, Anita. 2015. *Dying to Be Me: My Journey from Cancer, to near Death, to True Healing*. Carlsbad, Calif.: Hay House.

Westberg, Granger E. 2019. *Good Grief: A Companion for Every Loss*. Minneapolis, Minn.: Fortress Press.

BIBLIOGRAPHY

The Albert Team. 2019. "Biopsychosocial Perspective: AP® Psychology Crash Course Review | Albert.io." Albert Resources. December 4, 2019. https://www.albert.io/blog/biopsychosocial-perspective-ap-psychology-crash-course-review/.

Ashworth, Donna. 2022. *You Don't Just Lose Someone Once*. Facebook.com. 2022. https://www.facebook.com/profile/100044362152366/search/?q=Grief%20the%20Unspoken.

Atkinson, William Walker. 2023. *The Law of Attraction*. NYC: Macmillan.

Behrndt, Lexi. 2015. "How to Be Grateful When Life Is Hard." *Scribbles & Crumbs*. November 19, 2015. http://www.scribblesandcrumbs.com/2015/11/19/how-to-be-grateful-when-life-is-hard/.

Bernhard, Meg. 2021. "What If There's No Such Thing as Closure?" *The New York Times*, December 15, 2021, sec. Magazine. https://www.nytimes.com/2021/12/15/magazine/grieving-loss-closure.html.

Blake, John. 2021. "They Lost Their Loved Ones to Covid. Then They Heard from Them Again." CNN. June 20, 2021. https://www.cnn.com/2021/06/20/health/supernatural-encounters-pandemic-loved-ones-blake/index.html.

Carlos The Medium. "The 6 Clair Senses: Unlock the Key to Your Psychic Abilities." 2022. May 2, 2022. https://carlosthemedium.com/clair-senses/.

"Definition of Grief | Dictionary.com." n.d. www.dictionary.com. https://www.dictionary.com/browse/grief#:~:text=The%20first%20records%20of%20the.

Estes, Clarissa P. 2022. *Tears.* "Midwives of the Soul" 2022. Facebook.com. 2022 https://www.facebook.com/midwivesofthesoul.

Grewal, Narin. "50 Loss Quotes That Heal the Heart and Lessen the Grief." Dianne Bright. Reader's Digest. November 8, 2021. https://www.rd.com/article/loss-quotes/.

Halsey, Christopher G. 1975. *Macmillan Dictionary for Children.* Definition of "Hell." New York: Macmillan; London.

Harrison, Vicki. "Grief Is like the Ocean" n.d. Tiny Buddha. https://tinybuddha.com/wisdom-quotes/grief-is-like-the-ocean-it-comes-on-waves-ebbing-and-flowing-sometimes-the-water-is-calm-and-sometimes-it-is-overwhelming-all-we-can-do-is-learn-to-swim/.

Holland, Kimberly. 2018. "Stages of Grief: General Patterns for Breakups, Divorce, Loss, More." Healthline. September 25, 2018. https://www.healthline.com/health/stages-of-grief#7-stages.

"Ho'oponopono Course Certification by Joe Vitale, Dr. Ihaleakala Hew Len and Mathew Dixon." n.d. www.hooponoponocertification.com. Accessed July 29, 2023. https://www.hooponoponocertification.

com/?gad=1&gclid=CjwKCAjwzo2mBhAUEiwAf7wjkmoeGI-EYfE6NDjMT-462nGmjLuN1j1EXBVJKzcAqnClCr2bdoLgzxoCmWoQAvD_BwE.

Irving, Washington. "A Quote by Washington Irving." n.d. www.goodreads.com. https://www.goodreads.com/quotes/44057-there-is-a-sacredness-in-tears-they-are-not-a.

Kübler-Ross, Elisabeth. 1969. *On Death and Dying*. London: Routledge.

Milne, Alan Alexander. 1994. *The Complete Tales of Winnie-The-Pooh*. New York: Dutton Juvenile.

Munch, Edvard, "The Scream," Oil, Tempera, Pastel, and Crayon on Cardboard, 1893, The National Museum in Oslo, Norway, https://www.edvardmunch.org/the-scream.jsp

National Hospice and Palliative Care Organization. "Explanation of Palliative Care." n.d. NHPCO. Accessed July 28, 2023. https://www.nhpco.org/palliativecare/explanation-of-palliative-care/#:~:text=Palliative%20care%20is%20patient%20and.

National Institute on Aging, NIH. 2008. "Helping with Comfort and Care." https://www.adventhealth.com/sites/default/files/assets/end_of_life_helping_with_comfort_care_booklet.pdf.

Parker, Lyn, Irma Riyani, and Brooke Nolan. 2016. "The Stigmatisation of Janda in Indonesia and the Possibility of Agency." *Indonesia and the Malay World, UK* 44 (128): 27–46. https://etheses.uinsgd.ac.id/30385/.

"The Rainbow Bridge Poem." 2019. Rainbow Bridge Petloss Grief Suport Community. 2019. https://www.rainbowsbridge.com/poem.htm.

Research Institute of Molecular Pathology. 2012. "The Biology of Emotions." ScienceDaily. Accessed May 22, 2023. https://www.sciencedaily.com/releases/2012/09/120917111056.htm#:~:text=Summary%3A

Roman, Sanaya. "A Quote from Soul Love." n.d. www.goodreads.com. Accessed July 29, 2023. https://www.goodreads.com/quotes/757431-there-is-no-energy-more-powerful-than-love-love-creates.

Sakugawa, Yumi. "Yumi Sakugawa Quotes (Author of Ikebana)." n.d. www.goodreads.com. Accessed July 29, 2023. https://www.goodreads.com/author/quotes/7195747.Yumi_Sakugawa.

Seuss, Dr. (Theodor Geisel). "Dr. Seuss Quotes." n.d. BrainyQuote. https://www.brainyquote.com/quotes/dr_seuss_161986.

Shulman, Dr. Lisa M. 2021. "Healing Your Brain after Loss: How Grief Rewires the Brain." American Brain Foundation Webinar. September 29, 2021. https://www.americanbrainfoundation.org/how-tragedy-affects-the-brain/.

Sincero, Jen. "Gratitude Shifts Your Perspective." 2022. MotivateUs.com. Accessed July 29, 2023. https://motivateus.com/quote-of-the-day/gratitude-shifts-your-perspective/.

Sixth Sense "Collins English Dictionary | Definitions, Translations, Example Sentences and Pronunciations." n.d. Www.collinsdictionary.com/us/dictionary/english/sixth-sense

Tolkien, J.R.R. "A Quote from *The Lord of the Rings: Return of the King*." n.d. www.goodreads.com.

Accessed July 29, 2023. https://www.goodreads.com/quotes/701843-pippin-i-didn-t-think-it-would-end-this-way-gandalf.

Tonkin, Lois. 1996. "Growing around Grief—Another Way of Looking at Grief and Recovery." *Bereavement Care* 15 (1): 10–10. https://doi.org/10.1080/02682629608657376.

VanHaute, Mary. maxweb. 2020. "10 Inspirational Quotes about Grieving - Kenna & Turner." Kenna and Turner. March 26, 2020. https://kennaandturner.co.uk/blog/10-inspirational-quotes-about-grieving/#:~:text=.

Wilder, Jasinda. "A Quote from *Falling into You*." 2013. www.goodreads.com. Accessed July 29, 2023. https://www.goodreads.com/quotes/758398-feel-grieve-let-yourself-fell-the-anger-at-the-fact.

ACKNOWLEDGMENTS

Nickolas (Nick)—my beloved son, who helped me tremendously through the process of grief and healing. God knows I drove him crazy, yet he was my rock despite his own grief. He always offered words of wisdom. My magnificent son is a therapist, and he helped me process the brutal upheaval in my life from a clinical perspective. I truly appreciated his insights and kindness.

Victoria (Binks)—my loving daughter, who—despite her broken heart and her own grief taking her to her knees—always provided a listening ear. Her empathetic nature and kindness in my time of need helped me to keep rising. She was the patient light in my darkness, who rose to help me navigate grief and made decisions for me when I was unable. Her strength was unwavering.

Mitch—my son-in-law, who possessed inner and outer strength when I had none and was always ready to help at a moment's notice. He is a natural "giver" and was in tune with me.

Leah—my son's partner, who is a quiet, ever-present reserve of strength for me. She is a tremendous cook who always made sure my fridge was full of home-cooked meals.

Mom, Dad (Pops), and Husband Carl Bonofiglio—I know they were, and still are, with me as I travel this road of grief and rebirth. I love you all so much, and I was the luckiest woman to have you three in my life. My love for you is overwhelming. I was so blessed with you all.

Dana—Leah's sister, who prepared me vegetarian meals and who is a fantastic cook. I quit eating for the first few weeks, but knowing I always had food in the freezer was a comfort.

Tracy—my loving confidant and friend, who stayed with me for two weeks after my husband's death and continues to come weekly for my support. Having her to fill the emptiness helped my shattered heart. She has been perfectly present for me and lent support when needed.

Vivi—my best friend, who provided comfort and understanding and would make gifts (e.g., videos; artwork; etc.) for me that my husband would ask her (from behind the Veil) to design to ease my heartache. The heartfelt videos still bring tears to my eyes, bringing me so much love and comfort and helping me with my loss. I am so grateful she was open to this communication. Her expertise working as Graphic Designer and Illustrator on my book was paramount.

Dr. Dan—my chiropractor friend, who helped me organize, price, and liquidate Bono's clinic.. He was one of my most prominent helper Angels after my children. Always so patient and kind.

Dr. Josh Woggon and Dr. Dennis Woggon—two specialized chiropractors who helped me connect with doctors who also treated scoliosis patients through nonsurgical protocols and who were willing to fly across the country to help me with liquidating Carl's specialty equipment.

Brenda—a special friend and housekeeper, who covertly would check my fridge when she was there and tell me to eat. She was constantly checking in on me and my well-being. Her church made a prayer shawl that has provided me with incredible comfort, and I still use it for my tears.

Nurse Beth—my lifesaver, who helped me with the "end of life" for my parents. We forged a strong friendship during that time, and

Acknowledgments

she continued to check in on me constantly when my husband died. I still have such cascades of emotions whenever I think of her and what we experienced together. I have been truly indebted to her during this whole process.

Michael—a magnificent person, who also suffered a horrible, personal loss. He saw and felt my searing pain online, and he reached out to help me process my grief. He kept me from spiraling down the rabbit hole and mollified me—soothing the beast of grief residing in my heart. His words and advice were always comforting, and he became my anchor during the turbulent seas.

Farley Cat—a close friend, who I have been friends with for nearly thirty years and who also lost her husband. She always provided a kind and loving shelter when I cried, spiraled down, or had no faith and confidence in myself. She never negated me or made me feel less of myself.

Brian Louis Mayer and Carston Quinn—my Editors. So grateful for these two men, who helped me during this rough and stormy time of my life. They edited my book, kept my voice, and helped bring my message forward to share with the world. I am forever indebted to them. Their knowledge and expertise are unparalleled, and I strongly recommend them as editors.

All the quiet helpers and friends who supported me in the background—whether it be flowers, food, notes of kindness, gift certificates for restaurant meals, texts, or anything else helpful, you took care of me continuously. I am brought to my knees by your grace, and I have an infinite appreciation for your caring and help. I am incredibly blessed with my tribe.

All my friends on social media—for taking the time to put me in your prayers and encouraging me during my darkest, bleakest days. All of you truly helped me along this death, grief, and trauma journey. I am forever indebted to you. You offered support, wisdom, love, and kindness, which helped my heart to heal and restore me—bit by bit—back to my former self.

SPIRIT BOX #26: "LOVE WILL NEVER END":

"I Will Always Be There for You" in Spirit

"Encore. One more so long for now, readers. It's been a pleasure rocking out and tackling grief for your growth with you and my wife, and this Spiritual form will rest easy knowing he may have played even a minor role in helping you cope with your losses. But I can't say goodbye to Karen; I promised my wife I'd never truly leave her. Instead, I have this to say to you, my Love:

"I leave you, but I am not gone. I am the sunshine on your face, the love in your heart, the smile on your lips, and the laughter from your soul. I am forever with you.

"I love you, Karen. With every part of my being.

Peace out, readers." Vroom vroom

ABOUT THE AUTHOR

Karen Bonofiglio is a writer, teacher, mother, and friend who has been immersed in spirituality for decades. *Whoever Dies First... Wins* portrays her devastation-to-triumph journey, which was prompted by the sudden death of her husband within months of losing her parents. Her subsequent downward spiral into depression and despair left her completely lost and traumatized. She learned to thrive again by connecting to the dead—beyond the veil. Karen continues to share her unique perspectives about spirituality and life through her experience as an entrepreneur, teacher, trainer, partner, and parent.

www.ingramcontent.com/pod-product-compliance
Lightning Source LLC
Chambersburg PA
CBHW060511080526
44586CB00012B/453